Australian Urban Planning

Australian Urban Planning

New challenges, new agendas

Brendan Gleeson and Nicholas Low

ALLEN & UNWIN

Dedicated to the memory of Peter Self and Ruth Crow

First published in 2000
Allen & Unwin
9 Atchison Street, St Leonards NSW 1590 Australia
Phone: (61 2) 8425 0100
Fax: (61 2) 9906 2218
E-mail: frontdesk@allen-unwin.com.au
Web: http://www.allen-unwin.com.au

National Library of Australia
Cataloguing-in-Publication entry:

Gleeson, Brendan, 1964– .
   Australian urban planning: new challenges, new agendas.

   Bibliography.
   Includes index.
   ISBN 1 86508 238 4.

   1. City planning—Australia. 2. Urban policy—Australia.
   3. Local government—Australia. I. Low, Nicholas, 1941– .
   II. Title.

307.12160994

Set in 11/13pt Bembo by DOCUPRO, Sydney
Printed and bound in Australia by Brown Prior Anderson

Contents

Boxes, tables and figures

Figures

Acknowledgements

This book is the result of much discussion and debate going back many years. More influences have come to bear on it than can be adequately acknowledged. Some indication can be gained from the length of the Bibliography. Still, here we want to mention a few. We have dedicated the book to the memory of Peter Self and Ruth Crow, who both died in 1999. Peter was always a mentor, full of wisdom and common sense and a passionate commitment to good governance, and Ruth, with her partner Maurie, made an enduring contribution to planning thought and practice of the kind we would like to promote.

Patrick Troy has made so many contributions to Australian planning, personally, through his work, and through one institution he helped to create: the Urban Research Program at the Australian National University (now the Urban and Environmental Program). His remarkable and unique contribution is to make possible an *Australian* perspective and vision of planning. We also want to acknowledge Ruth Fincher, Brian McLoughlin, Max Neutze, Leonie Sandercock, Frank Stilwell, Paul Mees, Rob Freestone, Bruce Moon and Ed Wensing, to whose work and advice we often turned; and, in the field of political science and public administration, Anne Capling, Mark Considine, Michael Crozier, Martin Laffin, Martin Painter and John Paterson.

Two institutions especially helped us. The Urban and Environmental Research Program at the Australian National University provided an intellectual home for both authors. Brendan Gleeson was a member of the program between 1996 and 1999 and benefited enormously from interaction with the other program members. The program hosted a conference in 1998 on 'Renewing Australian Planning' which stimulated much thought. Nicholas Low spent four months as sabbatical scholar in the program in 1999, a fulfilling time which enabled him to contribute to the book's completion.

At different times both authors were helped by the Faculty of Architecture, Building and Planning at the University of Melbourne and its Dean, Professor Ross King. We thank the faculty for financial assistance at the time we most needed it: to pay for illustrations, ABS tabulation and the invaluable editorial assistance of Penny Hanley. Ruth Fincher, Professor of Planning in the faculty, patiently read and helpfully commented on our text. We also found stimulating insight in the discussions that took place during the series of conferences on 'The Regulation of Australian Cities', which Ruth organised and hosted in 1998 with the help of a grant from the ARC. Nicholas Low acknowledges the role of the ARC in funding research on 'Shaping Melbourne', part of whose findings are reported in this book. Brendan Gleeson is also grateful for the support and encouragement given to him by Professors Bill Randolph and Jane Marceau at the University of Western Sydney. Graeme Thomas of the ABS provided patient help with the production of maps for chapter 3. John Iremonger and the staff at Allen & Unwin were helpful and flexible publishers. The authors, of course, take full and sole responsibility for the text. An anonymous reader provided very useful comments on a draft of the manuscript.

On a personal level the authors acknowledge the positive and vital support of their partners Ulrike Gleeson and Elizabeth Low. Our children were always an inspiration. Parents are also always present in the shape of inherited value systems. Nicholas acknowledges the strong influence of Tim (Harold) and Cynthia Low who, in England, endured the appalling horror of World War II and yet provided strong foundations of love, security and a sense of justice. Brendan is grateful to his parents, Brian and Mary; Elizabeth and Terry, for the moral examples they have been to him throughout his life.

Abbreviations

ABS	Australian Bureau of Statistics
ACCC	Australian Competition and Consumer Commission
ACT	Australian Capital Territory
ACTU	Australian Council of Trade Unions
ALGA	Australian Local Government Association
ALP	Australian Labor Party
ANZ	Australia and New Zealand (Banking Group)
BCC	Brisbane City Council
CB	colonial bureaucracy
CBD	central business district
CCT	compulsory competitive tendering
CF&L	(Department of) Conservation, Forests and Lands
CL	corporate liberalism
CO_2	carbon dioxide
CPI	Consumer Price Index
CJC	Criminal Justice Commission
CSHA	Commonwealth State Housing Agreement
DAF	Development Assessment Forum
DURD	Department of Urban and Regional Development
EARC	Electoral and Administrative Review Commission
ESD	ecologically sustainable development
GATT	General Agreement on Tariffs and Trade
GOE	government-owned enterprise
GTE	government trading enterprise
HIA	Housing Industry Association
HURA	(Department of) Housing and Urban and Regional Affairs

ICLEI   International Consortium on Local Environmental Initiatives
ILAP   Integrated Local Area Planning
IMF   International Monetary Fund
MAV   Municipal Association of Victoria
MMBW   Melbourne and Metropolitan Board of Works
MP   Member of Parliament
MPE   Ministry of Planning and Environment
MTP   Melbourne Transport Plan
NATSEM   National Centre for Economic and Social Modelling
NCP   National Competition Policy
NGO   non-governmental organisation
NSW   New South Wales
NT   Northern Territory
NIMBY   not in my backyard
OECD   Organisation for Economic Cooperation and Development
PALM   Planning and Land Management Group (ACT government)
PCA   Property Council of Australia
PEDA   Planning and Environment Development Assessment (Bill)
PPEG   politics, philosophy, geography and economics
POG   Planning Officials Group
PSMC   Public Sector Management Commission
QDOT   Queensland Department of Transport
Q'land   Queensland
RAPI   Royal Australian Planning Institute
SA   South Australia
SAFA   South Australian (government) Financing Authority
SA Inc.   South Australia Incorporated
SBSA   State Bank of South Australia
SCAG   Southern Californian Association of Governments
SDM   social democratic managerialism
SEIFA   Socio-Economic Indexes for Areas
SEQ   southeast Queensland
SLA   statistical local areas
SPA   State Planning Authority
Tas   Tasmania
TCPA   Town and Country Planning Association
TOADS   temporarily obsolete abandoned derelict sites
UK   United Kingdom (of England, Scotland, Wales and Northern Ireland)
VGC   Victorian Grants Commission

Vic	Victoria
WA	Western Australia
WA Inc.	Western Australia Incorporated
WCED	World Commission on Environment and Development

Researching urban policy

Hard copy

The most useful hard copy resources for urban researchers are the scholarly and professional journals on planning and spatial governance. Some journals, such as *Urban Policy & Research* (Australia), contain both scholarly research articles and policy-related discussion papers. Geography journals are often a good additional source of information about urban policy and planning. Some journals have websites (see below).

For Australia, we recommend the following journals: *Urban Policy & Research, Australian Planner* (see also the newsletters of the RAPI's state divisions), *Just Policy, Australian Geographical Studies, The Australian Geographer, Australian Journal of Public Administration, Australian Journal of Politics and History* (contains useful descriptions of political and administrative changes and events in the states called 'Political Chronicles').

The key international journals are: *International Journal of Urban and Regional Research, Planning Practice & Research, Planning Theory, Environment and Planning A, B, C & D* (this is a series of four distinct journals: A has no subtitle, B is 'Planning and Design', C is 'Government and Policy', D is 'Society and Space'), *International Planning Studies, Cities, Journal of Environmental Planning and Management, Town Planning Review, Urban Studies, Housing Studies, Journal of Planning Education and Research*.

The Internet

We offer here a selection of some of the more informative web addresses relating to Australian and overseas urban policy. Be aware that web

addresses often change. For example, the periodic reorganisation of state and Commonwealth government departments often leads to changes in web addresses for public urban policy agencies. Be prepared to use search engines to track the websites you are looking for and to update the addresses you already have. Here is a web page with information that will help you develop your Internet research skills:
http://www.albany.edu/library/internet/search.html

Note also that government departments often release key policy papers—especially in draft form—through their websites. This offers a fast and free way of obtaining key documents. Documents are usually supplied in electronic formats that can be accessed by most web users, including 'portable document format' (.pdf) and/or 'rich text format' (.rtf).

Journal websites can also offer useful information, including the contents pages of current and recent issues and, with some, abstracts of published papers.

Commonwealth government agencies

At present there is no Commonwealth agency with a direct interest in urban policy. Some Commonwealth departments maintain an indirect interest in planning-related issues, including transport, local government, the environment, heritage and regional policy.

The Department of Transport and Regional Services is at:
http://www.dotrs.gov.au/
This department also deals with local government issues.

Environment Australia handles heritage and environmental issues:
http://www.environment.gov.au/

State government planning agencies

All state and territory planning agencies have a website. In New South Wales, the Department of Urban Affairs and Planning is at:
http://www.duap.nsw.gov.au/index.htm

In Victoria, the Department of Infrastructure is at:
http://www.doi.vic.gov.au/

In Queensland, the Department of Communication and Information, Local Government and Planning is at:
http://www.dcilgp.qld.gov.au/

In Western Australia, the Ministry for Planning is at:
http://www.wa.gov.au/planning/

In South Australia, the Department for Transport, Urban Planning and the Arts is at:
http://www.planning.sa.gov.au/

In Tasmania, the Resource Planning and Development Commission is at:
http://www.rpdc.tas.gov.au/

In the Northern Territory, the Department of Lands, Planning and Environment is at:
http://www.lpe.nt.gov.au/home.htm

In the Australian Capital Territory, the Department of Urban Services is at:
http://www.act.gov.au/urbanservices/index.html

Other government-related sites for Australia

The best web source of information can be found at the Australian Local Government Information Network site:
http://www.algin.net.au/

For information on local government in overseas countries, go to:
http://www.geocities.com/Paris/9925/ and *http://www.iula.org/*

The Australian Housing and Urban Research Institute is a national research organisation whose members include Australian governments and universities. It is at:
http://www.ahuri.csiro.au/index.htm

Professional and advocacy organisations

The main professional organisation for planners in Australia is the Royal Australian Planning Institute. It can be found at:
http://www.ozemail.com.au/~rapi/
     Follow the links through to the state divisions' pages.

Victoria's Town and Country Planning Association draws from a broader, community base and seeks to promote good urban and rural planning. It can be found at:
http://home.vicnet.net.au/~tcpa/

The Australian Institute of Urban Studies is an independent non-profit organisation that is concerned with all aspects of urban affairs. The AIUS is at:

http://home.vicnet.net.au/~aius/welcome.htm

Planning journals

Urban Policy & Research is at:
http://www.arts.unimelb.edu.au/projects/upr/

Information about the *Australian Planner* is at
http://www.ozemail.com.au/~rapi/

The *Journal of Environmental Planning and Management* can be found at:
http://cherubino.oclc.org/titles/09640568.htm

The *Environment and Planning* journals can be found at:
http://www.pion.co.uk/ep/

Urban policy research overseas

The 'Cyburbia' page is richly endowed with links to all sorts of very useful web addresses. It can be found at:
http://www.arch.buffalo.edu/pairc/

The 'RUDI' site contains many links to other pages with planning and urban design information. It is at:
http://rudi.herts.ac.uk/

The International Council on Local Environmental Initiatives can be found at:
http://www.iclei.org/
http://www.iclei.org/iclei.htm

In the USA a useful website is at the Center for Urban Policy Research at Rutgers University, New Jersey:
http://www.policy.rutgers.edu/cupr/cuprlite/newindex.htm

In Europe a useful site is the Urban Environment Expert Group of the European Union at:
http://www.iclei.org/europe/expert.htm
Information on the work of the Expert Group can also be supplied by:
Mr Eric den Hamer
European Commission
DGXI, Urban Environment Unit
Rue de la Loi 200
B–1049 Brussels

The European Sustainable Cities & Towns Campaign aims to promote the development of local Agenda 21 action plans in Europe. It was launched at the first European Conference on Sustainable Cities & Towns, which took place in Aalborg, Denmark, in 1994. European local authorities can join the campaign by signing the 'Aalborg Charter', which commits them to creating local Agenda 21 action plans. At present more than 300 local authorities representing more than 75 million people have joined.

The campaign is backed by the European Commission through DGXI (Directorate General Eleven), which provides financial assistance and links to the European Commission Expert Group on the Urban Environment. The WHO Healthy Cities network supports the campaign and forms part of the coordinating committee.

The European Sustainable Cities and Towns Campaign can be found at:

http://www.who.dk/tech/hcp/eurosust.htm

Local Agenda 21 plans in Europe can be found at:
http://www.iclei.org/la21/eurola21.htm

1 Introduction: new challenges for planning

He sees hope
In asking me about cities. How can I tell him
the cities are debris driven by explosions
whose regulation takes a merciless cunning?

Les Murray, 'Toward the Imminent Days'

This book describes and analyses the various theoretical, political and institutional forces that have shaped and reshaped public urban planning in Australia since World War II. It is written at a low ebb of planning in Australia. In practice, planning has been outsourced, marketised and stripped of the knowledge and confidence that informed its founders. Also, theoretical and political perspectives have emerged in recent decades that posit new political-ethical grounds for the regulation of urban development. Planning has powerful opponents, but many of its supporters are also calling for recognition of a broader range of cultural and ecological values in urban **governance**. If public planning is to regain its place in the proper regulation of a market society it must be rethought and reconstituted. We need to argue the case for planning most urgently if this form of governance is to survive in the new millennium in any meaningful form.

In arguing for more and better planning, our intention is to explain the historical purpose of planning in Australia and the nature of the diverse recent changes that have both reshaped and threatened this purpose. We argue for a political view of planning as a form of urban governance. We argue that Australian planning can be renewed through the articulation of a new set of political-ethical ideals. This renewed vision for planning must reassert the justification for spatial regulation while opening itself once again to the ideal of social justice and taking up the challenge of ecological sustainability.

This book attempts three things, contained respectively in Parts I, II and III. The first part of the book considers what has happened to Australian cities and their governance over the past 20 or so years. The second part considers the main sets of ideas that have informed planning theory over the period. The final part sets an agenda for the future of planning. In this introduction we both set the scene for the discussion that follows in the chapters of the book and briefly foreshadow the line of argument to be developed.

Australian cities and their governance

This book is primarily about the planning of cities. Part I analyses how Australia's cities and their governance have changed since World War II. There is simply not the space in this volume to include an adequate review of non-metropolitan regions and their planning needs. Most Australians live in cities, but the regions are enormously important to the cultural, economic and environmental health of the nation. We deplore the withering of Australia's regions that governments at all levels have allowed to occur in recent decades. Australian governments have undertaken regional planning and development in the past (notably the Whitlam federal administration 1972–75) but in recent decades have washed their hands of this vital planning function. We agree with Peter Self (1995) that a return to regional planning is necessary if social and environmental health is to be restored to the nation's dying rural settlements and regions.

Colonial/postcolonial cities

It is as well to remember, as we embark on the 21st century, that the settlement of Australia involved grave injustices: of invasion, displacement, racism and class warfare. Following the main European invasion in 1788, Australia's original inhabitants were quickly and brutally displaced. For the original settlers, and their successors, it became evident that, while British institutions would provide the framework for the colonial order, the realities of isolation from Europe ('the tyranny of distance') and environmental dissimilarity would require new approaches to social and economic development. Not surprisingly, then, the six separate colonies quickly established patterns of settlement and development that were quite different from those evident in Britain

(Neutze 1977). The colonies, established at various dates between 1788 and the 1830s, all eventually gained responsible, autonomous **government** before their Federation in 1901 to form the Commonwealth of Australia.

Australians from the first showed a preference for urban life: by 1891, some 49 per cent of Australia's populace lived in urban settlements of over 2500 inhabitants (Frost 1990). Culturally speaking, urban life was overshadowed but not completely maligned by class consciousness and economic cleavages (Cannon 1975). A mood of social egalitarianism had settled early in the colonies, though this was often more of an ideal than a well-observed practice. And, critically, many people had a material stake in the cities—by 1900 approximately 50 per cent of Australians were owner-occupiers of housing, compared with only 10 per cent in Britain (Forster 1995). This characteristic of high home ownership was an important source of material security and wellbeing for Australians during the later colonial period and afterwards. High levels of home ownership also mitigated class divisions.

Apart from economic class, there were other forms of cultural diversity, but these were rather heavily repressed beneath a closely regulated Victorian social order. Ethnically, colonial Australians were a diverse mixture of Europeans, with some other groups, such as Aborigines and the Chinese. However, the bulk of the population was drawn from Britain and Ireland, and an Anglo-Celtic cultural outlook dominated both official and popular life. Fears of racial diversity emerged early on, ranging from a mild oppression of the Irish to a more violent subjugation of Aboriginals and the Chinese.

In the capitalist world until the 1930s the engine of economic development had for 100 years, with a few cyclical disturbances, produced spectacular if environmentally appalling results. Urban planning was seen mainly as a way of mitigating the unsatisfactory byproducts of success. In the Great Depression (1929–34), however, the engine stalled, seemingly permanently. The Depression did not immediately act as a stimulus to planning. On the contrary, the deteriorating economic conditions, with some notable exceptions, tended to confirm governments in their belief that yet stricter application of current economic orthodoxy was required. In Australia, strategic urban planning, which had begun to catch the public attention in the 1920s, was largely rejected by governments in the 1930s. The Depression, however, had indirect *political* consequences.

The values that grew out of the Great Depression and World War II favoured planning: the deliberate reconstruction of society and economy under the hand of popular, democratically elected governments. The strong lesson imparted by both the initial economic successes of fascism and the conduct of the war economy by the allies was that large-scale resource planning by governments was a highly effective means of achieving strategic national goals (Hobsbawm 1995; Schumpeter 1943). This new strategic thinking was applied in the postwar reconstruction programs that helped countries such as Australia attain unheralded levels of economic prosperity and social security. Stemming from earlier traditions of thought and practice, urban and regional planning was provided after World War II with a fertile bed of ideas in which it could flourish. In chapter 2 we revisit and recover these ideas, and we argue that, for planning to succeed in this new century, it must today uphold and renew them.

In chapter 3 we explore how over the past 20 years Australian cities have broken out of the mould of more or less socially enforced cultural homogeneity. Australian cities have become more diverse. This new diversity has both a cultural and a geographical dimension. It is essential to distinguish clearly between *cultural pluralisation*, which we regard as healthy, and *spatial polarisation*, which is ultimately dysfunctional for a society. By 'cultural pluralisation' we mean shift in the social make-up of Australia towards a more complex, plural society. 'Spatial polarisation', on the other hand, is the geographic manifestation of extreme forms of social inequality.

Urban governance

A city, especially a city that already exists rather than a new town on a 'green field' site, already consists of almost all the elements of a society with all its various sources of power. Planning a city, therefore, means nothing less than planning a society. Given the undesirability (if not impossibility) of such a totalitarian undertaking, planning can change in one of two directions. Either it can be reduced to something much more modest in its aims: for example, the management of conflict over land use, or the protection of property values through zoning schemes. Or it can be reconceived in more politically sensitive terms: for example, as making a city, with all its freedoms and powers, work better and more fairly for its citizens. The idea of planning has therefore somehow to be subsumed by politics and governance without losing the noble ideals to which the forebears of planning aspired.

'Urban governance' means the structures of legitimate authority which provide the laws, rules and public services that make for a peaceful, just and prosperous urban society. Our view of planning is that it is both a *domain* of urban governance—that part of governance concerned with the provision of services to a city—and an *approach* to urban governance which seeks effective, equitable and democratic steering of the state apparatus for the benefit of citizens. We will have more to say about both planning and urban governance in the next chapters.

Changing the form of governance is not just a matter of changing the government by voting it out of office. The coming and going of political parties in office is an important source of change in urban governance—but so are shifts of beliefs and attitudes within the public service. We view the project of 'planning' in rather broad terms as the activity of governance required to make sure that all the services that people need in a city are provided, when and where the need occurs and at a price they can afford. Just as importantly, planning must ensure that a good environment is provided for all, both locally and globally. This conception of planning has become dominant over the past 20 years and has tended to supersede the idea of planning as a self-contained bureaucratic function. It is an *institutional* view of planning. Urban policy plainly comes up against the limits of the governmentality of the time. But urban governance is no more 'impossible' than is democratic governance itself.

How absurd it is that, as Troy (1999: 2) remarks, 'students of the city . . . have little literature which provides a critical framework within which they can assess the way their city is governed or its services administered'. But the literature is growing, and Troy himself and the Urban and Environmental Research Program he heads have contributed much to it. We explore the changing form of urban governance in Australia in chapters 4 and 5. In chapter 4 we consider how the form of urban governance was reshaped from the colonial system (colonial bureaucracy—CB) by social democrat governments at state level into social democratic managerialism (SDM). The social democrat vision for cities was promoted by increased political control of the public service. In chapter 5 we chart the growing impact of neoliberalism on urban governance and the gradual advance of a new form of liberalism we term corporate liberalism (CL). The CL model combines handing over the social functions of government to the private sector with strong direction from the political level and close relations with business.

Urban governance and globalisation

The story of planning in Australia over the past 20 years has also been a story of *globalisation*. The most important lesson to be learned from this story is that globalisation is not monolithic. Globalisation has at least four different dimensions. First, there is the real technical change in information processing and communication that has made possible new structures of management and control of business corporations— transnational corporations, a global financial market, electronic trading and free information on the Internet. Second, there is the ideology that accompanied the freeing up of capital and justified the expansion of the power of business owners and managers at the expense of workers: neoliberalism. Third, as well as economic globalisation there is ecological globalisation—the discovery that the exploitation of the Earth under present regulatory conditions is rapidly approaching its limits. Fourth, globalisation refers to the institutional change at global level that has occurred in response to both economic and ecological globalisation.

Australian governments at federal and state levels have negotiated the terms of their engagement with the different spheres of globalisation. What is remarkable is that, even while the terms negotiated have been portrayed as *inevitable*, there have throughout the world remained *wide differences* among countries in their responses to the changing global political economy and ecology. Even within Australia there have been considerable differences among the states in their response—and at different times depending on electoral political process. Planning has thus been affected by globalisation not as a simple mechanical response to a structure dictated at global level but as multiple responses to the changing growth model at national level (the national–global interface) and the various models of urban governance mediated by the states. As we shall see in chapters 4 and 5 there are alternatives in institutional response at both national and state levels.

Neoliberalism is not the only set of ideas to which planning has responded. Our intention in this book is to show something of the multiplicity of theoretical positions that exists. If we have choice, we may choose something different from our present path.

Forces for change

We want to see planning renewed, but it is equally important to avoid a misty-eyed view of the past. Postwar planning may have helped to construct a new social order and a new economy from the ravages of the Depression and the ruins of war, but it demonstrably failed to satisfy a broad range of human and environmental values. There have been many theoretical perspectives and political movements that have questioned various aspects of planning theory and practice in the postwar era. Generally speaking, these forces for change in planning were international in character, taking broadly similar forms in Western (especially English-speaking) countries. The key critiques—Marxism, environmentalism, feminism, and neoliberalism—were sourced in international theoretical and social movements. 'On the ground', however, there were marked differences in how the various critical forces were interpreted theoretically and organised politically. In Australia, there were important radical initiatives undertaken by urbanists and activists that influenced the course of overseas debates about urban policy.

Our intention in Part II is to trace the origins and character of the main forms of planning critique, and then consider how they were manifested and applied in the Australian theoretical and policy contexts. We begin in chapter 6 by considering the urban political economy critique of planning. Chapters 7 and 8 review in turn the criticisms and policy alternatives forwarded by radical democratic interests and environmentalists. Environmental and democratic interests sought to change rather than remove planning. By contrast, the managerial and neoliberal critics, reviewed in chapter 9, have set out to recast planning's role in capitalist societies in favour of the market. In chapter 10 we consider the impact of these various forms of critique on planning institutions and practice in Australia.

New agendas for planning

It is now conventional wisdom that critical scrutiny of history is necessary if we are to avoid repeating the mistakes of the past. We argue for the *renewal* of public planning, not a simple revival of the institutions and practices of the past. In our opinion, this renewal must reflect the lessons about planning's successes and failures that are recorded in Part II. In Part III, we outline a new value framework (chapter 11) and a new set of policy priorities (chapter 12) that might together form the agenda of a renewed planning effort.

One important lesson for planning that emerged from feminist and postmodern criticism was that there is no superior, all-knowing analyst among human beings. We acknowledge the limits to what we know about planning issues and therefore the particularity of our priorities. Our proposals in Part III are intended not as a complete program for action but as a starting point for discussion. Of course we would vigorously defend our values and policy priorities, but we would also welcome their refinement and enlargement through deliberation and argument.

Conclusion

We believe passionately in the need for planning, and in the potential it has to better our lives and the lives of those who will follow us. This book is intended to communicate to a broad readership the rational basis for our position, based on a historical reading of why planning emerged and why it now seems submerged in criticism and hostility. But we also hope that something of our *passion* emerges in the pages to follow. We even dare to hope that our enthusiasm for planning might be infectious, that this book might help to encourage others to feel strongly about the need for democratic governance of space. Passion need not blind us to the truth. We know that deeply held feelings bind us together in relationships and in society. Passion therefore is a quality of democracy and its servant principles justice and liberty. Liberty inspires fervour and justice requires compassion. It follows that planning, a servant institution of democracy, requires an emotional as well as an intellectual commitment. We hope that this volume imparts to the reader a real sense of the spirit and purpose of this most vital public endeavour.

Part I

Australia's changing cities and their planning

2 Planning values and 'the Australian Settlement'

We begin our review of Australian planning by tracing its development in the second half of the 20th century, and by relating this to the broad sociopolitical shifts that reshaped capitalism during this time. Though urban planning in various forms had been contemplated, debated and even experimented with within the industrialised world throughout the first half of the 20th century, it did not become firmly embedded in national regulatory systems until after World War II.

In this book we will argue that urban planning must now be viewed as a form of institutional governance, 'urban governance' (to be elaborated in chapters 4 and 5). Planning takes its place within a variety of overlapping and discrete state activities and regulatory frameworks that together form the institutional basis for urban governance. This institutional framework has been shaped over a considerable period by political values. To comprehend planning and urban governance, we must first understand political values and their embedding in institutions. More than this, if there is to be a renewal of support for planning in contemporary Australia we must recover the values and ideas that attended its birth. Yet, if we are to move on, we must also understand the limitations of institutions that have supported planning in the past.

In this chapter we first explore the values of planning that emerged in postwar Europe. We then show how these values came to be inscribed in the specific form of welfare state that emerged in Australia: the 'Australian Settlement', and its geographic extension and cultural expression. Finally we consider the ways in which the Australian interpretation of urban policy in the Settlement underpinned the planning of Australian cities.

The necessity and value of planning

What is planning?

Planning means different things at different times and in different places. Below are some terms for 'planning' whose meaning is more or less self-evident but which possess different nuances:

- urban planning, or town planning, or city planning;
- urban and regional, or town and country, planning;
- land use planning, statutory planning, or regulation of land use;
- urban policy—with varying emphasis on, for example, transport infrastructure or housing or both;
- corporate or strategic planning;
- urban governance.

'Planning' is a dialectical concept rather than an 'analytical' one. An analytical concept is one that can be perfectly and finally defined in such a way that we can know what it *is* and what it is *not*. A dialectical concept, on the other hand, is one which overlaps with other concepts and even with its opposite. It is a concept, like 'justice' or 'democracy' or 'money', crucially important for social life, but one which can never be pinned down in a unique, perfectly encompassing definition. Descriptive and normative meanings also overlap—what planning *is* and what it should be. Dialectical concepts are discussed by Herman Daly (1996: 2), who says, 'If all our concepts were analytic we could not deal with change and evolution'. Planning is a contested public activity, which sits uncomfortably with today's dominant assumption that the market can solve all social problems. But planning is also necessary for 'market' society. A society without the political steering and balancing implied by planning would destroy both its social and ecological foundations.

When we talk about 'planning' in this book we will use several of the above terms in our descriptions because of the various ways in which planning has been interpreted in practice. Our own view of what planning should be (and sometimes aspires to be) is as follows: *'The activity of governance required to make sure that all the services people need in a city are provided when and where the need occurs'*. Of course it is not the only activity of urban governance: economic policy, budgetary control, industry policy, electoral and participation processes, public auditing, the judicial system, policy for social justice and ecological responsibility, intergovernmental relations (both vertically between levels and horizontally with 'neighbouring' governments) are all domains of governance which overlap with, but are not identical to, the provision of services to a city. What planners can do is in part dependent on what the forms of governance (situated in time and place) permit. But planners and their ideas and institutions can also influence the forms of governance. Indeed, the political economist Kees van der Pijl (1998: 165) argues that planners, as a class, have the leading role in reshaping the world as a 'planetary community of fate'.

The terms of this definition will become clearer as the book unfolds. But we consider them briefly now.

- *Governance:* the activity of governing, directing, achieving goals and also representing the people of a place or territory. We can talk about 'corporate governance' which is not place-specific; here we are talking about the spatially constituted governance usually undertaken by a hierarchy of authority vested in the nation-state; we say usually, but not necessarily and not always, as any group of people can assemble to engage in the mutual act of governance, and such unofficial planning can shape societies and cities (see Sandercock 1998; Burgmann & Burgmann 1998).
- *Services:* houses, shops, offices, pipes and wires etc.; transport and communication services; social services such as education, health, public safety (police), childcare, care of the vulnerable (homeless, disabled); environmental services such as non-conflicting land uses; and, absolutely crucial today, ecological services—resources and sinks which must not be depleted.
- *People:* people defined in space, time and culture. A multi-tiered concept which includes the idea that people yet unborn also count. A question we do not address in this book (but do elsewhere: Low & Gleeson 1998: 141) is whether beings other than humans also count.
- *Need:* need rather than demand; planning is not about meeting demand. That is the function of firms in a market. Planning is necessary to ensure that a certain socially agreed and necessary base level of service is provided.

In this book we are looking back to the past—about 50 years—and forward to the future—also about 50 years. In the past, in the immediate aftermath of the Depression and World War II, we find an idea of planning much more like the one we are now proposing.

Planning for freedom

Planning by the people of a municipality, of a city, of a nation, acting together through democratic political institutions and processes, is an idea rooted in socialist and social democratic thought (see Box 2.1). It is an idea that opposes the culturally homogenising force of the capitalist system of production. Planning is equally opposed to the economic polarisation induced by the market. The concern for public health from which the idea of modern urban planning first sprung has close links with social democracy. Most especially, the idea of planning acknowledges that land and labour cannot be reduced to 'property', and cannot justly be treated as tradable commodities. Not surprisingly this is an idea loathed by people whose power in society is derived from the ownership of property, the exploitation of labour and the trading of commodities.

BOX 2.1 THE ENLIGHTENMENT, MODERNITY, SOCIALISM AND SOCIAL DEMOCRACY

ENLIGHTENMENT

What is called 'The Enlightenment' represents the growth of doubt among the intellectual communities of Europe about religious dogma. It began with discoveries about nature and the universe that contradicted literal interpretations of the Bible. It developed with the growth of the systematic exploration of the natural world: 'science'. It embraced a view of humanity whose focus was the human individual, whose conditions of existence in this world were at least as important as the hereafter. Each individual was seen to have equal intrinsic value: hence, as Rousseau remarked, humans were born free but everywhere they were in chains—enslaved by the power of aristocratic hierarchies. The principle of democracy, the rule of the people by the people, took shape, and the idea spread from the rule of the church to the rule of the state.

MODERNITY

This movement was powered by the growth of trade between places and peoples. The places of trade were mainly the cities and their markets. From the cities came a new class of traders, who lived in and presided over the walled cities, in French 'bourges', hence the 'bourgeoisie'. The wealth of this class was held not in the form of land, castles, servants and serfs but in money, or capital—the wherewithal of trade. Capitalism developed and threw up its own structures of power, reinforced by new forms of state in which the traders were represented alongside the older powers of the aristocracy. Thus new forms of social life emerged and shaped new institutions, production systems, class systems, knowledge and values. All this is called 'modernity'. Anthony Giddens (1990: 1) writes: 'modernity refers to modes of social life or organisation which emerged in Europe from about the seventeenth century onwards and which subsequently became more or less worldwide in their influence'. With these new modes of social life went the growth of industry, world trade, the application of science (technology), industrialised and socialised warfare, the separation of time and space, and reflexivity: 'the fact that social practices are constantly examined and reformed in the light of incoming information about those very practices' (Giddens 1990: 38).

SOCIALISM

Socialism was born from the realisation that individuals could not be free unless they were equal, not merely in principle but also in reality. Karl Marx and Friedrich Engels (Marx 1976/1846: 31) argued that people create themselves through the process by which they transform physical objects for their use: production. Marx subjected the dynamics of production and the forms of social life of his day to minute examination, bringing the term 'capitalism' into the vernacular with his three-volume work *Capital*. Capitalism enchained individuals in a new way: in wage labour, factory discipline, and the transfer of a surplus from the labourer to the owner of 'capital'—enriching the few while the masses were kept at subsistence level. Socialism held that people acting together as a society (or 'collective') should govern the conditions of their lives. Marx concluded that people will not even understand the depth of their own exploitation until an alternative is realised in which they collectively control the process of production: 'The veil is not removed from the countenance of the social life process, i.e. the process of production, until it becomes production by freely associated men and stands under their conscious and planned control' (Marx 1976/1867: 173). Socialism, thus, entailed collective ownership, planning, and control of the means of production.

SOCIAL DEMOCRACY

Marx advocated revolutionary seizure of the state (which at the time was not democratic but controlled by the bourgeoisie and aristocracy) by the mass working class. By the end of Marx's life, however, democracy had been widely extended and the working class had become organised in trades unions which, acting collectively, were able to put pressure on companies to pay better wages and provide improved working conditions and shorter hours. All over Europe a compact developed, taking different forms in different countries, between the two major classes: private ownership of the means of production and market exchange would be permitted, in exchange for democratic control of the state which would provide the means of support and advancement for the mass of the people. This compromise, which has been the subject of struggle throughout the 20th century, is called 'social democracy'.

The modern Western world that grew during the 19th century through imperialism and capitalist economic expansion was largely based on the principle that the self-regulating market was a law of nature. The Great Depression (1929–34) and World War II (1939–45) occurred in succession and nearly resulted in the destruction of global capitalism. These dreadful events shocked the elites of many nations into a realisation that a government-planned program of reconstruction was the only way in which democratic, market-based, capitalist societies could be saved (Hobsbawm 1995). That moment of reconstruction was the defining moment for planning. In that moment the background political values were elaborated under which the planning of cities could be seriously contemplated in a capitalist society.

The Great Depression dealt the first shattering blow against laissez-faire capitalism. In the aftermath of the global slump it was evident to all that this system, and its values, had catastrophically failed. This failure was perceived to lie not in specific political events such as the rise of fascism, or even war itself, but in the socially destructive power of the unfettered market. In particular it was clear that the theoretical lynchpin of market capitalism, Say's Law, which held that **unemployment** will be eliminated if wage levels fall to low enough (i.e. to 'market clearing') levels, was untrue. As Polanyi (1975/1944: 249) observed, laissez-faire capitalism was 'annihilated by the action of the self-regulating market'. Its dramatic collapse in the 1920s exposed 'the conflict between the market and the elementary requirements of an organized social life' (Polanyi 1975/1944: 249).

Capitalist modernity contains powerful homogenising forces. People are encouraged to express their desires in the individualised and atomised ways appropriate to the market economy. Capitalist production systems entrain populations in disciplines of labour—factory labour, agricultural labour, and individualised competitive labour. As Gramsci (1971) pointed out, capitalism becomes hegemonic when its norms become accepted by a large majority of the population. Of course it would be wrong to overstress this homogenising tendency in capitalism, just as it would be wrong to deny that bureaucratic planning has also been a homogenising force (see below). Critics of planning like to point to the supposed dull social and physical uniformity of planned settlements. But when planning is being blamed for erasing sociocultural differences, it is worth remembering that homogeneity was *not* its aim.

Earlier this century, Bertrand and Dora Russell wrote: 'In a thoroughly industrialised community, such as the United States, there is little appreciable difference between one person and another; eccentricity is hated, and every man and woman endeavours to be as like his or her neighbours as possible' (Russell 1923: 42). The Russells wanted, through socialism, to make industry and the market the servant of the community. Planning was required to liberate 'the non-material side of human life' (Russell 1923: 50); to make time and space for the flowering of individuality and difference. Planning was thus seen as a means not of subjecting people to the discipline of bureaucratic norms, or bringing people down to the 'lowest common denominator', but of *freeing* people from the grinding poverty and capitalist work disciplines to develop their individual and cultural differences. 'Planning for freedom' (see Mannheim 1951) is not the contradiction it appears to be.

To pursue freedom and develop difference, of course, required certain basic supports: food, shelter, social inclusion (see Doyal & Gough 1991). The objective of planning as portrayed by the socialist George Soule (1933: 282) must 'naturally be to raise the lowest standards of living, not to speak of providing everyone the assurance of enough to eat and wear'; but when that modest goal has been achieved,

> We may be more interested in the quality of our satisfactions than the quantity. We may want more beautiful communities in which to live, more chance to get back to the woods, to have camp fires, to swim, to fish, to hunt. We may want to paint pictures, to act in plays, to grow gardens, to read, to make our own furniture.

It would be easy today to mock the ethnocentric romanticism of such a vision. Yet surely the satisfaction of basic needs—for all—is the key to human freedom, including freedom of cultural expression? Put differently, postwar socialists and social democrats realised that cultural differences would become cultural antagonisms if minimum standards of economic and environmental welfare were not secured for all people. The market had failed to ensure minimum standards and security and it was self-evident that economic and spatial planning was not only desirable but even obligatory in a civilised society.

Planning for reconstruction

The new conceptual landscape that developed in non-fascist Europe during the war centred on planning for reconstruction. The idea took root that democratic governments would make 'blueprint' plans for many different policy domains. Urban or 'town' planning was one such domain. The extent of damage caused by war to cities and landscapes provided a powerful physical reason for planning. As one planning luminary, Britain's Sir Patrick Abercrombie, put it in 1942, 'Re-planning and re-building is inescapable: it can be done methodically and progressively or it can be left to the overwhelming rush at the close of the war' (Abercrombie 1943: 27). Planning was to be government-led and not left to the overwhelming rush of markets freed up by the end of the war economy. Only democratic governments would have the economic power, administrative scope and political authority to undertake the necessary programs for reconstruction. As decisive leadership was required, planning would necessarily be a rather centralised and 'top-down' process. The process was conceived in the linear terms of the model of science and technology: scientific survey and analysis would lead rationally to the plan (Geddes 1968/1915). Public ownership was to be considered a tool for implementation; and the underlying rationale was one of public need and improvement in the 'standard of living'.

The broad system of values that came to predominate in the postwar period was shaped by three main politico-theoretical influences. These influences were: class-based analysis, stemming originally from Marx and Engels, which affirmed the value of 'social justice' (see chapter 6); economic reform, emphasising the role of the public sector in creating full employment; and administrative reform, leading to democratically directed 'planning' rather than simply performance of bureaucratic function. Of course these values were plainly at odds with traditional market-oriented capitalism. The challenge for social democrats was to reconcile radical philosophical and political values with the reality of market capitalism. From this compromise was born the new order of the 'welfare state' and the 'mixed economy'.

Let us recall three statements that sum up in a certain way the core values and assumptions that underpinned the philosophy of planning. The first statement comes from the famous economist Maynard Keynes (1883–1946). Keynes is remembered today because he was in a real sense the architect of the postwar recovery of Western economies (though, as we discuss in chapter 6, this recovery did not bring prosperity for all). According to Keynes (1931/1926: 312, original emphasis):

> It is *not* true that individuals possess a prescriptive 'natural liberty' in their economic activities. There is *no* 'compact' conferring perpetual rights on those who acquire. The world is *not* so governed from above that private and social interest always coincide. It is *not* so managed here below that in practice they coincide. It is *not* a correct deduction from the Principles of Economics that enlightened self-interest always operates in the public interest. Nor is it true that self interest generally *is* enlightened . . .

Keynes argued that there was a legitimate, permanent and necessary place for the state, embodying the collective will, in modern capitalist society. Keynes said that public collective planning was necessary for prosperity and that full employment was quite consistent with, and indeed a requirement of, individual liberty. John Rawls (1971) later elaborated the philosophical implications for liberal democracy of this general standpoint. The need for economic security embodied in the 'difference principle' became the cornerstone of the Rawlsian architecture of the social contract and led Rawls (1971: 277) to identify the core functions of government as follows:

i) *allocation* of resources to check the formation of unreasonable market power on the part of individuals and firms and to correct market failure,

ii) *stabilisation* of the economy to achieve full employment,

iii) *transfer* of social resources to provide for the social minimum to enable all people to participate in markets, and

iv) *distribution*, through the raising of taxes, 'gradually and continually to correct the distribution of wealth and to prevent concentrations of power detrimental to the fair value of political liberty and fair equality of opportunity'.

Class analysis was presumed by Marx and later Lenin to indicate political and social revolution. But revolutionary politics had been largely abandoned in representative democracies in favour of shopfloor action and parliamentary struggle by social democratic movements (including labour parties) that united intellectual socialists, social democrats and the trades unions. Nevertheless, class politics remained a powerful theme which infused the political thought of the time. The second statement, therefore, comes from the English socialist Richard Tawney, who had this to say about the liberty that liberals claimed to be the great virtue of the capitalist system (Tawney 1981/1944: 87):

> It is constantly assumed by the privileged classes that, when the State refrains from intervening in any department of economic or social affairs, what remains as the result of its inaction is liberty. In reality, as far as the mass of mankind is concerned, what commonly remains is, not liberty, but tyranny. In urban communities with dense populations, or in great productive undertakings employing armies of workers, someone must make rules and see that they are kept, or life becomes impossible and the wheels do not turn. If public power does not make them, the effect is not that every individual is free to make them for himself. It is that they are made by private power—by landlords interested in increasing rents or by capitalists interested in increasing profits. The result, in either case, is not freedom, but a dictatorship . . .

Tawney thus concludes 'The economic system is not merely a collection of independent undertakings, bargaining on equal terms with each other. It is a power system . . . a hierarchy of authority . . .' (Tawney: 89).

Third, the idea of planning posed an immense administrative challenge for the parliamentary systems of national states. The idea of societal planning, hitherto associated with dictatorial regimes, had to be reconciled with democracy. The great Weberian sociologist Karl Mannheim sought a solution in the construction of an institutional framework of law and regulation, shaped by open parliamentary deliberation, in which freedom would be inscribed for the expression of individual needs and initiatives. Mannheim showed a remarkable grasp of the problems that lay ahead, as a form of planning took shape in the postwar years consistent with the institutions of representative democracy. Unfortunately, his insights were not followed up in the realm of urban planning (Mannheim 1951: 29, original emphasis):

> Our task is to build a social system by planning, but planning of a special kind: it must be *planning for freedom*, subjected to democratic control: *planning, but not restrictionist* so as to favour monopolies either of entre-preneurs or workers' associations, but 'planning for plenty', i.e. full employment and full exploitation of resources; *planning for social justice* rather than absolute equality, with differentiation of rewards and status on the basis of genuine equality rather than privilege; *planning not for a classless society* but for one that abolishes the extremes of wealth and poverty; *planning for cultural standards* without 'levelling down'—a planned transition making for progress without discarding what is valuable in tradition; *planning that counteracts the dangers of a mass society* by coordination of the means of social control but interfering only in cases of institutional or moral deterioration defined by collective criteria; *planning for balance* between centralization and dispersion of power; *planning* for gradual transformation of society in order to encourage the growth of personality: in short *planning but not regimentation*.

Mannheim saw planning as primarily a matter of morality and, as he put it, 'a creative politics'. He was writing at a time—World War II—at which the future of society was a matter of life and death. He said: 'it is not worth dying either for a sham democracy that favours only restriction and extremes of poverty and plutocratic wealth, or for a sham planned society in which all human freedom vanishes forever' (Mannheim 1951: 30).

Such ideas provided the touchstone for public sector planning all over the English-speaking world (Warner 1966; McConnell 1981). Yet with very few exceptions they are not explicitly stated in the urban planning literature of the time, nor have they been since. Perhaps planners wanted to be seen as objective and value-free scientists. Evans (1997: 3) points out: 'Once established the TPI [Town Planning Institute, the British professional body] was careful to keep its distance from the Garden Cities Association which it considered militant, "propagandist" and political'. McLoughlin (1969)—and he was not alone—argued that planning should be founded on the science of location theory (a branch of geographical science). Systems theory, popular in the 1970s, provided the illusion of rational analysis of complex political processes (Chadwick 1971; Faludi 1973). Town planning and 'administration' were seen as separate and often conflicting activities (Keeble 1983: 155). Though Marxist urban geography, prominent in 1980s planning theory, provided an explanatory framework, it failed to elaborate its own political or institutional value system (see chapter 6 on this). Perhaps planners wanted to distance themselves from political controversy. Perhaps the virtues of planning as a political practice were more or less taken for granted. At all events, the justification of town planning was not based on sound theory. Reade (1987: 156) claimed starkly that planning in Britain had no theoretical basis. His analysis applies equally to Australia. 'Planning', he wrote, 'can only be justified to the extent that a case is made for intervention. Why, then', he asks, 'has the case not been made?' (Reade 1987: 156, original emphasis).

In this part and in Part II we explain the political crisis that has beset planning in Australia today. We argue that this crisis can be attributed, in part, to the absence of understanding among politicians, professionals and the broader public of the need for planning. Planning emerged in the 19th century to counter the social and environmental problems that free markets inevitably impose on capitalist societies. In a sense, planning's very success in reducing, if not solving, the problems caused by capitalist land markets has been its undoing. As time passes, people often forget what living in unplanned cities was like and question the need for planning and, more generally, urban governance. If we are to understand why planning first emerged and why it remains a vital part of any civilised society we must take a broader view of Australian history and its political institutions. It is to this broader perspective that we now turn.

The Australian Settlement

With the birth of the Commonwealth of Australia in 1901, a new balance was struck between capital and labour that sought to reduce socioeconomic differentiation by ensuring a minimum level of welfare for the working class. This has been termed a tradition of 'social liberalism' (Capling et al. 1998: 25). Kelly (1992) depicted this new national resolution as the 'Australian Settlement', a loose but powerful compact between the social classes and their political parties, which enshrined the ideals of justice, fair employment and security (see Box 2.2).

BOX 2.2 THE AUSTRALIAN WELFARE STATE

The main features of the Australian welfare state as it developed during the 20th century included:

1. a compromise between capital and labour following the bitter confrontations of the 1890s which resulted in what has been described as 'wage-earner defence' (Castles 1985), a form which both maintained wages and provided a minimal safety net for those who fell out of the workforce;

2. a politics of compromise termed 'arbitral pluralism' (Dunleavy & O'Leary 1987: 243–8). Through independent quasi-judicial bodies created to arbitrate basic disputes between capital and labour, the government was enabled to distance itself from such disputes—a stance which lasted until 1983 when the newly elected federal Labor government adopted a more engaged corporatist approach. Davis et al. (1988: 33) list 'arbitrator and distributor' among six functions of the state in Australia: 'The high level of state involvement in the adjudication of interests is a characteristic of Australian public policy'. The concept of 'arbitration', the supposedly impartial 'umpire's decision', to use a characteristically Australian sporting expression, can be found in many fields of public decision-making;

3. a powerful bureaucracy initially situated at the level of the colony—subsequently the state. Municipal government, while predating 'responsible' state government, was part of the colonial administrative infrastructure and, though locally elected, remains entirely subject to the command of state governments;

4. vested interests in land, many contending organised interests, rowdy and public debates in Parliament, public scepticism about bureaucratic (originally military) rationality, and the early entry of labour into the party political arena;

5. the centralisation of policy-making: the Commonwealth government has acquired a steadily expanding role in determining policy over a range of domains which were formerly the exclusive preserve of the states. These domains included education, public health and the environment. At the same time, particularly in the postwar period, the political executives of state governments throughout Australia have attempted to capture as much

control as possible over their bureaucracies with forms of 'corporate' or 'strategic' planning.

This model of welfare state was the target of much neoliberal dismantling during the 1990s. (We explain and discuss the neoliberal reform program in chapter 3.)

FURTHER READING

Wilson et al. (1996).

This compact was implemented in law and institutional action through a set of carefully integrated policy settings. These settings included immigration legislation that sought to maintain racial purity (the 'White Australia Policy'), high tariffs to encourage the growth of domestic industry, a system of wage arbitration that guaranteed fair incomes, the state provision of infrastructure and key economic lifelines (notably, energy, communications and transport), and finally a close alignment of foreign and trade policy with those of a superior, protective state (first Britain and later the USA). The reconstructive fervour in the immediate aftermath of World War II breathed new life into the Settlement; and, importantly, spatial planning now became a feature of the policy settings.

The main intent of these measures was to encourage the development of a 'raw' and underpopulated land in a manner that would guarantee security and a high standard of living for all within capitalist parameters. The errors of Europe—especially its class antagonisms—were not to be repeated here. Nor was America to be regarded as a perfect model for emulation. The exaggerated enthusiasm for individual freedom and the market in the USA was not to be adopted in Australia. The Australian nation, from its inception, was rather suspicious of the ideal of liberty; in too great a measure it seemed the antithesis of the national preference for cultural homogeneity, economic fairness, quietude and orderly development. In addition, there were other authoritarian political sentiments that resented, and occasionally resisted, even the modest ideals of British liberalism and liberal democratic governance. For example, a number of neofascist organisations thrived in Australian cities during the 1920s and early 30s, feeding on the social and political resentments of idle returned servicemen. D.H. Lawrence's (1923) celebrated novel *Kangaroo* provides a fictionalised, but highly accurate, account of these groups.

Regardless of its ethical and political shortcomings, the Australian

Settlement achieved a long period of political stability and economic security for many Australians, which lasted from Federation in 1901 to the 1970s. The period was marred by two convulsions—the Great Depression of the 1930s that brought unprecedented hardship to Australian cities, and the two world wars. The duration of the wars was marked by disruption and delay of city growth but, at the conclusion of each, new periods of rapid urbanisation were unleashed (Neutze 1977).

Fortuitous external conditions helped to ensure the strategy's success: from the end of World War II until the early 1970s, Australia shared in the 'Long Boom', which brought sustained economic growth to Western countries (see Box 2.3). While some observers (e.g. Kelly 1992) have debated the precise impact of the Australian Settlement on aggregate growth rates and national income levels, it cannot be doubted that the Settlement achieved a relatively fair distribution of wealth by international standards. More than this, it delivered a labour market characterised by consistently strong demand—much of which had to be met through immigration—and a high proportion of good-quality jobs (i.e. full-time and well-paid).

Full employment was the key dimension of the secure and confident outlook of many in Australia's cities: at the end of the Long Boom in 1971, less than 2 per cent of the labour force was jobless (Forster 1995). Manufacturing and agriculture thrived under the tariff regime. Industrialisation was concentrated in the capital cities and reinforced their primacy. Strong labour markets and rising real incomes benefited all, but especially the working class, which was able to gain increasing access to home ownership (with state encouragement) and other key consumption goods (e.g. motor cars).

BOX 2.3 WHAT WAS THE 'LONG BOOM'?

The term 'long boom' has been used by a variety of commentators to describe a period of sustained economic growth in advanced capitalist countries that followed World War II. A key international agreement between developed nations—signed at the Bretton Woods Conference in 1944—provided a sound basis for management of this growth by closely regulating currency exchange rates and national banking systems. This 'golden age' of growth ran out of steam in the early 1970s (Fagan & Webber 1994: 7, 10):

Until the early 1970s growth rates averaged nearly 5 per cent per year in OECD countries as a whole; there were downturns in 1954, 1957, 1967 and 1970, but rates of economic growth were reasonably well maintained throughout the fifties and sixties. Since then, three recessions have occurred throughout developed capitalist countries—in 1974–75 (an effect of the steep rises in oil prices), 1982 and 1991–92 . . .

The histories of individual countries, however, are not especially similar . . . The long boom or 'golden age' was not uniform. If we define a golden age as a period of rising and then of sustained high rates of growth, the golden age in [selected] individual countries has been:

USA   1956–1964
Japan   1956–1967
Australia   1958–1969.

FURTHER READING

Webber & Rigby (1996).

In short, both living standards and the quality of life were raised for the middle and lower orders during the period of the Settlement. Security was won for all, but at the cost of freedoms for many: the social order settled around the restrictive model of a nuclear family. Employment and housing markets, government policies and cultural mores reinforced the economic dependency of women on men and the exclusion of alternative household forms, especially those based on 'unconventional' identities (e.g. unmarried, gay) (Harman 1988; Murphy & Watson 1997).

During the 1950s and 60s, high rates of natural increase and immigration, combined with the mass consumption of motor cars and other new technologies, brought major economic, demographic and spatial changes to Australian cities (Neutze 1977). Cities grew explosively during the Long Boom (Table 2.1). Between 1947 and 1971, the proportion of Australians living in urban areas with at least 20 000 residents grew from 68.7 to 85.6 per cent (Wettenhall 1994: 4). In this same period, Perth expanded its population by a staggering 132 per cent, Adelaide doubled its size and Brisbane's growth was not far behind. Importantly, migration was a major contributor to capital city growth. Migrants from other parts of Australia were an important component of the growth in Adelaide, Perth, Hobart and especially Brisbane, but made no net contribution to the growth of Melbourne and Sydney. People born overseas were the most significant migrants in terms of numbers in all cities, and immigration played a key role in overall expansion of the capitals. Between 1947 and 1971, Sydney and Melbourne each received over 600 000 settlers from overseas countries.

The improvement in national economic fortunes was reflected in

Table 2.1 Components of capital city growth, 1947–71 (percentage)

| | Total growth | Natural increase | Net migration | |
			Aust. born	Overseas born
Sydney	65	45.4	−1.7	56.2
Melbourne	86	43.5	−0.07	56.6
Brisbane	90	40.4	26.4	33.4
Adelaide	105	32.5	12.5	54.9
Perth	132	36.3	15.5	48.0
Hobart	82	53.5	15.3	31.3

Sources: derived from Neutze (1977, table 3.3) and National Population Inquiry (1975, diagram IV.3).

increasingly rapid **suburbanisation** of working- and middle-class families (Neutze 1977). Inner-city areas were changed in part by slum clearance programs, and also by progressive waves of non-British settlers, initially refugees from Northern and Eastern Europe, followed by migrants from Southern Europe and, later still, people from the Middle East and Latin America. Urbanisation came to reflect broadly the classic model of succession, first identified in the 1920s by Chicago School urbanists, as Anglo-Celtic working- and middle-class families moved progressively from the crowded, inner localities to new middle and outer-ring suburbs comprised mainly of detached dwellings in low-density patterns. In turn, the new immigrants took the inner localities vacated by suburbanising households. Immigrants from Britain and Ireland tended to follow Australian households into suburban locations. Although criticised, even maligned, by a number of contemporary observers, suburbanisation realised important gains for working- and middle-class families: 'Life in the new suburbs—poorly designed or not—was infinitely better than the traditional working class areas . . .' (Forster 1995: 14).

The new suburban landscapes were characterised by (outward) social homogeneity and a uniformity of dwelling type, and they often lacked basic urban services for several, even many, years following their establishment. Nonetheless, Australians showed a strong preference for the suburbs, shifting to them in great numbers and in time transforming them into well-serviced, pleasant landscapes (Horne 1987). Also, jobs moved to the suburbs. Manufacturing industry increasingly shifted to suburban locations, spurred by expansion in production and encouraged by new transport technologies (notably, the introduction of trucks and road transport), which freed firms from dependence on the rail networks that clustered in inner-city and port locations (Frost & Dingle 1995).

In time, a distinct pattern of ethnic residential segregation emerged in the major cities, with the Australian-born and those from Northern

Figure 2.1 'Australian Settlement' Postwar suburbia built in the 1950s and 60s at Moorabbin in southeast Melbourne: single-family houses, backyards with Hill's hoists, sports ovals and pocket-handkerchief parks

Source: National Library of Australia, reproduced with permission from *The Age.*

and Eastern Europe settling in the expanding suburbs, while marked enclaves of Greek, Italian, Yugoslav and Maltese settlers emerged in the inner-city areas. Later, these enclave communities would mostly shift to suburban locations, and new immigrant groups, and later gentrifiers, took up the housing they vacated.

Culturally, Australian cities by the 1960s were characterised by a degree of social and even geographic homogeneity. In the suburbs, a class geography was evident, but the social and environmental differences were modest by international standards. Even the poorest often had adequate, if rudimentary, housing, while a majority of households enjoyed the benefits of home ownership, good and improving urban services, and high residential amenity. Forster (1995: 23) writes: 'by 1961, the percentage of households which owned or were buying their dwelling had reached 68 per cent in Sydney and 75 in Brisbane: some of the highest levels of home ownership in the world'.

The potential for many forms of cultural expression was limited, both by the dominant Anglo-Celtic mores and by a physical urban form that was overwhelmingly suburban. There was some open ethnic diversity, but it was contained in the inner-city enclaves of certain national communities. Critically, racial diversity had been consciously limited and suppressed; Aborigines had been greatly reduced in numbers and were largely ignored, and the White Australia Policy had prevented the settlement of non-European migrants in any numbers. Thus, given that economic diversity had also been limited by the Settlement, the Australian metropolis of the Long Boom was quite different from its North American equivalent. In the USA, economic inequalities were severe and often overlapped with cultural differences, producing marked residential segregation and pockets of extreme disadvantage ('ghettos'). Moreover, Australian inner-city areas never declined to the extent that US equivalents did, and Australian CBDs maintained their economic pre-eminence long after the decline of North American 'downtowns' (Mees 1998).

A fortuitous combination of national policies (the Australian Settlement) and international conditions (the Long Boom) reinforced the love affair between Australians and their cities. With few interruptions cities grew and their inhabitants acquired a quiet confidence that rested on two main pillars: economic security and social stability. What role did Australia's urban policy frameworks play in shaping the cities of the Long Boom?

Australian urban policy

In Australia, planning values and those of the Australian Settlement shaped the thinking of the wartime Labor government and occasionally became explicit in the writings of far-sighted reformers like H.C. Coombs and Oswald Barnett. Barnett and his fellow reformers, W. Burt and F. Heath (Barnett 1944: 8), talk about reconstruction, meaning: social security for all, the absence of poverty and unemployment, equality of opportunity, better housing and no slums. Barnett refers to the gulf that separates those who want to return to the old order and those who desire the planning of a better order:

> Some may fear an attempt to regiment the people according to a rigid Fascist plan. Our purpose is just the opposite. The State must make the necessary provision to enable each citizen to fulfil his or her own particular individual talents to the uttermost.

In 1945, L.H. Luscombe of Melbourne, writing under the pseudonym of 'Veritas', boldly outlined the postwar reform hopes in his book *Australia Replanned* (Barnett contributing an introduction). Luscombe wanted nothing less than a comprehensive national planning program that would repair the environmental and social damage caused by economic depression, world war and unfettered markets. By embarking

The Curtain Falls

The Curtain Rises

"Evicted"

"The Dawn"

Figure 2.2 In his reformist tract *Australia Replanned* (1945), L.H. Luscombe provided imagery that dramatically contrasted the evils of free market capitalism with the virtues that would flow from social democratic planning. In these pictures 'the curtain falls' on the evil of eviction for non-payment of rent (a common fate of the poor in prewar Australia), while 'the curtain rises' on a new dawn of social democratic prosperity and civility

Source: Luscombe (1945).

on comprehensive economic and spatial planning, Australia would usher in 'a new dawn' of natural abundance and shared prosperity (Figure 2.2).

Decades later, Hugh Stretton echoed these sentiments—spatial planning, for him, was the foundation of social democratic improvement. Stretton explicitly appealed to Rawlsian philosophy in identifying the functions of government that urban planning should serve. He observed that 'city planning can't really be separated from general economic policy' (Stretton 1970: 2). His analysis contains a host of specific recommendations on how planners might manage the land market (Stretton 1976: 237–42):

> Land and housing should be traded in managed markets, with public agents operating wherever possible as competitive rather than monopolist suppliers, and using their tougher powers sparingly, under legal and political safeguards. They should work to distribute land and housing

first, money second; but both equitably. Their dealing should aim to make owner-occupation of houses, workshops, small shops and other smallholdings as secure and widely available as possible, at prices as close as possible to building costs; and to make absent ownership and business investment in land as such less attractive than productive investment in building, manufacture, commerce or services. Most of the unequalizing type of capital gain and rent-taking from property should cease.

Gordon Stephenson, joint author (with Alastair Hepburn) of Perth's first metropolitan plan (1955), published a thoughtful essay linking the rise of town planning to the compassionate philosophy of observers, both radical and conservative, of societies racked by capitalist greed, economic depression and war (Stephenson 1995).

Urban policy and regulation was slow to develop, and it was not until after World War II that a set of explicit town and country planning regimes emerged at the state level. Throughout the 20th century, Commonwealth and state governments tended to shape the growth and character of cities through indirect means, such as housing, taxation and financial policies, immigration schemes, and the provision of social services and infrastructure (Forster 1995).

This is not to imply that the course of urbanisation was left simply to be determined by economic growth cycles and market forces: on the contrary, the 'shadow' urban policies of colonial administrations, and later Commonwealth and state governments, provided a strong guiding hand in the development of cities. For example, the involvement of colonial, and later state, administrations in the provision of infrastructure (e.g. transport, sewerage and water) grew with time and was an important influence on the growth and nature of urbanisation. In addition, the states provided education, health and welfare facilities on the basis of explicit physical planning principles that increasingly favoured residential suburbanisation (Troy 1995). In time, also, municipalities came to regulate health and housing standards, and in the postwar period began to adopt town planning as a regulatory function (though not always willingly).

At the federal level, the Labor government during World War II became strongly inclined towards central intervention for purposes of reconstruction. The Commonwealth government accepted responsibility for housing policy, and especially for low-income housing. The most important federal housing initiative was the long encouragement given to home ownership as a means of securing a general level of economic and environmental welfare for working-class and middle-class Australians. To do this, the government deliberately made home ownership an attractive, not to say compulsory, tenure form for most households through a range of financial and institutional policies, thus encouraging the process of low-density suburbanisation that has shaped Australian city development, especially since 1945 (Frost & Dingle 1995). The taxation system was made to treat home ownership favourably, and interest rates were made attractive to Australians through a variety of controls and schemes. The 'Great Australian Dream' of homeownership was very much an aspiration encouraged by the state.

At the conclusion of World War II, the Commonwealth government established a housing compact with the states—the Commonwealth State Housing Agreement (CSHA)—which encouraged the growth of the small but significant public accommodation sector. This agreement provided for loans from the central government to the states for the erection of housing for low-income families (Neutze 1978). The loans were made conditional upon each state legislating to enable it to control throughout the state rental housing projects, slum clearance and town planning (Harrison 1974).

Public housing was established and administered largely by the states, while the Commonwealth provided large amounts of funding for this purpose. The establishment of a public housing sector was intended to reduce housing poverty in the large cities and extend the earlier slum clearance efforts of the states. State housing provision became an important influence on urbanisation: the South Australian Housing Trust, for example, built over 30 per cent of the new houses constructed in Adelaide during the 1950s and 60s (Forster 1995). The public stock was usually established in large, new estates, often close to new suburban factories on the urban fringes. In the inner cities, pockets of slum clearance produced several high-rise housing estates, mostly in Melbourne and Sydney.

Poorly maintained urban environments were designated 'slums', the solution to which was demolition. The Commonwealth Housing Commission coordinated 'slum clearance' with the cooperation of the states. The Commission considered slum clearance to be a major part of its housing program. Designated 'clearance areas' were defined as those places needing extensive demolitions and replanning, including inner-metropolitan localities such as Carlton (Melbourne) or Woolloomooloo (Sydney). Large areas of towns were to be replanned to fit the 'town plan'.

As was noted, the CSHA was used by the Commonwealth to encourage the development of formal town and country planning systems at state level. Although its introduction was not always received with enthusiasm by the private sector and conservative political interests, town and country planning in Australia began with many of the same hopes evidenced in other, antecedent planning systems in developed countries, most especially in Britain (see Cullingworth 1964). Town and country planning, according to the Minister introducing Victoria's first Town and Country Planning Bill, was 'the science of guiding and shaping the growth of our cities, towns and rural areas'. The aim and purpose of town planning is 'the health and happiness of every member of the community'. The problems of land use on the periphery of cities he saw as being created by land speculators. Coordinated planning was necessary to ensure that these problems did not recur.

Eventually all the mainland state governments, apart from Queensland, produced master plans for their capital cities, while municipalities adopted zoning regulation to ensure orderly urban development and protect basic residential amenity (Neutze 1977). Some were more ambitious than others. Sydney's County of Cumberland Planning Scheme (1948) aimed to rationalise urban growth largely through the imposition of a greenbelt (Stilwell 1993a). Population growth and private sector resistance, however, undermined the plan and it eventually collapsed as 'owner-builders, developers, speculative builders and the Housing Commission vied with each other to cover the landscape with freestanding houses' (Spearitt & DeMarco 1988: 23). As Forster (1995) observes, the city master plans generally aimed to rationalise, rather than prevent or slow, the processes of suburbanisation, largely through negative controls which sought to improve the efficiency of urban development, while reducing the potential for major environmental pollution, large socioeconomic imbalances and natural hazards. More ambitious concerns—such as equity, service coordination, and the preservation of rural and scenic landscapes—were expressed, though always fiercely contested by the private development sector and by conservative political interests.

Thus, the social goals of planning were uncomplicated, centring on the rational control of suburbanisation and, to some extent, the preservation of CBD importance (see Moser & Low 1986). Planning was certainly about improving social welfare, but it was generally accepted that the entrenched processes of suburbanisation would achieve this goal if well regulated. It was assumed both by the states and by the business sector that public and private interests converged neatly in the goal of suburbanisation.

The election in 1972 of a new Labor federal government led by Gough Whitlam at the end of the Long Boom saw the first serious attempts by the Commonwealth to develop explicit urban policies. A Department of Urban and Regional Development (DURD) was established in 1972, with the intention of addressing increasingly evident problems in the major cities, notably declining access for low-income earners to housing, infrastructure and urban social services (Neutze 1977). DURD also undertook a bold program of decentralisation, attempting to direct settlement growth into newly designated regional centres. However, the Labor government was dismissed in 1975 by a conservative political coup, and DURD was quickly abolished (see Troy 1978). As we explain in chapter 5, subsequent Labor governments (1983–96) attempted, with limited success, to re-establish a national urban policy framework. Just as with the earlier Whitlam framework, these efforts were rapidly undone after the election of a new conservative government in 1996.

In summary, it can be said that in contrast to some overseas experience (e.g. that of Britain and Sweden) urban policy played a rather diminished, though appreciable, role in Australian urbanisation from Federation until the end of the Long Boom. But this is not to say that Australian governments failed to shape the process of urbanisation. Quite the reverse: governments, especially at Commonwealth and state levels, used a range of powers and activities to ensure the creation of cities that embodied the social democratic ideals that emerged in the aftermath of the Great Depression through much of the Western world. The goals were simple—the expansion of collective welfare through rational suburbanisation, and the protection of the most vulnerable through a modest public housing sector—but they were seriously pursued. Although the actual redistributive capacities of the state town and country planning systems that emerged after World War II were modest, the commitment to welfare was sincerely registered in spatial policies that sought to regulate, if not command, urban land markets for the common good. By the late 1960s, the Australian Settlement was manifested physically and socially in Australia's settlements.

Conclusion

Planning by a community of people through their local political institutions was the idea that legitimised government in the face of the immense sacrifices asked of peoples by their governments during World War II. It was the idea that inspired reconstruction. The planning of cities was an integral part of that great idea: planning for freedom. These ideas were absorbed, albeit imperfectly, into Australian society and were modified in accordance with Australia's local cultural mores and political traditions.

Inevitably the idea of planning contained contradictions which, in policy practice, would work to move society on to a new phase. The tension between collective planning and the freedom to assert difference was one. The gap between the idea and its realisation—a failure of adequate implementation—was another. Even more importantly, the contradiction involved in rescuing capitalism (with its associated class politics, turbulent dynamism, and democratic freedoms) through economic planning began to assert itself ever more forcefully. Capitalist organisational techniques and the information technology developed to fight World War II worked together to free capitalist production from territorial restraints. The impact of globalisation both as a story and as a reality began to produce profound changes in the Australian Settlement and in Australian planning. Chapter 3 brings these changes into focus.

Unsettling Australia: new forms of urban diversity

As we explain in chapter 2, Australians have long shown a preference for urban life. Today, the vast majority of Australia's 18 million citizens live in the coastal metropolises that ring the island continent (Table 3.1). In 1996, four out of 10 Australians resided in the two largest cities, Sydney and Melbourne. Cities provide the centre stage for Australian cultural and economic life.

In recent decades Australian cities have been transformed by a variety of local and international forces. Political observer Paul Kelly has described the 1980s as 'the end of certainty' for Australia. Another influential commentator, the social psychologist Hugh McKay (1993), believes that Australia, like other Western nations, entered in the 1980s an 'age of redefinition', a time when established sociocultural institutions became ambiguous for many Australians. Kelly agrees, observing that the 1980s witnessed 'the collapse of the Australian Settlement, the old protected Fortress Australia' (Kelly 1992: 13).

Kelly here stresses various axes of political-economic change that combined to enhance the *economic diversity* of Australian society. Just as profound were the deep transformations that enhanced Australia's *cultural diversity*. In particular, the shift in the 1970s from **assimilation** to **multiculturalism** as policy ideals in official immigration and cultural programs was a profound source of social change. Other sociocultural shifts deeply affected gender roles, sexual expression and identity, and spiritual and ecological values.

Kelly's story of the 1980s charts a transition, beginning in the 1960s, from a relatively stable, homogeneous society towards a more volatile, more sophisticated, and certainly more diverse social formation. It would be wrong to portray pre-1980s Australia as a simple, homogeneous

Table 3.1 Major city population size and state share, 1996

Capital city[b]	No.	% of state/territory popn[a]	% of national popn[a]
Sydney	3 881 136	63	21
Melbourne	3 283 278	72	18
Brisbane	1 519 994	45	8
Adelaide	1 079 112	73	6
Perth	1 295 092	73	7
Hobart	195 718	41	1
Darwin	82 232	45	0.4
Canberra	307 917	99	2
Capital cities	11 644 479	—	64

[a] Rounded to nearest tenth. [b] All capital city figures are for statistical divisions.
Source: Adapted from ABS (1998a, figure 1.4).

society. We do not completely go along with this perspective. In recent years historians and other social scientists have shown that Australia has actually been a rather diverse and complex society from the very beginnings of European settlement (e.g. Grimshaw et al. 1994). Badcock (1997: 244) reminds us that our 'cities have always been divided and, up to a point, spatially polarised'. Nonetheless, as Kelly points out, the pace of sociopolitical change in Australia grew rapidly from the 1960s, and especially during the 1980s. These rapid and profound changes undermined the bases of social certainty (both real and imagined) in Australia, and fostered new senses of diversity and insecurity in the popular imagination.

'Diversity' and 'insecurity' may mean different things for different people. Thus for some, admittedly large, sections of Australian society, the growing *cultural diversity* of the nation from the 1960s brought a greater sense of unfamiliarity and uneasiness. Paradoxically, for other social groups, this cultural diversification and its official recognition brought greater social and psychic security. By contrast, the growth in *economic diversity* in Australia during the 1980s—literally, a widening gap between rich and poor—introduced or deepened a basic material sense of insecurity across many different sociocultural groups.

This chapter will focus on the theme of diversity, exploring how Australian cities have become more diverse social formations in recent decades. Of course, there must be sensible limits to such an analysis: urban social diversification has taken a great many forms, and has occurred at a variety of geographic and cultural scales. Our discussion will highlight what are arguably the two most important forces for diversification in Australian cities: 'spatial polarisation', and 'cultural pluralisation'. Before we continue, it will be useful to define these two types of urban social diversity.

By 'cultural pluralisation' we mean a progressive shift in the social make-up of Australia towards a more complex, plural society. Importantly, our sense of 'culture' refers to more than simply the ethnic grouping or national affiliation assumed by individuals or communities. Here, a cultural form is simply the social expression of any human identity, including outlooks informed by racial, sexual, ethnic and gender differences (see Milner 1993). Cultural pluralisation therefore indicates a process of growing diversification in the social identities assumed by individuals and groups in Australia.

'Spatial polarisation' in broad terms is simply the geographic manifestation of extreme forms of social division. In this chapter, polarisation refers to the tendency of economic processes to widen the relative division between poor and rich localities. In short, polarisation means the spatial sorting of city dwellers into areas of relative privilege and disadvantage. Here spatial 'privilege' and 'disadvantage' can refer to social geographic differences that arise both from structural sources (e.g. employment, income, education) and from the qualities of particular places (e.g. environmental and social conditions, access to 'goods', proximity to 'bads').

The chapter is divided into four main parts. We begin by considering the political and social impacts of economic globalisation on Australia. After this we examine two major consequences of globalisation and associated social and cultural changes for Australia's cities: spatial polarisation and cultural pluralisation. Then we pause to consider whether the changes described have 'postmodernised' Australia's cities.

Globalisation and the rise of neoliberalism

The Australian Settlement, and its institutions, eventually broke apart for two main reasons. First, it collapsed under the weight of its own contradictions: Australia was always a more diverse society than the guardians of orthodoxy were willing to admit. A variety of unconventional identities were lived and explored outside the margins of social acceptability. Eventually, many 'unconventional' social groups, such as gays and lesbians, disabled people and Aboriginal Australians, were able to resist and eventually shift outwards the boundaries of acceptability that had long labelled them abnormal or even criminal. The second major force that undermined the Australian Settlement was the set of shifts associated with the imposition of a new global economic order. The political-economic changes wrought by globalisation profoundly altered people's relationship to work, governments and their environments. In examining these broad shifts, we turn first to the process of globalisation which, although largely political-economic in character, tended to reinforce many of the cultural changes that were unsettling the social patterns that had been set after World War II.

The end of the Long Boom

A global economic crisis began to grip advanced capitalist nations from the early 1970s. The Long Boom that had begun to ease the painful memories of the Great Depression now foundered. The world economy slowed down as the demand for mass-produced goods began to be satisfied. The slowdown was punctuated by sudden economic shocks, notably the oil crises of 1974 and 1979. The Bretton Woods agreement (Box 2.3) broke down in 1971, triggering an enormous growth in international financial transactions. This caused the growth of a 'large global investment pool of financial capital which could be circulated rapidly through a highly-connected international banking system' (Fagan & Webber 1994: 19). The new surge of footloose investment capital fuelled a rapid expansion of world trade. Also, industrial capital in the form of transnational corporations began to free itself from the West and flooded into developing nations. Information technology developed to control distant industrial plants and to manage money markets. Globalisation emerged as a technological and political-economic system of control, integrating far-flung cities, regions and even nations in new international production and financial exchange systems (Wiseman 1998).

This crisis contributed to a series of deep political shifts. In the developed world, Keynesian interventionism seemed unable to control the parallel growth of unemployment, inflation and interest rates ('stag-flation') and was increasingly discredited. 'New Right' or neoliberal interests took advantage of the sense of crisis to promote radical political reform programs that sought to dismantle much of the welfare state's institutions and regulatory regimes (Box 3.1). The Soviet empire, for all its political, social and environmental deficits, had provided a working model of planning. When it began to collapse finally in the late 1980s under the weight of its economic and political legitimacy crisis, there were hopes that a new form of democratic planning might evolve from the ruins of centralised Soviet-style communism. This was not to be. New and shaky postcommunist governments were often seduced by the simplistic, free-market reform programs advocated by some Western economists and the many right-wing 'think tanks' that had been set up with vast funds by big business all over the world to

BOX 3.1 NEOLIBERALISM OR 'ECONOMIC RATIONALISM'?

The 1970s saw the revival of a political ideology that many people had regarded as dead and discredited. Going by a variety of names—neoliberalism, libertarianism, New Right ideology, free market radicalism, and, in Australia, economic rationalism—this theory is basically the laissez-faire doctrine of the 19th century. Neoliberals argue for a radical program of deregulation and privatisation that reduces the influence of governments in people's everyday lives. The market is presumed to be the best mechanism for organising economic affairs and even social life.

Neoliberalism is also a model of economic growth, and its prestige in the USA coupled with the apparent economic success of that country's growth policy in the past 20 years have led to its adoption worldwide. As a growth model, the neo-liberal argument is that unconstrained growth (i.e. growth of business activity measured by GDP) will be maximised by policies that facilitate specialisation in products in which the country has at least a potential comparative advantage. According to the model, these products are revealed only by the working of unfettered markets and free trade.

The key neoliberal thinkers have been Friedrich von Hayek, an Austrian economist, and Robert Nozick, an American political theorist who provided a moral justification. Neoliberalism has come to dominate right-wing thinking, and has swept aside alternative right perspectives, such as conservatism, which allowed a greater role for the state in society. But what has really been remarkable about neoliberalism is the extent of its influence on centrist and left-wing thinking, evident, for example, in the enthusiasm of the Australian Labor Party since the early 1980s for deregulation and privatisation. Michael Pusey's widely cited 1991 book *Economic Rationalism in Canberra* tells the story of neoliberalism in Australia, charting its rising support among key bureaucrats, politicians and academic thinkers from the late 1970s. It is important to note, however, that while neoliberalism has been influential in Australia, Britain, the USA, Canada and New Zealand, other developed and developing countries have shown much less enthusiasm for this ideology. Indeed, Michael Pusey, a severe critic of neoliberalism, recently described it as the 'English-speaking disease' (Bennetts 1997).

promote neoliberalism (Self 1993: 64–5). These movements and forces produced the well-known ideological reform trilogy of competition, deregulation and privatisation.

Importantly, globalisation was not simply an economic phenomenon. The globalisation of right–wing political theory—under various guises (Box 3.1)—was intimately related to the broader process of deregulation that created the global economy. The economic globalisation described above was only partly attributable to technological advances, such as the development of computerised telecommunications that could link distant places and, more importantly, far-flung national economies. It was the explicit neoliberal policy agendas pursued aggressively, especially by states in the English-speaking world from the late 1970s, which encouraged global economic integration. The liberalisation of trade and financial markets was a deliberate policy choice of governments, admittedly under pressure from powerful lobby groups, rather than simply a 'natural' response to technological changes.

As Wiseman (1998) reminds us, globalisation is a social creation and not an inevitable outcome of technological change. This fact, however, has rarely been acknowledged by the policy elites in national governments and international financial institutions (e.g. IMF, World Bank, OECD), which have promoted economic integration and neoliberalism as part of the one inseparable reform package. In the English-speaking world, especially, governments have used simplistic interpretations of globalisation to legitimise radical free market reform agendas and to foreclose on debates about policy alternatives. However, most mainstream political discussions of 'globalisation' tend to oversimplify what is a complex and by no means inevitable set of shifts within divergent policy systems (cultural, economic, social, ecological). The (erroneous) view that globalisation and its socioeconomic consequences are inevitable and therefore unstoppable was captured in Margaret Thatcher's famous dictum: 'There is no alternative!'

The ending of the Long Boom affected Australia more profoundly than most other Western economies. Australia was a peripheral player in the postwar Western economic system, and was heavily reliant on trade with a few key nations, notably Britain and the USA. The emergence of global economic crisis in the 1970s, combined with the refocusing of British trade on Europe, delivered a series of shattering blows to the fragile 'developed dependency' which Australia had cultivated, and benefited from, during the Long Boom. As trade problems mounted, unemployment and inflation soared, and pressure rose dramatically on state finances. In a climate of 'stagflationary' recession, neoliberal politics gained ascendancy, offering bold and readily packaged 'solutions' to the twin crises that had beset the state and the economy.

From the late 1970s, the protectionist-interventionist pillar of the Australian Settlement was replaced by neoliberalism as the new national economic orthodoxy (Kelly 1992). Although successive Commonwealth and state governments have differed in their zeal for many aspects of the neoliberal agenda, there has been, since the late 1970s, a broad consensus between the major political blocs—Labor and the Liberal/ National coalition—on fundamental aspects of trade policy and state financing (Argy 1998). In short, neoliberal prescriptions for trade liberalisation, public fiscal conservatism and deregulation have become new articles of faith in the Australian political system. In a recent assessment of these changes, Bell (1997) has described the neoliberal project in Australia as the 'ungoverning of the economy'. His book catalogues the progressive deregulation of most areas of public intervention since the early 1980s.

The impact of globalisation on Australia

Two decades of neoliberal economic restructuring have not solved the problems of the Australian economy. Since the 1970s, successive Commonwealth governments have imposed a broad-ranging set of reforms on the Australian economy whose main features have included: rapid tariff reductions; deregulation of the finance sector; cutbacks to budget outlays; wage restraint strategies; and restrictive monetary policies (Stilwell 1993b). While not necessarily amounting to a coherent reform program, these policy changes have helped to reshape the economy dramatically, encouraging a substantial decline in primary (rural) and secondary (manufacturing) industries while promoting growth in the tertiary (services) and quaternary (information) sectors (Fagan & Webber 1994).

The consequent shift in employment from manufacturing to services has been dramatic: between 1981 and 1991, manufacturing employment contracted by 16 per cent, while jobs in finance, property and business services grew by 48 per cent (Badcock 1995). Service employment has continued to grow rapidly: between 1993 and 1996, the amount of jobs in the finance, property and business services sector grew by more than 24 per cent (ABS 1993, 1998b). Victoria, a traditional heartland of Australian industry, lost 170 000 manufacturing jobs between 1974 and 1996, 'while financial, property and business services doubled in size' (Buxton 1998: 3). Deindustrialisation has occurred at a rapid rate in some localities and regions. In another key industrial centre, Adelaide, employment in manufacturing dropped from 20.7 per cent of the city's workforce to 15.3 per cent between 1991 and 1996 (Hamnett et al. 1997: 30).

To survive in the new competitive global scenario, some manufacturing sectors turned to exploitative labour practices, notably the use of outworkers based in private homes. By 1999, it was estimated that the textile, clothing and footwear industries employed over 300 000 outworkers, outnumbering factory-based workers by about 15 to 1 (Australian Council of Trade Unions 1999). Wages were often very low—sometimes as little as $2 per hour—and working conditions were often substandard. Migrant women from non-English-speaking backgrounds were heavily represented among the outworking workforce. Many outworkers were drawn from the newer ethnic enclaves located in middle and outer-ring suburbs of the larger cities.

Nationally, service employment growth has been concentrated at two extreme ends of this labour submarket, producing mostly high-paid and low-paid jobs, with not much in between. This growth has also been characterised by a high proportion of insecure, non-full-time positions. As with other labour submarkets, 'class capacities'—the education, skills and social resources that vary with individual and household wealth—largely determine the assignment of people to good and bad service jobs. Thus, for McGregor, service employment growth is recasting existing class divisions, this time based on a new division of labour between (1999: 6, emphasis added)

> . . . the *Underclass Infoproles*, the new information proletariat which has been locked out of the century by lack of the skills/education/resources that the new era demands, and the *Global Surfers*, the techno-elite who surf the Internet, the computer world and post-industrial society with consummate ease.

While one may question the use of the term 'underclass' in the Australian context (see Box 3.2), McGregor's colourful depiction of the new class divide within the service sector illustrates how globalisation and technical change have produced new forms of socioeconomic difference in Australia.

How has industrial and labour market restructuring affected the distribution of employment and wealth in the 1990s? First, unemployment levels continue to be high, while the quality of working life has deteriorated generally. In 1997 the Australian Bureau of Statistics (ABS) believed that 1.9 million Australians were either unemployed or underemployed. The underemployed included many of those who were forced to take part-time or casual jobs because full-time employment was not available (Australian Council of Social Services 1997).

For those employed, there has been an increase in income dispersion during the 1980s and early 1990s (McKay 1993). Although Australia's dispersion in earnings has been relatively mild in international terms, the trend has been appreciable and has set the course for further inequality (Figure 3.1). Between 1980 and 1991, for example, this shift left men in the lowest earnings decile 7 per cent worse off, and men in the highest decile 5 per cent better off (Badcock 1995). Average earnings have also been under pressure, falling in real terms during the 1980s decade. One economic reason for women's rising workforce participation during this period has been the need for households to offset declining income. Many women have been drawn into the highly casualised service sectors, where the wage levels and work conditions have progressively declined in recent years. Wealth has also become more unevenly distributed. Long reports that, between 1993 and 1999, 'the share of the nation's wealth held by the richest 10 per cent . . . increased by almost five percentage points, from 43.5 per cent to more than 48 per cent . . .' (Long 1999: 21).

The broad middle class, the social bulwark that benefited from and supported the Australian Settlement, has been undermined by structural adjustment: incomes are under pressure, savings and assets are eroding, jobs are increasingly insecure and degraded, and access to declining public services increasingly threatened. Indeed, the very survival of the middle class seems at stake. McKay (1993) estimates that between 1976 and 1992 the middle class shrunk from 65 per cent of households to just 40 per cent.

Below this, things are very much harder. Blue-collar employment has been devastated, and the number of households without a bread-winner has increased dramatically. By 1992, it was estimated, for example, that 600 000 children lived in families with no employed parent (McKay 1993). These economic adjustments have combined with demographic and social changes to produce new and growing forms of disadvantage. Social deprivation has become concentrated among single-parent families, which have burgeoned since the mid-1970s (ABS 1998b). Women head most single-parent families (Mullins 1995).

Recent analysis by King (1998) shows that poverty has increased markedly in Australia since the early 1970s. The ABS estimated that up to 3.4 million Australians were living in poverty in 1995/96: of these, about one million were children (Wright 1998). Citing analysis by the National Centre for Economic and Social Modelling (NATSEM), the *Canberra Times* (15 June 1998: 10) reported that:

> In the early 1980s, the richest working families in Australia were earning eight times as much as the poorest. By the mid-1990s they were earning 13 times as much. Worse, the poorest families had actually gone backwards, earning 26 per cent less in real terms . . . than they had a decade earlier, while families at the top end of the salary spectrum were earning 22 per cent more.

Working poverty has also grown. A separate study by NATSEM found that low-wage workers comprised 16 per cent of the workforce in 1994,

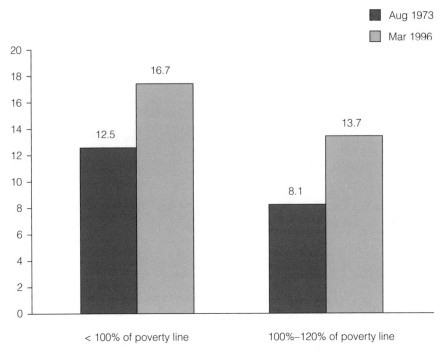

■ Aug 1973
☐ Mar 1996

Figure 3.1 'The 'very poor' and 'rather poor': August 1973 and March 1996. This figure measures the rate of poverty among 'income units' in Australia. As King (1997: 3) explains, 'The **income unit** is the basic population grouping used in the analysis. It is a restricted definition of a family, which is best described in terms of the four forms it can take: a couple without dependent children, a couple with dependent children, a sole parent with dependent children, and a single person'.

Source: King (1997: 6).

up from 11 per cent in 1986. According to NATSEM, the typical low-wage worker is 'female, poorly educated, married and works part-time' (*Canberra Times* 29 July 1998: 5). The numbers of men on low wages, however, had grown rapidly since 1986, and by 1994 comprised 49 per cent of the low-wage workforce.

If we accept, for now, Kelly's thesis that the 1980s witnessed the demise of the Australian Settlement—what were the effects of this dramatic shift for Australia's settlements, in particular, the main cities? The short answer is that the complex set of far-reaching, and sometimes contradictory, changes that Kelly and McKay refer to have engendered a profound transformation of the Australian urban system, and the entirety of these shifts cannot be adequately captured here. As stated in the introduction, this necessarily selective account of recent urbanisation in Australia will focus on two important dimensions of change: spatial polarisation, and cultural pluralisation.

Spatial polarisation and locational disadvantage

We have noted that the political and economic shifts associated with globalisation have produced deep changes to Australian society: notably, a relentless worsening of social polarisation. This growing disparity between social groups has been mirrored geographically, evident in deepening spatial divides between privileged and disadvantaged communities (Fincher & Wulff 1998). The clearest trend in polarisation has been a growing residential segregation by income within major cities. Spatial segregation is also worsening when measured by other 'social well being' factors—including occupational grouping, educational attainment, language skills and employment status (Hunter & Gregory 1996; Moriarty 1998; Walmsley & Weinand 1997). Badcock notes that a combination of economic shifts and the contraction of government activities has produced new 'pockets of hard core poverty and inequity within the cities' (Badcock 1995: 196). Australia has not been alone in this regard: a general trend towards worsening economic polarisation was also evident in Britain and the USA during the 1980s and early '90s (Hall 1998).

In the major cities, globalisation has produced new geographic patterns of employment and industry (Stilwell 1993b). While all of Australia's major cities are now dominated by service employment, the effects of this structural adjustment in workforce patterns have been spatially uneven (O'Connor & Stimson 1995). The benefits of globalisation have been concentrated—though not exclusively—in some parts of the larger mainland capital cities, especially Sydney (Stilwell 1997). Long reports that 'Some 30 000 new jobs have been created in Sydney's CBD during the past 5 years [McGregor's (1999) 'information age elite' or 'Global Surfers'], 20 000 of them going to professional women . . .' (Long 1999: 21). The growth of this new group of affluent professionals and service workers has been mirrored by a concentration of wealth and economic opportunity in better-off residential areas, such as Sydney's North Shore and harbourside localities. Brain (1999: 217) notes that the average household income in Sydney's high-income areas was 45 per cent greater than that of the poorest major group—the provincial towns—in 1986, and 83 per cent greater in 1996. By 2004 the difference will be 100 per cent.

Historically, manufacturing was concentrated in the larger centres—

Sydney and Melbourne and, to a lesser extent, Adelaide. Between 1986 and 1996 all three cities experienced large declines in their share of national manufacturing employment, while Brisbane and Perth made gains in this labour market sector. Stimson et al. (1998) characterise parts of Sydney, Melbourne and Adelaide, plus the smaller industrial urban areas (e.g. Wollongong, Newcastle, Geelong) surrounding these cities, as Australia's 'rustbelt regions'. The urban 'rustbelt' has experienced the devastating consequences of industrial restructuring, in the form of high levels of unemployment, deep social dislocation and a slowing in population growth. Badcock (1994) describes such cities— especially the regional centres—as 'stressed out communities'. Apart from social dislocation, environmental malaise is another source of stress. In Newcastle, for example, the management of abandoned industrial spaces—or TOADS (temporarily obsolete abandoned derelict sites)— has emerged as a significant environmental planning problem (Dunn et al. 1995).

The explosive city population growth rates witnessed in the Long Boom have subsided. Extremely high rates of population and dwelling growth, however, are still recorded in smaller, emerging urban centres, often at the fringes of the major metropolitan areas and along the coastlines of New South Wales and Queensland. Nationally, the centre of gravity of urban growth has shifted to the 'sunbelt' states, Queensland and Western Australia. Badcock (1995: 199–200) writes: 'whilst Sydney and Melbourne grew by about 10 per cent between 1981 and 1991, the corresponding growth rates for Brisbane and Perth were 30 per cent and 27 per cent respectively'. While population growth has slowed dramatically in many declining or 'rustbelt' cities, metropolitan expansion has often continued in these same places through additions to dwelling stocks. In Hobart—'the capital of a State that has lost out in the globalisation stakes' (Long 1999: 22)—Graham (1994: 264) characterised city development through the 1980s and early 90s as 'explosion without growth'. As this author argues, stalled population growth and even economic decline do not necessarily restrict the rate of urban expansion, challenging traditional planning assumptions about the relationship between demographic shifts and changes in the built environment. In contemporary Australia, population growth is not a precondition for physical expansion in many towns and cities.

In the 1980s, new population growth centres emerged— Queensland's Sunshine and Gold Coasts, for example, grew by approximately 70 per cent in the decade to 1991. Between 1991 and 1996, seven of the 10 fastest-growing urban centres were located in Queensland. Again, the Sunshine and Gold Coasts featured prominently, and here some urban centres recorded growth rates well in excess of 100 per cent (ABS 1998c). However, as Walmsley and Weinand (1997) observe, Brisbane and Perth may have the fastest population growth rates among the major cities but it is Sydney and Melbourne that have benefited most from new levels of capital investment stimulated by economic globalisation.

Unemployment rates differ substantially within metropolitan regions, producing mosaics of work advantage/disadvantage. In 1996 unemployment rates in Brisbane ranged from as high as 12.8 per cent in Redcliffe City to as low as 6.5 per cent in Pine Rivers Shire. In Melbourne, Dandenong City (14.5 per cent) had nearly three times the unemployment rate of Boroondara City (5.5 per cent) (ABS 1998b). Generally, unemployment has remained highest and most concentrated in suburban localities that have hosted significant manufacturing activity, especially the proletarian tracts developed in the 1950s and 60s. Forster (1995) reports, for example, that in working-class suburbs such as Melbourne's Broadmeadows and Adelaide's Elizabeth, nearly a quarter of the labour force is unemployed, and many others have been discouraged from seeking work altogether.

Forster cites research by Daly et al. (1993), which has shown that in some deprived working-class suburbs of Sydney, notably in the outer west, youth unemployment was about 50 per cent in the early 1990s. More recently, Lagan (1999) reported a youth unemployment rate of 36 per cent in northern Adelaide. Moreover, as Badcock (1995) explains, cutbacks to government social services and infrastructure provision have affected such communities disproportionately, adding a further source of disadvantage to structural sources of deprivation. In particular, many outer-suburban working-class communities have had to bear the dual burdens of high structural unemployment and 'locational disadvantage' arising from poor access to jobs, services and infrastructure.

Locational advantage refers to the set of social, economic and environmental benefits that location confers on households (Maher et al. 1992). The growth of income polarisation has converged spatially with a deepening segregation between locationally advantaged and locationally disadvantaged suburbs. Increasingly, 'disadvantaged people and disadvantaged localities tend to go together' (McDonald & Matches 1995: 17), though there are some important exceptions to this trend. Locationally advantaged areas, such as the coastal suburbs of Sydney and Perth, and the 'access-rich' inner areas of most cities, have increasingly become the preserve of higher-income households (Moriarty 1998). Conversely, lower-income households have increasingly concentrated in the locationally disadvantaged middle and outer suburbs that often lack infrastructure, social facilities, public transport access and employment (Stilwell 1993a). Some residential areas on urban fringes of major cities have emerged as particular concentrations of locational disadvantage, because jobs and services have generally begun to suburbanise more slowly than residential populations (Moriarty 1998). Environmental quality is another dimension of locational advantage/ disadvantage. Locationally disadvantaged suburbs may be characterised by poor environmental amenity and low access to valued natural resources, such as waterways, parks and undulating landscapes.

Locational advantage/disadvantage is not determined simply by distance from a city's CBD (Maher et al. 1992). Urban fringes, for example, also contain pockets of wealth, including exclusive housing estates that are richly endowed with high-quality physical and social infrastructure. Nor is there always a neat convergence between wealth and locational advantage (Maher 1994). It is important to recognise that 'locational advantage' is in fact a composite variable comprising a range of environmental and social 'goods' that a household or community may desire access to. Thus, some relatively affluent outer-urban communities may be characterised as locationally disadvantaged if certain key social and physical 'goods' are emphasised. In such areas high-quality schools, community facilities, shops and parks may be supplied in abundance (sometimes supplemented through private means), but residents may still have to travel considerable distances to workplaces or to other important social and cultural facilities (see National Housing Strategy 1992: 37). As with poorer outer-urban communities, 'public' transport may be limited to an infrequent and expensive private bus service. While wealth obviously reduces the impact of locational disadvantage for a household in such an estate, its members may feel isolated from key places of social and economic interaction. In less privileged fringe communities, these problems are obviously compounded both by strained household finances and by inadequate levels of social and physical infrastructure.

In some instances, disadvantaged places can be highly localised, nested within relatively privileged and well-resourced areas (Maher 1994). One example of this 'nested disadvantage' is highlighted (McDonald & Matches 1995: 18) by:

> . . . the situation of people living in high-rise public housing in the inner parts of Melbourne and Sydney. These people have affordable housing in areas of high amenity, but a relatively poor immediate environment and standard of housing, limited employment opportunities and little freedom to move . . .

Moriarty summarises how changes to locational attributes and spatial segregation have overlapped in recent years (1998: 217):

> Higher income/work status households are increasingly concentrated in the inner suburbs. Conversely, low-income households, once over-represented in the inner city, now comprise a growing share of outer urban residents. This trend was less important when jobs and services were more rapidly suburbanising and car costs were more affordable. But there are now signs . . . that suburbanisation has reached its limits. Throughout Australia, the burden of car ownership and operation is rising, which will be a particularly serious problem for outer suburban residents.

Murphy and Watson (1997) show how the relentless economic restructuring in Sydney since the 1970s has deepened existing patterns of suburban residential segregation. Their analysis charts the emergence of 'two Sydneys', revealed as a worsening socioeconomic divide between an affluent north and the increasingly deprived outer-western and southwestern suburbs. The shifting geographies of several key socioeconomic variables demonstrate this widening gulf (Figures 3.2 and 3.3). By 1999, unemployment, single-parent families and public housing were relatively concentrated in the outer western and southwestern suburbs; while in the north, median incomes were higher and the proportion of workers employed in well-paid service occupations was greater (McGregor 1999; Morris 1999). Moreover, the north had locational advantages, being well supplied with social services and physical amenities.

Rising housing costs have imposed additional hardship on middle-income and working-class households in middle and outer-suburban communities (National Housing Strategy 1991). Mowbray (1994: 93) notes that there has been a 'long term decline in housing affordability, with those on low and moderate incomes most affected'. Many such households in the later 1980s and early 90s experienced the loss of their homes through mortgage foreclosure (Forster 1995). While recent declines in both housing prices and interest rates have lessened affordability pressures generally, many households—particularly sole parents, single aged people and low-income private renters—continue to experience various forms of housing poverty. Housing poverty can be both economic and environmental: the 'housing poor' may both struggle to pay rents or mortgage costs while also being forced to accept inadequate and/or substandard forms of accommodation.

People living in public housing have been adversely affected by changes in government policies (Troy 1996a). Funding for public housing has been declining since the 1970s, and the sector has been

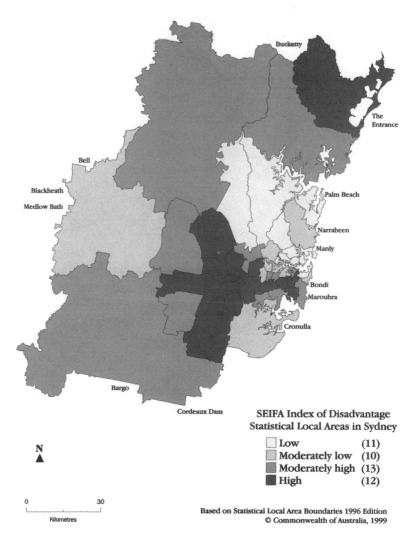

SEIFA Index of Disadvantage
Statistical Local Areas in Sydney

☐ Low   (11)
▨ Moderately low   (10)
▨ Moderately high (13)
■ High   (12)

N
▲

0   30
Kilometres

Based on Statistical Local Area Boundaries 1996 Edition
© Commonwealth of Australia, 1999

Figures 3.2 (above) **and 3.3** (right) Measuring patterns of socioeconomic disadvantage in Sydney and Perth, these figures are based on the ABS Socio-Economic Indexes For Areas (SEIFA) that were derived from 1996 census data. SEIFA summarises a variety of social and economic variables, including low income, low educational attainment, high unemployment and jobs in relatively unskilled occupations. Both maps reveal significant socioeconomic differences between statistical local areas (SLAs) in both cities. The contrasts are marked at the regional scale. In Sydney, high disadvantage is concentrated in SLAs in the south (e.g. Campbelltown) and west (e.g. Fairfield). Perth's disadvantaged areas are mainly in the south (e.g. Armadale) and the north (e.g. Stirling)

Source: Australian Bureau of Statistics.

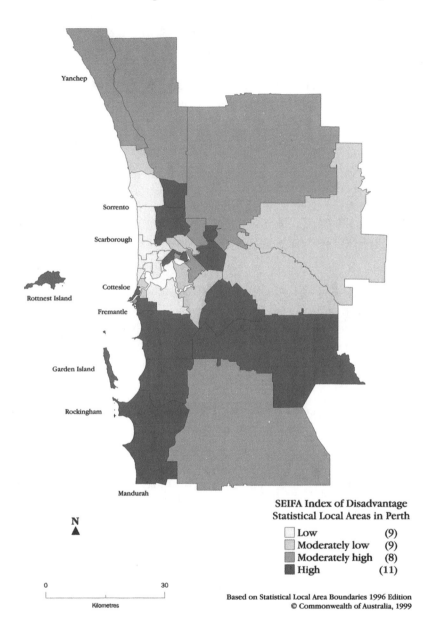

Yanchep

Sorrento

Scarborough

Rottnest Island

Cottesloe

Fremantle

Garden Island

Rockingham

Mandurah

N
▲

SEIFA Index of Disadvantage
Statistical Local Areas in Perth

☐ Low   (9)
▨ Moderately low   (9)
▨ Moderately high   (8)
■ High   (11)

0   30

Kilometres

Based on Statistical Local Area Boundaries 1996 Edition
© Commonwealth of Australia, 1999

increasingly downgraded, accommodating rising numbers of welfare-dependent households (Peel 1995). In Sydney and Melbourne, the concentration of public housing stock in inner-city high-rise, and suburban low-rise, estates has meant that such localities have emerged as new poles of deprivation (Fincher & Wulff 1998). New forms of absolute disadvantage have also surfaced, notably homelessness and poverty in the private rental sector. In 1997, the Council to Homeless Persons estimated that at least 147 000 people had sought help in the previous year with emergency or urgent shelter needs from accommodation services and welfare groups (Fannin 1998: A4). Nationally, homelessness grew by 11 per cent in one year between 1996/97 and 1997/98. The highest rate of homelessness is in Victoria, where 49 000 people sought emergency accommodation in 1998 (Brady 1999). Many went without shelter overnight.

Declining affordability in the private rental market has placed increasing economic stress on many poorer households (National Housing Strategy 1991). Within this housing submarket new evidence is emerging of highly localised concentrations of poverty in marginal accommodation forms, such as caravans and other relocatable dwellings. A study by Mowbray and Stubbs (1996) found that long-term residency in inferior dwelling types—especially caravans and factory built 'manufactured homes'—has been rapidly growing during the 1980s and 90s. For these authors, the conversion of short-term stay caravan parks to long-term 'manufactured housing estates' has in many instances produced low-quality residential environments, characterised by poor dwelling design standards and a lack of physical and social infrastructure.

At the opposite end of the income spectrum, households in relatively wealthy suburbs have tended to weather the economic storm comfortably. In addition, the growth of producer services and allied functions has helped sustain the employment bases of CBDs, while the surge in high-paying jobs in such sectors has boosted the demand for housing in inner-city areas. This development intensified the process of **gentrification** that had emerged in the major cities in the 1960s. Gentrification of inner suburbs has caused steep rises in property values and displaced significant numbers of lower-income households, many of whom have had to relocate to poorer-serviced fringe suburbs. Badcock (1995) argues that the steepening of price gradients for residential land in the major cities has caused a redistribution of real wealth from outer-area to inner-area home buyers. Polarisation *within* the inner suburbs has worsened due to: first, gentrification, which has replaced poorer private renters and home owners with richer households; and second, a rising proportion of residents on older public housing estates who are poor and/or dependent on welfare (Fincher & Wulff 1998). This fact has led Forster (1995: 99) to describe, with a hint of irony, the inner suburbs as 'typifying the economically polarised diversity and disorder of the postmodern era'.

In summary, a combination of economic shifts, public sector cutbacks and changes to household composition have produced a new geography of segregation in Australian cities. The inner suburbs have become more polarised, between gentrifiers and public housing tenants, while in the middle suburbs 'the patterns of large-scale segregation inherited from the long boom remain, and the differences between rich and poor areas appear to be growing' (Forster 1995: 112). In the new and growing outer suburbs the picture is mixed, and includes both poorly serviced concentrations of low income earners and relatively wealthy, well-resourced communities.

BOX 3.2 'URBAN GHETTOS' IN AUSTRALIA?

There is compelling evidence to show that spatial segregation by income is worsening in Australia's large cities. But does this signal the Americanisation of the Australian city? In the early 1990s, the economists Hunter and Gregory (1995) argued that 'urban ghettos' of unemployment were appearing in Australian cities. Their views attracted a lot of media attention and produced many colourful headlines about the supposed 'ghettoisation' of Australian cities. In 1995, the *Sydney Morning Herald* trumpeted: 'Urban ghettos loom as social divide widens' (29 April). An earlier study (Falk et al. 1993) had begun to stir the pot of public concern by suggesting that an urban 'underclass' existed in Australia's cities. If their problems were not tackled, the report intoned ominously, 'social disruption, often manifested as "violent riots", [would] result' (Falk et al. 1993: viii-ix). Birrell (1993) added a cultural characterisation, alleging that ethnic ghettos had begun to form in the larger Australian cities.

Can terms such as 'ghetto' and 'underclass' be used meaningfully to describe spatial disadvantage in the Australian context? We, with many Australian urban scholars (e.g. Whiteford 1995), argue that they cannot. Both terms are drawn from debates that describe social phenomena that are unique to cities in the USA. Moreover, both terms have been subjected to heavy theoretical and social criticism in overseas debates, though this is rarely acknowledged when they are translated, often uncritically, to the Australian context.

The term 'ghetto' actually originated in Europe during the Middle Ages to describe the areas of cities in which Jews were forced to live. The term was adopted in the USA by sociologists of the Chicago School from the 1920s to describe economically deprived urban communities characterised by ethnic or 'racial' homogeneity. As Jary and Jary (1991: 258) note: 'The term is often used in emotive, racist and imprecise ways'. It is certainly misleading to describe Australia's lower-income urban areas as ghettos, as they do not have the cultural homogeneity implied by the term. Analysing the concentration of Vietnamese people in Sydney, Burnley et al. (1997: 39) point out that 'The Vietnam-origin population is itself heterogeneous. It therefore cannot be suggested that the Vietnam population in Sydney is ghettoised'. Levels of residential segregation between indigenous and non-indigenous Australians may have risen in recent decades (Hunter 1996), but this process has not produced the sorts of entrenched pockets of disadvantage described as ghettos in the USA. The use of the term in Australia therefore only serves to stigmatise poorer urban communities.

'Underclass' is an ambiguous and even insidious term. Overseas, the term has been used by some commentators to describe a mixed group of social and economic 'underperformers', including the working poor, single mothers, migrant workers and people from certain ethnic origins (Jary & Jary 1991). It is often assumed that the underclass is 'welfare-dependent'. Hovering around the term is the implied accusation that members of the underclass are unable to attain economic independence largely because of their 'personal shortcomings'. Not surprisingly, the term has been controversial and it is arguable that its use serves only to cloud, not clarify, understanding of how social disadvantage arises.

As Forster (1995) and Stilwell (1997) both note, this heightened segregation, while of great concern to contemporary Australians, is still nowhere near as severe as that experienced in North American and European cities. Australian cities contain neither gated communities of the rich nor impoverished ghettos of the poor. (Since the 1980s exclusive, even walled, new residential developments have appeared in Australia, but local governments have generally not permitted the gating of suburban streets.) But there is a climate of popular opinion that increasingly believes that such horrors will inevitably appear in Australian cities (Peel 1995)—partly encouraged by the colourful and misleading proclamations of some urban researchers in recent years (Box 3.2). Moriarty, adopting a more moderate though deeply concerned tone, forecasts a worsening of social and spatial polarisation, unless 'changes in Federal government policies soon occur . . . such as reversing the trend towards globalising the Australian economy' (Moriarty 1998: 217).

Cultural pluralisation

The demise of the Australian Settlement also saw a far-reaching cultural pluralisation in Australia that can be attributed both to the growing social heterogeneity of national (especially urban) society and to the struggles of social movements to liberate non-orthodox identities and social values. Another cause of pluralisation has been technological change, especially the rise of global media and popular cultural forms that have increased social understanding of, and tolerance for, new identities and values. Heretofore, Australian social conventions and culture had been moulded by a rigidly Anglo-Celtic outlook (Horne 1987). This outlook tended to suppress the underlying (if often invisible) heterogeneity of Australian society, and established a social orthodoxy that was heavily derivative of British, and later American, culture.

The white, Christian nuclear family was the cellular form of the society idealised by the Australian Settlement. This family form was certainly an important social reality, and indeed remains so. In mainstream culture, however, this ideal tended to fix a set of restrictive and culturally enshrined identities—the breadwinner father, the housewife mother, and dependent children. Deviations from this social form were discouraged by social convention and cultural practice, and even forbidden in law. For some, including the conservative postwar establishment, this ideal was threatened by continuing (if sporadic) immigration from countries of non-British culture. This source of social change was therefore regulated through the interdependent policies of White Australia and cultural assimilation. By the 1950s, even after significant postwar intakes of (European) refugees, outside observers were struck by the outward homogeneity of Australian society, as expressed in the relatively uniform social geography of its cities.

In the 1960s, everything began to change. As with other Western countries—especially the USA—this decade unleashed the political energies of alternative and non-orthodox cultural forms, often through urban social movements linked ideologically, and even organisationally, to international struggles and debates. In the main, the claim was not for the radical overthrow of all social conventions—though this ideal was advanced by some progressive currents—but for official toleration of, and cultural respect for, non-orthodox identities and lifestyles. Politically and institutionally, the feminist movement had the greatest early successes, evidenced in new legal guarantees of sexual equality in most areas of social life and in the growing participation of women in public realms. In all Western countries, decades of feminist thinking and activism have been central to the processes of cultural pluralisation that have produced what Fincher and Jacobs term 'Cities of Difference' (Fincher & Jacobs 1998). Other identity causes were pursued, including those of gays, youth, Aborigines, disabled people, and non-Anglo-Celtic peoples and cultures. In time these struggles met with varying degrees of success, measured by increasingly broad legal protections against cultural forms of discrimination in administrative realms and in civic life.

The emancipation of suppressed identities both coincided with and encouraged profound changes to the composition of Australian households. Average household size has fallen dramatically in recent decades: from about 3.25 persons in 1976 to around 2.6 persons in 1996 (ABS 1998d). The decline in household size is attributed to two main social changes: the growth in single-person households, due largely to the ageing of the population; and falling fertility rates.

One important source of household change was the passage of the Commonwealth *Family Law Act* in 1974, which made divorce easier and long-term marriage less likely. Combined with rapid demographic changes, notably falling fertility rates and population ageing, these changes undermined the concrete and ideological significance of the nuclear family. Between 1971 and 1996, couples with dependent children declined significantly as a proportion of all family units (Table 3.2).

Multicultural cities

A major source of cultural pluralisation was the demise in the 1960s of the White Australia and assimilation ideals in Commonwealth law and policy. Although initiated without much official enthusiasm, this change created the way for a deeper commitment to more inclusive immigration and cultural policies by later Commonwealth and state governments. By the 1980s, multiculturalism was the new ethical-political ideal guiding the immigration policies of the Commonwealth and the social objectives and functions of the states (Castles et al. 1988).

Multiculturalism encouraged, and was in turn reinforced by, an increasingly diverse migrant profile. Importantly, the major new immigrant groups of the 1980s and 90s were drawn from non-European countries, especially Southeast Asia. Just as importantly, the size of the migration intake ensured that this was a major source of cultural and social change. Australia recorded during this time some of the highest immigration levels in the developed world. Burnley (1998: 49) writes: 'Between 1947 and 1991, 5.3 million immigrants . . . settled in Australia, and in 1991 Australia had more immigrants per capita than any other country in the world except Israel'.

An important internal source of cultural differentiation has been the rapid rise in the population of indigenous Australians. Between 1961 and 1997, the number of indigenous Australians grew from approximately 100 000 to around 333 000 people (ABS 1997a). This growth has reflected in part the reassertion of Aboriginal identity in recent decades, a cultural awakening that has encouraged more people to identify themselves officially as indigenous Australians.

How has cultural pluralisation manifested itself in the cities? We examine in turn two important manifestations of cultural change: shifts

Table 3.2 Family type (%), 1976–96

	1976	1981	1986	1991	1996
One parent with dependent children	6.5	8.6	7.8	8.8	10.1
Couple only	28.0	28.7	30.3	31.4	40.2
Couple with dependent children	48.4	46.6	44.8	44.4	34.7
Couple with non-dependent children	11.1	10.0	10.9	9.5	8.8
Other	5.9	6.0	6.2	5.9	6.3
Total	100.0	100.0	100.0	100.0	100.0

Source: ABS (1998d: 146).

in the ethnic composition of cities; and the emergence of new spaces of sexual identity.

The tendency of most immigrants to settle in the state capitals, particularly Sydney and Melbourne, meant that Australian cities became far more ethnically diverse during the 1970s and subsequent decades. In this time Sydney overtook Melbourne as the major recipient of overseas migrants. As Burnley (1998: 49) tells us: 'Prior to 1971, Melbourne had been the primary immigrant city in Australia, but after that date more immigrants settled in Sydney'. Overseas migrants were increasingly drawn from 'non-traditional' sources. All state capitals, with the exception of Hobart, registered significant rises in the proportion of residents born in 'non-traditional' migrant countries between 1971 and 1996 (group 2, Table 3.3). Conversely, the proportion of residents born in 'traditional' sources of migration, the UK, Ireland and New Zealand, declined in all capitals during the same period (group 1, Table 3.3).

Murphy and Watson summarise some of the consequences of this shift for Sydney (1997: 4–5):

> Sydney was once a city predominantly of British immigrants; now people come from all over the world. For most of its first two hundred years of white settlement Sydney looked to Europe and the United States, while now its orientation is shifting to East and South-East Asia . . . In many ways Sydney has become a more attractive and diverse city to live in, particularly in comparison with many other large cities in the world . . . Yet even its much-vaunted attractions mask an underbelly of poverty, pollution and prejudice . . .

Overall, the most significant cultural change has been the emergence of new ethnic geographies in the cities (Burnley et al. 1997). Newer, non-European immigrant groups have made their presence felt by developing distinctive 'enclaves'. Importantly, these new and visible ethnic communities have established themselves outside the inner sub-urbs, which have proved increasingly expensive and spatially restrictive for immigrant groups (though some significant concentrations of new

Table 3.3 Percentage of overseas-born in state capitals, 1971 and 1996, grouped by origin

	1971			1996		
	Group 1	Group 2	Total	Group 1	Group 2	Total
Sydney	10.0	14.8	24.8	7.4	23.3	30.7
Melbourne	9.5	17.9	27.4	6.7	22.4	29.1
Brisbane	9.6	6.4	16.0	9.9	10.4	20.3
Adelaide	15.2	12.9	28.1	11.3	13.4	24.7
Perth	18.5	13.2	31.7	16.4	15.9	32.3
Hobart	7.2	5.6	12.8	6.0	5.8	11.8

Notes: Group 1 denotes people born in the UK, Ireland and New Zealand; Group 2 denotes people born in overseas countries other than the UK, Ireland and New Zealand.
Sources: ABS (1971; 1997b).

settlers have occurred in the public high-rise estates). Burnley (1998) cautions us against making too much of this pattern of ethnic concentration. As he points out for Sydney, while there are certainly strong residential concentrations of *recent* immigrants, there is no evidence here of the enduring cultural segregation that is a common geographical feature of North American and European cities. Although there is a long history of ethnic enclaves in Australian cities, almost all have tended to be ephemeral in character.

Ethnic concentrations have developed in the proletarian and lower-middle-class suburbs of Sydney and Melbourne, joining earlier (European), postwar immigrant groups who had moved from the inner localities. In the northern suburbs of Melbourne, for example, Turkish and Lebanese immigrants have mixed with earlier settlers from Southern Europe: the area has an increasingly Mediterranean ambience, contrasting with its earlier Anglo-Celtic character. New migrants from Southeast Asia and South America have transformed other working-class suburbs, such as Footscray and Springvale in Melbourne. Typically, these localities contained tracts of cheap and public housing, and were also situated close to migrant hostels, the entry points for refugee groups, especially the Vietnamese.

One notable example of a new suburban ethnic enclave is Sydney's Cabramatta, a locality transformed by migrants from East Asia, especially Vietnam (Dunn 1993). In 1996, people born in East Asia and their immediate descendants comprised about 32 per cent of the population of Fairfield, the local government area in which Cabramatta is situated. Cabramatta's built environment contains a dense concentration of Vietnamese restaurants, shops, religious institutions and community facilities. While to the outside eye an enclave such as Cabramatta can appear economically vibrant, patterns of disadvantage lie just below the

Figure 3.4 Multicultural suburbia Fairfield in Sydney's west contains a juxtaposition of old and new cultural forms in Australian suburbia. In the foreground we see a small weatherboard house, typical of early 20th century suburban landscapes. In the background, the minaret of a mosque signals the arrival of a different culture (see Box 3.3)

Source: Nicholas Low.

surface. As Murphy and Watson (1997) note, unemployment in Cabramatta is very high among recent settlers, and many of the employed toil in low-wage occupations, such as outwork for clothing manufacturers (see also Burnley 1998 on this).

Such enclaves can be islands in a sea of ethnic diversity. Cabramatta, for example, is located in the culturally diverse City of Fairfield. In 1996, 'Fairfield had an overseas-born population of 97 203—53.5 per cent of its total . . .' (Morris 1999: 4). Fairfield's migrant population included significant numbers of people from Italy, Malta, Lebanon and the former Yugoslavia. Many other working-class suburbs in the major cities have developed highly complex ethnic compositions. In addition, recent influxes of wealthier migrants from Asia, notably Malaysia, Hong Kong and Singapore, have clustered in higher-income suburbs and exclusive inner-city residential developments.

While some Anglo-Celtic Australians may have ambiguous feelings about the new suburban enclaves, older ethnic areas of the inner cities have become places highly valued for their aesthetic appeal and consumption opportunities. Melbourne's CBD and inner suburbs, for example, contain a 'Chinatown', a 'Saigon-town', a 'Little Italy' and a

'Greek Precinct'. Sydney and the other major state capitals have their 'ethnic showpieces'. Anglo-Celtic and other Australians flock with foreign tourists to the restaurants, coffee shops and cultural facilities that lend these areas their distinct ethnic ambience.

However, these new ethnic consumption spaces tend to be frequented by wealthier, Anglo-Celtic Australians. Their working-class compatriots are far more likely to meet recent and earlier migrants in their workplaces, schools and home neighbourhoods than in these consumption playgrounds. The suburbs are not always happy theatres of multicultural diversity. Tensions have risen as certain non-European cultural facilities have appeared in suburban landscapes. Mosques, for example, have attracted opposition from local residents and municipalities (Murphy & Watson 1997). For many, the mosque and the Hindu temple are disturbing motifs of the cultural pluralisation that is 'threatening' Australia's European social order.

BOX 3.3 CHALLENGING THE CULTURAL 'OBJECTIVITY' OF PLANNING

In October 1998, the ambiguity that many public officials, including planners, feel for new religions and their facilities was brought to light when a Sydney council refused permission for a former Christian church to be used as a mosque on planning grounds (Marsh 1998). The Bangladesh Islamic Centre that had wanted to establish the mosque lodged an appeal against the decision in the New South Wales Land and Environment Court and lost. The property had long been zoned for church use but the court ruled that a mosque was not a church.

Leaders of state ethnic groups expressed dismay at the ruling. The president of the Local Government Association observed that 'Decisions should be made on objective planning grounds. There must be no notion of racism in the decision-making process and everybody should think proactively about potential problems of reuse of church premises so solutions can be found before the event' (1998: p.5). The problem, it seems, was not racism, but a definition of planning 'objectivity' that had been framed around a cultural outlook that no longer reflected the social reality of metropolitan Australia. (In chapter 7 we consider the arguments made by postmodernists and others for a radical broadening of planning's cultural outlook.)

It is important not to exaggerate the extent of ethnic tension and conflict in Australia. Many observers have remarked on the success of multiculturalism in Australia, which by international standards is a relatively diverse, tolerant and peaceful society. Doubtless, part of the reason for this success has been the official encouragement given to multiculturalism, and the increasing regulation of social tolerance, by successive Commonwealth and state governments. The cities have become culturally heterogeneous environments, and most Australians have generally welcomed the new diversity of buildings, monuments and recreation spaces. As Murphy and Watson (1997: 28) have observed for Sydney, 'Despite sporadic conflicts over some sites there is no doubt that by the mid-1990s a far greater tolerance towards different architectural and cultural sites had developed'.

New gay terrains

Next to ethnic diversification, other new forms of cultural plurality have registered a presence in Australian cities. One important new cultural terrain to emerge has been the spaces and places inhabited and frequented by openly gay people (mostly men) in inner-city Sydney and Melbourne. Australia's most visibly gay terrain is centred on inner-Sydney's Oxford Street and adjoining residential areas, notably Darlinghurst and Paddington.

During the Australian Settlement era, homosexuality was forbidden in law, vilified in culture, and often violently suppressed (Thompson 1986). Since the 1970s, gays and lesbians have benefited from rising social tolerance (if not always acceptance) and the gradual replacement of legal proscriptions by new, codified guarantees of freedom from discrimination. Wotherspoon (1991: 211) depicts the gay and lesbian communities in Australian cities as an 'urban sub-culture' which has participated in the renewal of several inner-city residential and commercial districts. Many gays, especially male couples, have participated in the gentrification of inner cities (Wotherspoon 1991). Sydney's Oxford Street is both a focus of gay and lesbian gentrification and a centre of consumption and cultural activity by homosexual people. Over time, gender differentiation has emerged within inner-Sydney's homosexual landscape. According to Seebohm (1992: 4), 'A visible lesbian enclave now exists in the Glebe, Leichhardt and Rozelle areas'.

The Oxford Street area has been the stage for what is now arguably Australia's premier cultural spectacle, the Gay and Lesbian Mardi Gras. By the late 1990s the Mardi Gras was drawing the biggest crowd of any event in Australia, while highlights of the parade were attracting high ratings on prime-time television. In 1999 approximately 600 000 spectators lined the parade route. Clearly, Mardi Gras has come to represent both the political assertiveness of gays and lesbians in Australia

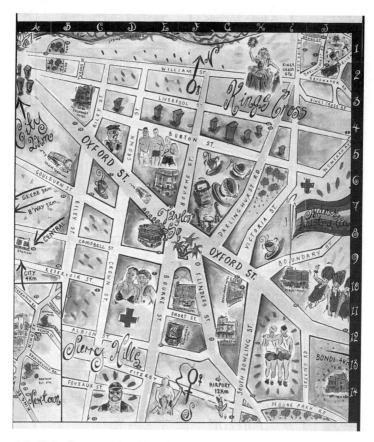

Figure 3.5 This Gay and Lesbian Sydney map marks out an area of inner Sydney that has become the focal point for accommodation, services and entertainment used by homosexual people. The surrounding residential areas, such as Surry Hills, contain substantial numbers of gay and lesbian residents. The map also indicates a 'satellite' gay and lesbian community in Newtown. Maps such as this should be read as a claim to identity rather than a territorial 'fact'. They are an important example of the public assertion of difference that has been a part of cultural pluralisation in Western cities. This map serves both as an assertion of spatial presence and as a source of information about services and entertainment for gay and lesbian people who do not live in the area

Source: Travel Maps Australia, Sydney.

and the growing acceptance of this identity form by 'mainstream Australia' (Murphy & Watson 1997).

However, the increasing cultural visibility and official acceptance of gays and lesbians must be considered against a backdrop of continuing, if often muted, animosity and violence towards homosexual people. Tolerance for the open expression of homosexual identity seems lowest in the suburbs, though this is undoubtedly where the bulk of gay and lesbian Australians live. Even in the gay heartland, Sydney's Oxford Street, this intolerance is expressed both through random acts of violence and frequent, if ineffectual, demonstrations against the Mardi Gras. Seebohm (1992: 8) has characterised Sydney's 'gay ghetto' as a centre stage of social tension—the point where 'Two ideologies, orthodoxy and heterodoxy [confront] one-another, symbolising a highly contested terrain'. While the Mardi Gras attracts enormous crowds, many come to watch rather than celebrate the event. Elements of the parade openly mock middle-class values, and the embers of social resentment towards gay assertiveness continue to glow in suburban and rural Australia.

New places and spaces: but are they postmodern?

The processes of cultural and economic diversification that we have described for the Australian city have been observed, to varying degrees, in most other Western urban systems. For many urban commentators these twin trends reflect a broader 'postmodernisation' of societies and places. Increasing urban cultural plurality coupled with worsening economic polarisation are often regarded as hallmarks of the so-called 'postmodern city'. Other associated features of the postmodern city have included the fragmentation of employment and retailing patterns, the progressive privatisation of public space, and the rise of new consumption/entertainment spaces for elites, ranging from 'urban spectacles' (e.g. city theme parks, harbourside redevelopments) to grand, enclosed shopping malls (Forster 1995; Hall 1998).

The popularity of postmodernism in urban studies has been associated with an increasingly common assumption among theorists and policy-makers that Australian patterns of urbanisation have copied those in North America. In many analyses, it is assumed that recent global forces—especially economic globalisation, the postmodernisation of culture and rising migration flows—have reshaped Australian cities along North American lines. In this view, such 'universal' shifts are creating postmodern cities and places in Australia. Special attention is given to the host of consumption 'theme parks' (multipurpose shopping malls, harbourside playgrounds) that are the familiar elements of the postmodern urban landscape. Others see the rise of the postmodern city in more pessimistic terms, fearing that Australian cities will one day mirror the chaos and social division of Los Angeles (Peel 1995). Both in Australia and overseas, urban analysis has centred on the alleged importance of the global postmodern city in the developed world and increasingly in developing countries. In fact, while the idea of the global city may have international significance, it hardly has universal relevance. Such analysis is usually fixed on the major national metropolises most integrated in the global economy, and therefore has limited relevance to most of Australia's large towns and cities.

While American urban analyses have had an enormous international influence in recent decades, some Australian commentators have questioned their relevance to cities in this country. In 1991, the American urban commentator Garreau (1991) pronounced that North Sydney qualified as an 'edge city' in his widely read—and to many, 'sensationalised' (Freestone 1996: 28)—depiction of new consolidated centres on the fringes of North American cities. Garreau was later taken to task by the Australian commentators Freestone and Murphy (1993, 1998), who urged a more cautious and empirically based assessment of the relevance of new American urban concepts. Certainly, as Freestone (1996: 29) has shown, the suburbanisation of economic activity in Australia's major cities 'has seen a breakdown in the classical monocentric urban form and a shift toward multi-nucleated metropolitan regions'. However, in contrast to the decentralising trends evident in the USA, the CBDs of Australia's major cities have continued to play a key economic role, with the larger centres benefiting from strong growth in the financial services sector (O'Connor et al. 1998: 208). Moreover, while the edge city in the USA is a 'free-wheeling, uncoordinated artifact of speculative capital', many of the new suburban economic centres in Australian cities have been consciously shaped by state and local planning policies (Freestone 1996: 29).

Burnley & Murphy (1995) argue that there is a need for 'culturally sensitive analyses' of metropolitan restructuring in Australia. Such analyses should subject international urban concepts to critical empirical scrutiny in Australian contexts. In this vein, Mees (1998) upbraids Spearitt (1995) for depicting Australian urban morphology as highly derivative of North American forms. A similar criticism can be levelled at other commentators who have predicted that the Australian city will inevitably follow the downward spiral of US urban areas into a dystopia of class and racial polarisation. Watson (1993), for example, musing on the dysfunctional social trends in US cities, comments that 'Australian cities are on a similar trajectory and that . . . the Los Angeles scenario may not be far away' (in Peel 1995: 40). While such comparisons are easily made, and appear to confirm—at least superficially—a widespread sense of cultural Americanisation in Australia, they are not easily substantiated. Indeed, as Mees (1998) shows, close empirical examination still yields evidence of profound differences in the patterns of urbanisation in Australian and North American cities. Australia's relatively strong state and local planning systems (at least historically) have produced distinct urban forms that have avoided many of the worst problems evident in North American cities. As Troy (1996b) argues, 'sprawl'—i.e. uncoordinated, unplanned metropolitan growth—has not been a feature of Australian urbanisation in the postwar era (though this fact has been largely ignored in recent urban commentary).

Certainly, as we mentioned above, recent decades have seen dramatic shifts in the cultural make-up and even the morphologies of Australia's major cities. The phenomenon of cultural pluralisation is one instance of this. However, most of these changes have mirrored North American trends only at the broadest scale: on closer inspection the shifts in culture, economy and physical make-up that have changed Australia's cities are unique and not simple reflections of a new universal postmodern model of urbanisation. As Forster (1995: 64) observes, 'our cities, though they have been subject to the same forces of global restructuring and technological change [do] not conform to the pattern suggested by North American writers'. There is no evidence to suggest that the much-discussed North American postmodern urban phenomena have been reproduced in Australian cities. The edge cities that so preoccupy urban commentators in North America in the 1990s have not emerged in Australia, any more than the inner-urban ghettos and abandoned CBDs on which urbanists focused attention in the 1970s.

Large suburban shopping malls, enclosing a variety of functions—retailing, entertainment and even social services—are certainly proliferating and growing in Australia's cities. Allan (1998: 121) reports that:

> Melbourne's Chadstone is now Australia's largest self-contained shopping centre with around 141 000 m² of lettable space. Other large malls include Parramatta in Sydney (127 000 m²) and the Marion Centre in Adelaide (109 000 m²). None of these, however, approach in size and character the giant 'postmodern' malls of North America, such as Canada's West Edmonton Mall (483 600 m²) and the Mall of America near Minneapolis (390 600 m²).

Overseas urbanists (e.g. Shields 1989) have categorised such 'mega-malls' as postmodern for two reasons: first, they often contain significant cultural activities, such as large theme parks that mimic external 'realities' (i.e. beaches, forests) and reproduce historical artefacts in fantasy form (e.g. Columbus' ship *Santa Maria*); and second, they function as superregional hubs of thriving suburban peripheries. On these criteria, Australia's suburban malls are hardly postmodern. Moreover, they are embedded within urban contexts that differ markedly from their North American counterparts.

Importantly, one reason that a number of commentators (e.g. Burnley & Murphy 1995; Freestone & Murphy 1998; Mees 1998) have advanced to explain the dissimilarities in North American and Australian patterns of urbanisation is the relative strength of urban and regional planning in this country. While the merits of planning outcomes may be debated, it is important to recognise that spatial regulation in Australia during the postwar era helped to shape cities that depart in significant ways from the North American model. Moreover, some analyses (e.g. Forster 1995; Mees 1998) would suggest that this influence has been socially beneficial, helping to prevent the emergence of many of the problems commonly associated with US cities in particular, such as severe sociospatial polarisation, ghettoisation and inner-city decline. In spite of its many critics, planning does seem to have been a beneficial influence on the development of our cities. (We return to this issue of 'planning and its critics' in Part II.) Since the 1980s, however, the focus of Australian urban policy, and planning in particular, has been shifted away from the *regulation* of markets towards the *facilitation* of economic development.

Conclusion: the prospects of cities

In this chapter we have traced in broad outline two of the important contemporary and recent forces for diversification in Australian cities. Can the dual patterns of social polarisation and cultural pluralisation be sustained? What are the policy and political consequences of these shifts?

Many commentators—including us—see social polarisation as a bad thing, because it deepens social injustice and weakens the bonds of social cohesion. Conversely, cultural pluralisation is generally to be welcomed as it enhances the possibilities for individual and collective expression, while also enriching the social and physical resources of any society. Unfortunately, there is evidence in contemporary Australian society that some people and groups are confusing these two *morally* distinct patterns of social change. In short, cultural diversification is sometimes seen as the cause of the worsening socioeconomic divides in cities and regions that we have surveyed.

To a large extent, this confusion can be blamed on the attitudes towards social and economic change taken by governments and business elites. Both groups insist that globalisation is an unstoppable process: the best we can do is shield the vulnerable from its worst consequences.

In this climate, resistance to globalisation and neoliberalism seems little more than 'noble hopelessness' (Wiseman 1998: 24). With so many avenues for political action and policy alternatives seemingly blocked by the globalisation juggernaut, it is perhaps not surprising that some sections of the community have pointed an accusing finger at new ethnic groups and newly liberated cultural practices as the causes of 'social demise'. The cultural counterreaction draws deeply from the wellsprings of social resentment filled by rising levels of economic insecurity and hardship. Observing these events, the sociologist Pusey remarked that (Bennetts 1997: 1):

> Insecurity is biting hard into Middle Australia and generating . . . social resentments . . . The ethnic lobby has been particularly concerned . . . because it is uncomfortably reminiscent of the situation in 1930s Germany and some parts of Europe today where politicians were able to focus resentment caused by genuine social and economic hardship onto racial scapegoating.

Is planning implicated in this confusion over the origins and consequences of social change? Cultural and economic security depends on the opportunities for a balanced, healthy life. This ideal has never seemed more distant to a large group of urban Australians for whom degraded forms of work, inaccessibility to services and environmental stresses are pressing realities.

As we explained in chapter 2, economic and social security were key values guiding postwar planning, both in Australia and in other parts of the developed world. However, as we show in the chapters that follow, planning has lost its way and appears unable to meet the challenge of satisfying these values. There are several reasons for this. First, it could be argued that the value set of traditional planning was too narrow and undervalued, or simply ignored cultural freedom and ecological sustainability. As these values became increasingly prized in Australia from the 1960s, planning for many seemed at best irrelevant and at worst an oppressive 'establishment' institution that made no space for cultural diversity and cared little about the environment. In short, this form of critique implies the need for a larger planning enterprise, which can encompass a broad range of social values and ensure their reflection in the built environment. Second, the institution of planning in recent decades has been under pressure from neoliberal interests, which have sought to reduce its political and institutional power. This form of critique is quite distinct from the first; neoliberal planning reform seeks the reduction, not the expansion, of public intervention in the land economy. Here one set of 'values'—free market liberalism—is prioritised over all others.

In chapters 4 and 5 we survey the evolution of Australia's planning systems in the past few decades in the wider context of the changing nature of urban governance and the new political economic agendas that have sought to reshape urban regulation. Our aim is to show how the transformation to planning within urban governance has both reflected and contributed to the changes in cities described in this chapter.

4 Changing urban governance I: social democratic managerialism

The changes in Australia's cities noted in chapter 3 have been wrought by many political, economic and social forces. Among these—and of special relevance to planning—is the changing way in which the cities are governed. In this chapter and chapter 5 we outline the changing nature of urban governance in Australia, drawing attention especially to the much-debated transition from managerialism to neoliberalism (Considine & Painter 1997).

To talk about 'urban governance' is to cast a very wide net—too wide to deal with fully within the confines of one book, let alone a couple of chapters. But planning can no longer be adequately thought of as a discrete package involving regulation aimed at avoiding conflict between land uses. As we argue in chapters 1 and 2, planning is part of urban governance. We postpone consideration of the theoretical issues surrounding planning until Part II when we place the discussion in a broader conceptual context. Here we try to bring into focus the general currents of change that reshaped urban governance within the different states and territories of Australia in recent decades.

This chapter has six main parts. We first explain the concepts that we use to describe the development of urban governance at state level in Australia. We address the form of governance we term 'social democratic managerialism'. Then we go on to explore in greater detail the key aspects of this form of governance. These are: reform of the public service to provide greater political control, a new relationship between economic planning and the management of urban development, and a desire to reform local government. Finally we explore how planning is situated within social democratic managerialism.

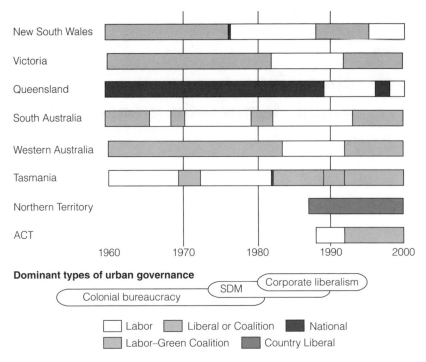

Figure 4.1 Parties in office in state governments, 1960s to '90s

Concepts of urban governance

Global material realities and currents of thought act on urban governance through a particular mixture of Commonwealth, state and local government institutions. The relationship between the three levels is not a simple hierarchy or set of nested boxes—federal containing state, state containing local. The principal actors in urban governance are the states, and it is important to keep in mind the flux of state politics and changes of the political party in office (see Figure 4.1).

The formal authority of state governments over the local governments within their jurisdiction is well known. But states sometimes assert their authority over local government and sometimes do not. On occasion, local governments can mobilise substantial community power, especially when they collaborate across local boundaries. The Commonwealth government, even though it wields formidable power over state budgets and through various provisions of the Australian Constitution, does not generally intervene directly in how state governments organise urban governance. However, there have been occasions when the Commonwealth has acted directly to influence urban policy, and

colonial bureaucracy began to break down and gave way to its recon-
ceptualisation—as urban management (see Paterson 1977: 13).

Paterson correctly observed that the blueprint plan implemented by
'planning' professionals was ill-equipped to achieve the necessary coordination of urban service delivery. But Paterson failed to problematise
the political sphere, viewing planning as a purely technical matter of
employing the appropriate instruments of coordination. Planning is about
the interaction between the political and the managerial which forms the
sphere of urban governance—how the political tier steers the state
apparatus, to what end and with what instruments, and how the ends and
the instruments influence one another. In this and the next chapter we
describe how these relationships in urban governance changed from *social
democratic managerialism* (SDM) to *corporate liberalism* (CL).

Social democratic *governance* assumes that governments can steer the
local economy with the help of the apparatus of the state to deliver higher
living standards and social justice. But *managerialism* has come to mean a
particular kind of governance—one which draws heavily on the ideas of
neoclassical economics and the management of private sector corporations (see Box 4.1). The style of management is described by Yeatman
(1994) as 'post-bureaucratic': that is, allowing for greater integration of
policy development and implementation with 'learning' and 'feedback'
between the two. It thus encourages a much closer relationship between
ministers and bureaucratic chiefs and their departments—this coupled
with increasing use of the market as a coordinating mechanism within
public bureaucracies 'to make them more cost-conscious and reward
them for enhanced productivity' (Yeatman 1994: 291).

BOX 4.1 MANAGERIALISM IN QUESTION

The idea of 'corporate management' began to influence thinking about governance in Australia in the early 1980s. Mark Considine (1990: 171) tells us that
managerialism had four main design features:

PRODUCT FORMAT

Public sector activities are defined as 'products' and thus as commodities to be
traded.

INSTRUMENTALISM

The organisation is viewed as a tool in the hands of management (hierarchical
and autocratic). The elected government, through cabinet, heads the state
apparatus as a whole, and ministers head its divisions.

INTEGRATION

The whole bureaucratic state apparatus is viewed as a single system whose integration becomes a central goal.

PURPOSIVE ACTION

Government uses its control of public service functions such as health, transport and planning 'as part of a larger concerted effort to steer the whole economy and other aspects of society in a deliberative way' (Considine 1990: 171).

The framework was soon challenged from a number of quarters and debates took place in the pages of such journals as the *Australian Journal of Public Administration*. Critics (Wilenski 1988; Cullen 1988) argued that managerialism simply failed to deliver what it promised, and politicians accused bureaucrats of confusing managerialism with good management (Kirner 1988).

Critics said that it was inappropriate to describe many activities of the public service as 'products' to be traded. Education, health and a good environment, for example, were best seen as public goods or services that were never intended to serve narrow economic purposes. They also pointed out that instrumentalism based upon tight central control militated against pluralism—the legitimate existence of many values and interests in a free society. They pointed to the growing costs of system integration. Limited capacity in time and effort often cause integration to fail (Considine 1990: 171). Moreover, specific tools of corporate management (program budgeting, corporate planning, and performance indicators) ignored the complexity of good democratic governance and imposed simplistic patterning on bureaucratic reporting and behaviour without altering underlying realities.

According to Considine (1990: 171) 'performance is viewed as an economic problem largely associated with the ratio of inputs to outputs'—technical efficiency. This neglects other desirable features of performance, such as equity and effectiveness (how well an action achieves its goals). 'Lamentably', he writes, 'Corporate management did not result from a systematic appraisal of the problems of the Australian public sector . . . The costs and benefits of these major restructures have not been openly assessed by those who speak loudest of the importance of the "bottom line"'.

FURTHER READING

Paterson (1988), Considine (1990)

Corporate liberalism adds to managerialism the assumption that the state must submit to the demands of global business to create the conditions that will attract investment: low taxes, financial stability and subsidies to business. Social justice and environmental protection are seen as irrelevant to this 'main game'. In style, CL reintroduces the principle of separation between policy and implementation: between 'steering and rowing' (Osborne & Gaebler 1993). CL, however, demands a strong state steered from the centre in order to radically shrink and 'hollow out' the public sector and reduce public expectations of the role to be performed by the state (Gamble 1988). While 'entrepreneurialism' has existed in most states in some form over quite a long period, CL brings entrepreneurialism to new heights, building on the foundations of managerial control bequeathed by the social democrats. The managerial reforms and bureaucratic restructuring aimed at giving Cabinet and ministers strong directive power over the bureau-cracy, together with the introduction of norms of commercialisation and corporatisation, paved the way for CL.

The managerialist project in social democrat hands sought to elevate urban planning in the bureaucratic hierarchy by linking it to strategic economic goals and to economic planning and management structures. The difficulties of pursuing such goals in the context of an increasingly irrational and erratic market, coupled with the abandonment of social democracy by the Commonwealth government, led to the collapse of the core of the project in the states (Hayward 1993). The quite unintended and unanticipated link, via economic planning, of Labor governments to entrepreneurial irresponsibility led to the 'Guilty Party' political advertising campaign which the Liberals used very effectively, not only to keep the Australian Labor Party (ALP) out of power but also to destroy the social democratic project within Labor. SDM, therefore, was associated with the ALP only for a fairly short period, and has to be sharply distinguished from the later acceptance by the ALP of a form of CL. Even so, the impact of SDM was substantial, and has had important effects on the cities and their governance.

Social democratic managerialism

Social democracy is both a *social* and a *democratic* program. The South Australian government led by Don Dunstan was the first at state level to articulate the social democrat project. Dunstan (1979: 18) described the agenda retrospectively with admirable clarity:

> As a social democrat government, the Labor government in South Australia emphasises as a key factor in its whole approach the security and fulfilment of the individual in the community . . . If a person is to play a full part in the life of the community, a premium must be placed on the provision of secure and stable employment, income, housing, health, hospitals,

education, protection from exploitation and oppression, access to justice and the general freedom of self expression.

Dunstan linked this program to urban policy aimed at providing services fairly to all within the state's jurisdiction. As Parkin and Pugh (1981: 91) observed, 'State governments are Australia's urban governments', so a major part of the state's program of planning and coordination was directed at metropolitan Adelaide. Parkin and Pugh (1981: 95) infer from 'a mixture of policies and ideas' four elements of Dunstan's vision for the social democratic city:

i) *The urbane city:* the 'metropolis as a vibrant, cosmopolitan centre, with cultural facilities, pedestrian walkways, high density mixed land uses, lively street life, outdoor cafes'.

ii) *The communal city:* promoting community and neighbourhood facilities as foci for social life in suburban areas.

iii) *The technological city:* stressing advanced planning techniques and the rational allocation of resources on the French model of technocratic planning.

iv) *The egalitarian city:* deliberate public intervention to correct the tendency of markets to polarise populations between rich and poor, good and bad living environments.

Although Dunstan pursued a social democratic program, his government did not at first attempt to change the form of urban governance much from the CB model. Instead he injected his ideas through a strong and intellectually well-equipped Premier's Department, to which the planning staff of the State Planning Authority (SPA) were annexed in 1971. However, change from CB to SDM began gradually from the mid-1960s. In 1965 the South Australian Housing Trust was placed under the direction and control of the Minister for Housing. The Corbett inquiry into the South Australian public service, commissioned in 1973, recommended reduction of the number of departments by at least 18 and the creation of a consolidated Department of Housing and Urban Affairs (later Housing and Urban and Regional Affairs, HURA) to coordinate planning and development. Such a department was formed in 1976 to assist the Minister in promoting more efficient and equitable urban and regional development. Its first Director-General was Mr John Mant, a Labor lawyer who later helped spread the managerialist gospel throughout the state systems of urban governance. Mant's philosophy was that planning should no longer be regarded as a 'professional activity to be carried out at arm's length from Cabinet and the political processes' (Mant 1978: 86). Rather, the selection of planning tools was a choice for the government itself.

Whereas Dunstan in South Australia carried the social democrat banner before him, Wran in New South Wales kept it discreetly hidden. Some argue that he placed it in permanent storage (Stretton 1987: 9–10). Nevertheless, it should be remembered that in 1976 the newly elected Wran government immediately cancelled major sections of the inner-city freeway system that would have destroyed large areas of the inner suburbs of Woolloomooloo and Glebe. His government then cooperated with the Whitlam government to rehabilitate these areas with the addition of much public housing. By 1987, 573 dwellings had been built in Woolloomooloo and Glebe, 75 per cent of which was public housing. The focus of attention for much of Wran's administration, however, was reform of the electoral and parliamentary system in New South Wales.

In the 1980s the SDM program came to turn on three major elements: reform of the public service; economic planning, to which urban planning became connected; and, to a lesser extent, local government restructuring. Public consultation played a variable role in the program. Through this form of urban governance a variety of urban projects was pursued: metropolitan regional planning, coordinated delivery of social services with budgetary processes, land release and housing, capture of the **land value increment** in rezoning, reform of transport infrastructure, heritage conservation, and environmental protection.

Reform of the public service

Public service reform was a major feature of SDM, not least because it offered new Labor governments the means of imposing social democratic goals on a public service long accustomed to serving conservative governments. The model of reform was pursued, albeit cautiously, in New South Wales by the Wran government. Following Dunstan's example, Wran created a strong Premier's Department with a Ministerial Advisory Unit to brief him on all matters of political sensitivity and to provide greater control over the budget (Painter 1987: 102).

In 1977 Wran appointed a one-person commission of inquiry into the NSW public service under Dr Peter Wilenski. Moore (1978: 189) writes: 'Of all the recent inquiries his [Wilenski's] is the one most committed to the ethic of the fair-go'. Wilenski was concerned about improving policy advice, devising a better budgeting system, introducing performance evaluation, and encouraging staff mobility and development. But most of his report was devoted to social issues, such as equal opportunity, worker participation, community access to services, freedom of information, public participation and regionalisation (Moore 1978: 190).

The Wran government also introduced major changes to the planning system, creating a new Department of Planning and Environment. The *Environment and Planning Assessment Act 1979* introduced the broad idea of 'development standards', which were put into effect by the 'State Environmental Planning Policy No. 1' of 1980. A specialist appeal court was created: the Land and Environment Court, which could enforce its own decisions and 'in which all remedies, both civil and criminal, would be available under one roof' (Hanson 1993: 9).

In Victoria from 1982, under the Labor government of John Cain, a more comprehensive managerialist restructuring was carried out. In the environmental sphere, on the advice of John Mant among others, the government decided to amalgamate a number of agencies: the Department of Planning, the Ministry for Conservation (having jurisdiction over national parks, fisheries and wildlife, soil conservation and air and water pollution), the Department of Crown Lands and Survey, and the Department of State Forests. Mant's philosophy was that the government had two distinct responsibilities: one to regulate the use of private land, and one to manage public land. Two new large ministerial departments were formed from various sections of the four existing agencies: the Ministry for Planning and Environment (MPE), and the Department of Conservation, Forests and Lands (CF&L). Following Mant's advice the planning functions of the Melbourne Metropolitan Board of Works, a typical CB agency, were also taken into the Ministry for Planning and Environment.

By 1986 then, for the first time since the statutory establishment of town planning in Victoria, land use control was now carried out at state level by a single ministerial department, the Ministry for Planning and Environment, responsible for the entire territory of the state. This ministry changed its name and structure several times during the Cain–Kirner administration, ending up amalgamated with the much larger Ministry of Housing.

Neoliberalism struck early in South Australia under the Tonkin (Liberal) government from 1979. HURA was disbanded and the South Australian Land Commission abolished, urban policy was reduced to 'narrowly conceived land use planning functions' under a new Department of Environment and Planning (Hamnett & Lennon 1997: 7). Tonkin's government was the first in Australia to move towards 'contracting out', instead of in-house provision of government services. In fact the size of the South Australian public sector had nearly doubled under the Dunstan government, financed by the sale of the state country railways to the Commonwealth and increased grants to the States by the Whitlam government. The public sector in South Australia arguably kept the state afloat in the recession of 1975 (Radbone 1992: 102).

Bannon (ALP) defeated Tonkin in 1982. John Bannon's approach to governance was well described by Parkin and Patience (1992) as 'the politics of restraint'. In contrast with Dunstan's 'bold and visionary' approach to planning, Bannon's was one of 'careful management within the established parameters' (Orchard 1992: 148) or 'planning as management' characterised by 'incremental growth, urban consolidation and by the idea that planners should cease to get in the way of adjustment and profitability' (Forster & McCaskill 1986: 106). Radbone (1992: 101) observes:

> The dominant theme of developments in the South Australian public sector under Bannon was cut-back management. These cuts were accompanied by the introduction of a managerialist philosophy which stressed the value of adopting private-sector management techniques in the public sector.

'Commercialisation' was brought to the public service but also a 'social justice' strategy which required all departments 'to examine the social justice implications of their programs and reserve budgetary funds for activities and projects nominated by agencies as having a social justice benefit' (Radbone 1992: 108).

More problematic was the Bannon government's control over its public enterprises and authorities. Bannon (Scott 1992: 84) insisted at the outset that public enterprises should have a 'commercial brief', that their only goal 'should be to make the highest possible profits consistent with the guidelines set down by government'. But in reality the government relied on these agencies to implement broad policy and did so increasingly. Kenny (1993) terms the approach of the government 'SA Inc.', cross-referring to the proven corruption in Western Australia in what became known as 'WA Inc.' (see below). But while the South Australian government used financial manipulation to raise revenue and minimise state taxes, there was in fact no evidence of corruption—simply a failure of government oversight.

The Western Australian government had already begun a process of managerial reform of the public service before the Burke (ALP) government took office, introducing business management concepts into rules governing the service. Burke continued and intensified the process of reform, bringing in ministerial advisers from outside the service, reorganising the Premier's Department and the Treasury, 'setting up a "Functional Review Committee" to examine all areas of government activity and initiating inquiries into areas perceived as needing change' (Gallop 1986: 85). Gallop comments on three themes in Western Australian reforms: increased political control over the bureaucracy, strengthened central coordination of the activities of the public sector, and rationalisation of departmental structures to achieve efficiency.

In Queensland the SDM project did not begin in earnest at state level until the Goss government took power. Goss adopted the technique recommended by Fitzgerald, of using independent reform commissions at arm's length from political influence. To the two proposed by Fitzgerald—the Criminal Justice Commission (CJC), and the Electoral and Administrative Review Commission (EARC)—Goss added a third, the Public Sector Management Commission (PSMC). Goss engaged in a process of 'careful reform', the main thrust of which was the managerialist formula: a senior executive service, economic steering by Premier and Cabinet, amalgamating and ministerialising departments (reducing departments from 27 to 18), reorganising cabinet committees to focus on policy development and coordination, and 'corporatisation and commercialisation'. As Smerdon (1992: 73) explains,

> Commercialisation . . . relates to agencies or activities which are intended to remain under the direct control of the minister . . . Commercialisation seeks to encourage rational economic choice in the use of resources and efficiency in the production of goods and services by subjecting service agencies, to the greatest extent practical, to market disciplines faced by the private sector.

Corporatisation related to government-owned enterprises (GOEs) and the primary objective was 'to strive for improved commercial performance' (Smerdon 1992: 76).

The planning function was amalgamated with housing and local government (in the Ministry for Housing, Local Government and Planning). Planning was reinterpreted as 'management' in the *Planning and Environment Development Assessment Bill (PEDA) 1995*, and its scope was extended to include 'the management of land use and development and how that promotes sustainable land use, development and the economic, social and physical wellbeing of people' (Wright 1995: 12). The Bill sought to abolish zoning, giving local councils discretionary power to 'assess' development (along the lines of the 1947 and 1968 UK Planning Acts), to introduce 'state' planning policies and to integrate state, regional and local levels of planning policy within a single legislative framework.

The introduction of managerialism was not confined to the state government nor to the Labor Party (see Wanna & Weller 1995). In Brisbane City Council (BCC), in the CB tradition, departmental managers were 'regarded as feudal barons in charge of engineering empires. They were the experts who controlled the flow of information, answered only to the lord mayor and brooked little interference in the decisions in their area' (Wanna & Weller 1995: 64). The Liberal administration of Sallyanne Atkinson in the 1980s, however, introduced a form of 'Civic Cabinet' (the Establishment and Coordination Committee) to centralise power, shape an overall policy direction, and to see that it was implemented by each arm of the local bureaucracy. For Wanna and Weller (1995: 68), 'Managerial techniques . . . increasingly became a priority of the BCC executive from the mid 1980s'.

David Corbett, who undertook the 1973 inquiry into the South Australian public service, reflects that these public service inquiries were a response by state governments to the emergence of new issues forced onto the public agenda by social change: 'slowly, like a tanker at sea, the administrative apparatus of the States has changed direction so that it can face at least some of the issues of planning, protection and social repair work which the 1970s and 1980s have brought to the fore' (Corbett 1987: 95). Unfortunately, though, the states faced new tasks, with increasingly reduced financial resources and growing demands on them to manage their domestic economies and create jobs. At every national economic crisis (in 1975 and in 1982), unemployment grew and the demand became more strident.

Entrepreneurialism, economic planning and urban development

States have never been able to control their own economies comprehensively, but this has not prevented their governments from engaging in concerted action to improve their economic position in competition with other states. These attempts have often been connected with major urban projects: 'mega-projects' (Berry & Huxley 1992). Sydney's Darling Harbour redevelopment (Box 4.2) and successful bid for the 2000 Olympic Games are examples. Others include Melbourne's failed attempt to secure the 1996 Olympics, and its successful bids for the Formula One Grand Prix car race and the 2006 Commonwealth Games.

BOX 4.2 CITIES IN COMPETITION I: DARLING HARBOUR

The state government of New South Wales had tried unsuccessfully in the 1970s to redevelop the Rocks and Woolloomooloo in Sydney against a strong coalition of working-class and middle-class residents and construction unions (see Box 8.3). The drive to develop Darling Harbour, an obsolescent waterside industrial area with no resident population, represented an effort by the state government of Neville Wran to claim for Sydney a significant place in a hierarchy of cities directing the operations of the global markets (Daly 1987). Daly points out that the NSW state government wanted to enable Sydney to gain a central place in the new world financial system, and that the development of Darling Harbour was seen as important in meeting this goal.

Wran first tried in 1980 to get Darling Harbour developed as a site for an international expo to be held in 1988. That did not attract federal (Liberal–National Party) support. The next attempt in 1983, following the election of the Hawke (ALP) Commonwealth government, was to form a partnership with private developers to turn Darling Harbour into a first-class convention, exhibition, market and tourist centre. Tourism became the key to the project's success and made it attractive to the Commonwealth government, which was trying to promote tourism as a growth industry.

The project announced in 1984 was for a public/private joint venture costing $1 billion. The Darling Harbour Authority was given powers greater than those of the City Council and the State Planning Department. The aim throughout the project was to get the development completed with maximum speed, in time for the 1988 Bicentennial—and the re-election of the Labor government. Planning objections were ignored. The minister responsible, Laurie Brereton, stitched together a pact with the unions to finish the job quickly. The project included an overhead monorail through Sydney's CBD to bring people to the site; this became the focus of furious public protests and demonstrations. But these were also ignored, setting a precedent for the Kennett (Liberal–National) government in Victoria. The project was to include a casino, costing $750 million, which would be the principal money-spinner for the government—a further precedent for the Kennett government. In the midst of the crisis, however, Wran retired from politics for personal reasons.

There were allegations of impropriety concerning both the monorail and the casino. As a result the government was forced to abandon the idea of the casino (later revived), leaving $450 million in public sector costs. The project ran into more union troubles, and the deadline of January 1988 was abandoned. The Labor Party lost the 1987 election—and the Darling Harbour project, which had become more and more controversial, was considered a major factor in that loss. The project was officially opened in May 1988 during the Bicentennial, but the site was only half-finished.

The Wran government in New South Wales relaxed planning controls and sold off public land to assist development: 'In the face of complaints from business about the proliferation of controls and the complexity of bureaucratic clearance procedures, deregulation became part of government's deal with business' (Thompson et al. 1986: 20). According to Thompson et al. (1986: 20): 'Economic circumstances are bad and the accompanying social problems seem intractable, so tinsel and glitter, sport and gambling and grand gestures in concrete and glass might serve to divert'.

In Queensland, entrepreneurialism was well established up until the change of government in late 1989. But the entrepreneurial tendency was somewhat checked by a fragmented CB bureaucratic system in which the state intervened only when it wanted to promote develop-ment, and by a clientelistic form of politics in which ministerial patronage was the name of the political game but not by any means ministerial *steering* of the public service. As the hold on power of the National–Liberal coalition government became shakier, so the govern-ment increasingly turned to spectacular projects such as 'resort' developments (covered by the *Sanctuary Cove Resort Act 1985*; *Integrated Resort Development Act 1987*) and the 'Korean Tower' (Box 4.3).

At local level, entrepreneurialism was institutionalised in 'negotiated planning', in which zoning controls had become a bargaining tool for the planner to parlay with a developer in order to obtain marginal improvements 'in the public interest' (landscaping, toilet blocks and the like). Brisbane City Council was a major planning authority with plenary powers over most of the metropolitan area, yet the Brisbane Plan remained a traditional zoning plan, with two main commercial zones.

BOX 4.3 CITIES IN COMPETITION II: THE KOREAN TOWER

In 1987 a South Korean development company in concert with the Queensland government proposed to build the world's tallest office building in Brisbane. Phil Day (1987b: suppl. page) writes of the proposal:

> The Bjelke-Petersen era may be coming to an end, but the tally of economic, social and environmental damage is not yet complete. There are several interventions in the Brisbane Town Plan now in the pipeline. But, if the time comes when Queenslanders burn effigies in the streets, the Korean Tower may very well loom large in Brisbane people's minds as the most disastrous and long-lasting of all the Petersen Govern-ment's legacies.

Certainly it will loom over Brisbane—and cast a winter morning shadow extending from Ann Street across the river and over the Cultural Centre. If it goes ahead, of course. Given an imminent over-supply of office space in Brisbane, it may yet join the billions of dollars worth of phantom projects announced by the Premier over the years which have been merely one-day headline wonders.

But, if it does go ahead (and the Government has in fact guaranteed that it will lease most of the proposed office space), its international (or even interstate) distinction will almost certainly be shortlived, and the price of temporary distinction will be saddling Brisbane permanently with a bizarre 445 metre edifice totally out of scale with its surroundings.

No public building this, symbolising the city's civic status, but a private commercial structure which will inject a massive additional influx of pedestrian and vehicular traffic into an already tightly constrained CBD. Tourists will be able to see the Gold Coast—on a pollution free day. Brisbane ratepayers (and the State's taxpayers) will foot the bill for the swathe of new radial roadworks needed to bring traffic to and from an overdeveloped city centre . . . The penile image is particularly appropriate— coupled with the diminution of the City Hall and the Cultural Centre, it symbolises the rape of Queensland by unrestrained private sector greed and the mindless pursuit of Development.

The project was dropped after sustained and vocal opposition on the part of the Liberal leader of the City Council, Sallyanne Atkinson. Eleven years later a proposal for the world's tallest office building was approved by the Kennett government of Victoria for the Docklands site in Melbourne. This too is now in question for financial reasons.

The Cain government in Victoria and the Bannon government in South Australia, however, went beyond entrepreneurialism. Both governments tried to use the state apparatus to resolve the fiscal crisis of the 1980s: fear of raising taxes coupled with cuts to Commonwealth grants. Both governments sought to improve the economic advice available to them with a view to intervening in the state economy on a broad front. In Victoria an 'Office of Management and Budget' was set up within Treasury which soon *became* the Treasury. The new Department of Management and Budget produced a neo-Ricardian strategy for economic development of the state. The aim was to identify and then encourage Victoria's competitive strengths. A major part of this strategy was developing and improving the central area of Melbourne. The strategy also included allowing the State Bank of Victoria, through its merchant banking arm 'Tricontinental', to join the speculative rush to property and commercial projects. The strategy ended with the property crash of 1990/91, a disaster which left Australian banks, in both private and public sectors, with huge losses, the largest accruing to the two biggest banks in Australia, Westpac and the ANZ (Sykes 1993).

Under Bannon, the South Australian Government Financing Authority (SAFA), a creation of the Tonkin government, became one of the largest financial institutions in the state. The purpose of the authority was to borrow on behalf of all South Australian authorities and, because of the size of its borrowings, thereby reduce the interest costs of the loans. SAFA borrowed money up to the limit of its Loan Council entitlement, whether the money was wanted by the public sector or not. The surplus funds were put into the money market. Thus SAFA, being a government-guaranteed agency, could *borrow* at a lower rate and *lend* at full commercial rates. About 19 per cent of SAFA's total assets were invested outside the South Australian public sector, mostly with commercial enterprises. SAFA was used also to help the government sell public assets like power stations and forests and then lease them back 'to take advantage of supposed federal taxation loopholes' (Kenny 1993: 63).

The State Bank (SBSA) also was encouraged to behave as a commercial enterprise, and like many commercial banks in the 1980s it loaned funds for projects which subsequently became, in the euphemistic jargon of the times, 'non-performing loans'. The bank grew spectacularly in the 1980s (at twice the rate of the State Bank of NSW and nearly 80 per cent faster than the State Bank of Victoria) from an asset base of $2.3 billion in 1984 to $17.3 billion in 1990. Just as spectacular was its crash in the late 1980s, when it was revealed that it had incurred losses of more than $3 billion from an asset base of $21 billion (Kenny 1993: 68).

The Queensland government, observing the agony of the Cain government in Victoria and the Bannon government in South Australia in the early 1990s, was confirmed in its belief that economic planning had to be treated with the greatest caution. Treasury was kept separate from economic development, which was handled by the Department of the Premier, Economic and Trade Development. Under the headline 'The 1990s: a decade for planning', the president of the Queensland division of the Royal Australian Planning Institute (RAPI) optimistically announced, 'At all levels of government, prominent politicians are placing issues such as urban form, urban consolidation, infrastructure financing, social justice, environmentally sustainable development and housing reform high on their agendas' (Vann 1991: 2). In 1990, Ellis (1990: 224) commented that state governments, and especially the Queensland government, are 'playing a role in helping firms to compete in the international market place'.

In Western Australia under the premierships of Brian Burke and Peter Dowding there developed 'an interlocking association of vested interests which had coalesced around the State government and, in particular, the department of Premier and Cabinet' (O'Brien 1991: 77). These close relationships between entrepreneurial business and government became known as 'WA Inc.' and resulted in a botched attempt to rescue a large merchant bank (Rothwells). The Royal Commission, set up (by succeeding Labor Premier Carmen Lawrence) to investigate allegations of impropriety, revealed corruption; several Labor politicians, including Burke and Dowding, were prosecuted and found guilty.

The economic failures in Victoria and South Australia were an inevitable result of the irrationality of the market, and more to do with managerialism than social democracy. Too much faith was placed in private sector managerial style. As Radbone (1992: 110) observes,

> The dominant ideology of the 1980s disparaged the ability of the public sector to add to the productive capacity of the community. In response, in South Australia, as elsewhere, either State activities have been economised or State activities have tried to ape the private sector as much as possible.

Unfortunately, the result was a loss of confidence not in the market but in the capacity of government, and this loss of confidence in the political sphere struck at the heart of the project of social democracy. 'WA Inc.' was a very different matter from the failures in Victoria and South Australia. Even in Western Australia the problem lay not with the social democratic project but with something much closer to corporate liberalism—albeit conducted by a Labor government (see Stone 1997).

State–local government relations

Social democratic philosophy placed considerable importance on the role of local government. One response to financial pressure on the states was to transfer some of their responsibilities to local government. The SDM project included enlarging local government units by amalgamation, to take advantage of economies of scale and to enable them to build up the staff expertise needed to take over the provision of a wider range of urban services. The degree to which such amalgamations were necessary or seriously pursued varied in the different states.

In New South Wales under the Wran government the setting of council boundaries was handled by an independent commission, the Local Government Boundaries Commission. In 1982, following the

South Wales and the Goss government in Queensland, where there is no upper house).

Urban governance and metropolitan planning

Many urban planning projects were pursued at the same time as SDM was taking shape as a form of urban governance. But, despite the managerial reforms, planning continued largely as a professional sectoral activity, producing strategic and local plans indicating the location, type and intensity of future development. Wilmoth (1987: 160) notes: 'The 1979 Environmental Planning and Asssessment Act [NSW] has enabled a number of planning policies with region-wide significance to be implemented, particularly those that have increased the range of housing choice in the existing urban area'. Metropolitan regional plans were published at intervals for Sydney, Melbourne, Brisbane, Adelaide and Perth. Notwithstanding the remaining compartmentalisation of planning, serious attempts were made to coordinate the provision of urban services (social as well as physical infrastructure) in New South Wales (Urban Development Program, Urban Development Finance Program), Victoria (Metropolitan Services Coordination System), and South Australia (Urban Staging Study).

Urban consolidation was pursued with vigour in most states. For example, in Sydney in 1980 and 1981 the Minister for Planning (Bob Carr—later to become Premier) introduced Environmental Plans 1 and 2 permitting dual occupancy subject to local council consent (Caulfield & Painter 1995: 238). Urban consolidation became a major theme in the Sydney metropolitan strategy of 1988 (*Sydney into its Third Century*). In Melbourne the planning authority—then the Melbourne and Metropolitan Board of Works (MMBW 1981)—was an early convert to the consolidation ideal, which was adopted in its 1981 amendment to the city's Metropolitan Planning Scheme (MMBW 1981: 3). Urban consolidation was an important part of the Planning Ministry's 1987 metropolitan strategy (*Shaping Melbourne's Future*).

In Victoria, under the *Environment and Planning Act 1987*, the Planning Ministry strengthened heritage preservation, adding many buildings to the Historic Buildings Register. Revitalisation of central Melbourne became a primary goal of planning policy and was written into the economic strategy. A 'Major Projects Unit' was set up in 1987 in order to separate the governmental role of arbitrator from its role of fostering and encouraging particular projects seen as beneficial to the state and to some extent '**fast-tracking**' such developments. The district centre policy which first appeared in the 1954 Melbourne Metropolitan Planning Scheme was implemented, resulting in a number of controversial decisions to reject applications from developers for shopping centre expansions and office developments outside the district centres.

The poorer western suburbs became a focus of attention. The Western Suburbs Action Program included controlling noxious industries and industrial emissions, dealing with pollution of the Maribyrnong River, and promoting residential and green space developments. Consultative processes played a considerable role in this program, as they did in some other Cain government initiatives, most notably the state's strategy for assessing the demand for electricity following the attempt by the State Electricity Commission to run a major overhead power line through residential inner-urban neighbourhoods. Areas for future growth were designated and funding provided for urban services and environmental conservation. The transport portfolio, however, remained resolutely uncoordinated with planning. Roads planners with the support of their minister continued to promote plans for freeway developments. A roads department, as Corbett (1987: 86) notes for Sydney, 'is not easily turned aside from a mission it regards as historically inevitable and preordained'.

In Queensland, environmental protection and sustainable development was at last introduced as a task of government—and integrated with planning, as it had been in New South Wales. Heritage protection was given proper attention (*Heritage Act 1992*), and the relationship between state, regional and local government spelled out (the State/Local Government Protocol). A major initiative was taken in regional planning for the high-growth area of South East Queensland (SEQ 2001).

As the idea of 'planning' on such a scale smacked of socialism, thought to be anathema to Queensland voters, the minister responsible, Terry Mackenroth, proceeded with caution and maximum consultation: with business and the unions, with social, cultural and environmental groups, professional and academic bodies, with other state government agencies, and with Commonwealth and local government. A strategy document emerged in 1995: *SEQ 2001 Regional Framework for Growth Management*. The process was thus not designed to be decisive but 'to motivate consensus' (Moon 1995: 24). State and local responsibilities were not clearly spelled out and it became clear that the state government was not going to intervene (on behalf of 'regional planning') in the plans of local governments in the region. On the other hand, the consultation coordinator for SEQ 2001 complained that, 'The objectives of the government in pursuing consultation are not clear, and there has been little evidence of demonstrated commitment to the resourcing responsibilities that accompany consultative processes' (Robinson 1993: 13). The strategy that resulted was not backed by an agency capable of implementing it. Moon (1995: 24) provocatively pronounced SEQ 2001 dead 'on the premise that it was once alive'.

One of the causes of the premature demise both of SEQ 2001 and of the Goss government was the failure of the government to curb the road-building ambitions of the Queensland Department of Transport (QDOT). When the former Main Roads Department was subsumed by QDOT, its road engineers remained a cohesive group within it. This group wanted to construct a new South Coast Motorway parallel to the Pacific Highway. The story of how the engineers fought within QDOT against local environmental groups, local government, negative economic assessments and the SEQ 2001 planning process to promote the road is a tortuous one (see Moon 1995 for a description). The stimulus to urban growth provided by the Commonwealth's *Better Cities* program announced in 1992 played a part in justifying the eastern transport corridor, for which no prior need existed. The outcome was that the government accepted the road proposal. In the election of 1995 the government barely scraped home, with a single-seat majority, losing several seats in the path of the South Coast Motorway. The government subsequently abandoned the road, but its majority was kicked away with the loss in 1995 of the Mundingburra by-election called following a disputed return. The PEDA Bill never became an Act. The succeeding National–Liberal government began to introduce CL over the top of Goss's aborted SDM.

Conclusion

SDM was, in fact, an unfinished project in every state. In Victoria, South Australia and Western Australia managerial reform itself occupied much of the time and energy of governments. In later years, from 1985, the increasing severity of cuts in Commonwealth support to the states made it difficult to pursue social democratic projects. Time and energy was turned to finding alternative sources of funds. Managerialist advice was to follow the model of the private sector, and 'let the managers manage'.

In the later 1980s the private sector responded to financial deregulation by embracing all sorts of high-risk ventures that promised enhanced returns. Little wonder then that state governments facing severe fiscal crisis were tempted to look for ways of taking advantage of such returns. In the end it mattered little to the electorate that every Australian bank had followed the same course, resulting in enormous losses. Losses incurred by state agencies have to be borne by taxpayers, who are not given the choice of where their taxes are invested—but who also have to hand at election time the means of rendering the government accountable. The scene was set for SDM's successor: corporate liberalism.

5 Changing urban governance II: corporate liberalism

Social democratic managerialism (SDM) transformed the activities and structures of urban governance across the states. Importantly, political control of the apparatus of government was greatly enhanced. The old fragmented professional structures of colonial bureaucracy (CB) were replaced by more centralised and integrated systems of government, steered by political priorities and attuned to what were widely portrayed as the imperatives of globalisation. Even so, as we saw in chapter 4, there were considerable differences among the responses of the states.

The *social democratic* aims of early managerialism faded in the 1990s as the political cycle turned and neoliberalism took command as the dominant ideology of government. Managerialism, however, rapidly adapted to the neoliberal ideology, finding common cause with the political aims of the right-wing governments that took control in most states in the 1990s. Indeed, as we discuss in chapter 9, managerialism and neoliberalism have much in common. What emerged in the 1990s was the form of urban governance we have termed 'corporate liberalism' (CL). We do not want to suggest that CL is a monolithic system. In fact, as is clear from the advance of environmentally and ecologically oriented planning legislation in New South Wales, Queensland and South Australia, a new paradigm of environmental governance is already taking shape. (This we discuss further in chapter 8.)

At federal level, by the early 1990s there was belated recognition by the Commonwealth government of the failure of new urban policy regimes to improve general welfare (Bunker & Minnery 1992). A *Building Better Cities* (BBC) program was instituted in 1991, promising significant investment funds—over A$800 million in the first five years—to address the problems of locational disadvantage, housing inaccessibility and declining infrastructure (Orchard 1995). Despite the political hopes invested in the BBC, the program failed to reduce, or even stall, the worsening problems of locational disadvantage and spatial polarisation (Stilwell 1993a).

As Spiller (1999: 2) explains, the BBC program contrasted strongly with the dominant government rhetoric but marked up some significant achievements, demonstrating the need for 'place-specific' rather than 'portfolio-specific' (or function-specific) management of government urban programs: 'But in the end only modest resources were dedicated to these programs, reflecting the true orientation of the Government of the day'. In 1996, a new conservative administration abolished what remained of the BBC and so ended altogether the federal government's hitherto desultory attempts to reanimate a national spatial policy framework.

In this chapter we first explain in more detail what we mean by corporate liberalism. We then expand on its impact on urban governance: the steady increase in liberalisation within the public sector during the 1990s, how planning tends to become **place marketing** under corporate liberalism, and the impact of CL strategies on local government. We conclude by considering the wider implications of CL for key aspects of urban governance.

Corporate liberalism

Corporate liberalism has three elements specific to the behaviour of Australian state governments in the 1990s: (a) a view of the state itself as a corporation, combining a group of subsidiary corporations—the departments or agencies; (b) the creation of markets as the institutional matrix for the delivery of services; and (c) selective enhanced entrepreneurialism, in which close relations are established with certain business elites.

The political leadership takes on a self-image as the directorate of a big corporation. State Cabinet begins to depict itself as a board of directors, with the State Premier as chair of the board. This involves the hierarchical and autocratic approach to governance of the business corporation, whose control over the corporation is a condition of its effectiveness for the purpose of profit. There is a major contradiction here between corporate governance, aiming at profit, and democracy, aiming at justice and the personal fulfilment of citizens. Markets are regarded as the most efficient means of delivering services. This is an article of faith which CL governments 'waste' no time testing. At the same time CL governments that already have close ties to business elites seek to use those ties to encourage investment. Through corporate liberalism the general project of removing urban services from the sphere of the state is pursued. At the same time private entrepreneurial ventures, and some public sector projects, are supported which (a) are supposed to improve the attractiveness and profile of the metropolitan city to capital investment, and (b) attract public applause for their entertainment and cultural value.

Corporate liberalism is theoretically an oxymoron. If there was anything Hayek, a genuine liberal, hated more than collectivism it was corporatism. Hayek believed in a market society in which the state would have a greatly diminished role. That the state should intervene to support certain kinds of businesses was appalling to him (Hayek 1944: 44). In practice, however, theoretical contradictions can be reconciled. The CL state, oriented to the appearance of economic success, demands intervention, and the form of intervention is built on entrepreneurialism rather than the economic planning of SDM governments.

The model has been most strongly pursued by the Kennett government of Victoria. Aspects of the model can, however, be found in most other states and, as an ideal type, the CL model is influential far beyond the borders of Victoria. As Des Moore (1993: 13), a neoliberal consultant, explained: 'Victoria should aim to exploit one of its most important natural advantages, viz, that of being able to provide government services at a lower cost per head than any other State'. How 'natural' this advantage is, readers may judge for themselves, but if the model is seen to give Victoria a competitive advantage, the pressure for it to be adopted in full in other states will grow.

A major effort of CL was further to 'reform' the management of the public service. This meant centralising power (as befits a corporation), and creating markets by 'corporatisation', 'commercialisation' (applying the profit criterion), and, on occasion, privatisation. Privatisation took a number of forms: actually selling publicly owned assets to private companies; and '**outsourcing**' and competitive tendering (getting services delivered by private companies rather than the public sector supplying them). Here we use the term 'liberalisation' (now in common use worldwide) for these strategies.

Liberalisation

Following the early attempt by the Tonkin government of South Australia to introduce some neoliberal measures, the Greiner (Liberal–

National) government in New South Wales from 1988 took the CL model a step further. The neoliberal reform agenda did not win votes (Laffin & Painter 1995: 9). Indeed, Greiner himself says that he had a drawer for issues that would help him get elected, and another for matters he would pursue once in government (Greiner 1994). The second drawer was not opened in public until after the election.

To generate public support for the cuts and managerial changes, Greiner used a Commission of Audit (the 'Curran' Commission in NSW) to portray the state of New South Wales in financial crisis. Cuts were made to the heartwood of state expenditure—the schools budget and the staffing levels of major public trading enterprises. Greiner acted quickly to implement unpopular reforms without consultation with interested groups. This strategy was in marked contrast to the 'deliberative consultative approach to public service reform pursued by Wran and Wilenski' (Laffin & Painter 1995: 8). The challenge was 'to create an institutional framework for government which resembles the market as closely as possible' (Greiner 1985). This challenge was to be met by commercialisation, corporatisation and privatisation.

Urban policy under Greiner demonstrated significant continuity with planning under Labor, but economic policies came to predominate over social and environmental concerns. The 1994 strategic planning document *Cities for the Twenty-First Century* reinforced metropolitan regional policies for peripheral growth ('linear expansion'), the concentration of commercial development at selected district centres, and urban consolidation (Caulfield & Painter 1995: 237). Urban consolidation policy, however, 'hardened in the early 1990s' (Caulfield & Painter 1995: 239) as the result of a shortage of funds for infrastructure brought on by a squeeze on public borrowings from the Loan Council, and financial reforms of the Greiner government designed to bring to the surface the relative costs of different settlement patterns: 'Indeed, these economic and financial considerations began to dominate the whole field of urban policy' (Caulfield & Painter 1995: 239). On environmental policy, Kellow (1995: 267) concludes that a program of change was consistently implemented: 'the separation of regulatory from trading functions and an increased reliance on financial incentives and market mechanisms rather than coercive powers of the state to produce better environmental outcomes'.

Greiner's CL approach, in retrospect, can be seen to be cautious compared with that of Kennett in Victoria, though the two had a similar agenda. There were also distinct continuities with SDM. 'Corporatisation' emphasised managerial principles such as clear objectives for managers, unambiguous assignment of management responsibilities, independent monitoring of performance against agreed targets, rewards and sanctions commensurate with performance, and competitive neutrality so that performance was not distorted by privileges to the corporation arising from government ownership (Painter 1995: 92). Government Trading Enterprises (GTEs) were to be treated as competitive corporations on the same terms as private corporations. But Greiner did not proceed from corporatisation to privatisation of the major utilities. And although Greiner made cuts in high-profile areas, R.G. Walker (1995: 129) comes up with the 'startling finding' that 'the perception of the Greiner government as a cost–cutting administration is false'. This was not the case in Victoria.

Kennett wanted revolutionary change and, as with Greiner, this required a heightened sense of crisis. So he appointed a Commission of Audit staffed by committed neoliberals (it was chaired by Professor Bob Officer, a member of the Institute of Public Affairs). The Commission, by including 'unfunded liabilities', discovered a rise in the level of debt from under $25 billion in 1989 to over $70 billion in 1992 (Victoria 1993a). This 'discovery' was then used to justify the major cuts to the public sector that Kennett had promised in opposition. The same strategy of appointing an ideologically driven expert committee to justify expenditure cuts was applied by incoming Liberal and coalition governments in Tasmania (1992), Western Australia (1993), South Australia (1994) and Queensland (1996).

The Kennett government cut staffing in almost every area of the public service, except those dealing with public order. Three years after winning office Kennett could boast of 'downsizing' the public service by some 60 000 personnel (Tullock 1996). During its first two years the Kennett government cut 8200 teaching positions (about 20 per cent of teaching staff in public education). Special needs staff in education were reduced from 2000 in 1992 to 310 in 1993. In all, 260 schools were closed (Marginson 1994: 8). Large cuts were also made to public hospital funding and staffing. Introduction of the 'casemix' approach to funding health care placed public hospitals in competition with one another for patients.

Under 'casemix', hospitals are funded according to the number of 'cases' they expect to treat. A 'case' is a patient with a specific illness—for example, an ingrowing toenail or prostate cancer. Such a 'case' is considered a consumer demand, just like the demand for hamburgers or Porsche cars. In 1993 when the system was introduced, John Paterson (1993: 93), then secretary of the Department of Health and Community Services in Victoria, announced 'Within a short time the economics of the operations of public hospitals, individually and as a system, will become indistinguishable from that of Target, Safeway, General Motors or McDonald's'.

Managerial control from the top was tightened and centralised. Zifcak (1997: 108) observes:

> Ministers brought to government a sharp sense of their right to prevail and a clear, ideological agenda that demands implementation. Control of this agenda is centred on the Premier who effects it politically through the cabinet and managerially through the State Coordination and Management Committee (SCAM), consisting of all the departmental secretaries and known within the public service as 'The Black Cabinet'.

Every departmental chief executive officer is employed directly by the Premier, not by the Minister. Each CEO is on contract, the terms of which 'directly reflect the government's strategic and budgetary objectives' (Zifcak 1997: 108).

Control of the state apparatus from the top has resolved the problem of coordination in a way that has had important effects in planning. The reshaping of Melbourne is now driven by control over the road infrastructure. Land use and transport planning have been brought together in a Department of Infrastructure, in which the road planners are completely dominant. The centralising and controlling tendency does not stop with the public service. The Kennett government has shown itself to be intolerant of criticism from any quarter, to the extent that civil rights have been severely eroded (Larritt 1996).

Kennett did not stop at corporatisation of public utilities but imposed full privatisation of the profitable sectors of public urban infrastructure, especially energy. The State Electricity Commission was broken up into a number of separate producer and distributor corporations (the latter covering different areas of the state) and sold to overseas interests. Privatisation of the gas industry has proceeded and, in 1999, the management of the entire public transport system was privatised (though physical infrastructure is to remain in public ownership). The biggest transport infrastructure project since the Snowy River Scheme, the City Link freeway circling Melbourne is privately financed, constructed and managed. Outsourcing and contracting has been applied throughout the sphere of government. We might, then, reasonably designate CL as the philosophy of the 'contract state'.

The Kennett government in Victoria developed close and organic relations with business. Even before winning government Kennett and the Liberal elite established regular informal meetings with business leaders (Figure 5.1). The Kennett government lent more than $1 million from the 'community support fund' to the owners of the Rialto building

Figure 5.1 The 'Rumour Tank': how Melbourne's *Herald-Sun* saw relations between business and the Kennett government

Source: *Herald-Sun.*

for the building of a theatrette (Brady 1995: 3). The former State Electricity Commission building bought by the government from Grocon Pty Ltd for $250 million in July 1994 was valued by the Valuer-General at between $40 million and $50 million (Auditor-General's Annual Report 1995, in Johnston 1995: 7). The close relationship between the developers of the Crown Casino and the Premier became the subject of much controversy and press speculation. Crown was allowed to raise the number of gaming tables at the casino from 200 to 350 in exchange for an extra $100.8 million in gambling taxes over three years (Brady & Miller 1995: 1). Crown chairman Lloyd Williams was reported as saying that the Casino could not have been built without the backing of the Kennett government (Gibson 1997: 1). The opposition continually tried to make political capital out of the alleged 'cronyism' but failed to uncover compelling evidence of improper conduct (Green 1994: 2). In the end, pointing the finger at alleged cronyism that could not be proved was no substitute for policies that differed noticeably from corporate liberalism.

Whereas the Victorian government has become the paradigm case of CL, other states have followed more cautiously. In Western Australia the Court government was elected in 1993 at the height of public protest in Victoria at the Kennett cuts. Although the odium of WA Inc. (see chapter 4) hung over the Labor government in 1993, Court was up against an astute and popular premier in Carmen Lawrence. He made effective use of the 'Guilty Party' slogan (borrowed from Kennett) against Labor but was careful to distance himself from the Kennett model, vowing not to cut public service staffing. His subsequent electoral success depended on a cautious approach. In WA the major public utilities have been corporatised but not privatised (though the State Bank and the Government Printer were sold), but outsourcing of public sector work has proceeded rapidly—growing from $365 million in contracts in 1994 to $671 million in 1995, the largest area of contracting out being in public health (Gallop 1997: 83). Gallop (1997: 83), the 1999 leader of the opposition, argued that such contracting out makes government dependent on business:

> What is clear, however, is that new and powerful partnerships develop between government and business . . . Although the theory has govern-ments in charge, the practice may very well see governments adjusting and responding to the needs of its private contractors, some of whom may be party benefactors.

In South Australia the government carried out significant cuts to the public service (though not on the scale of Victoria), privatised the management of the water industry (ownership of existing infrastructure remaining in public hands) and outsourced the government's informa-tion-processing systems. A number of state-owned enterprises were also sold off, including the State Bank, the State Insurance Commission, and many smaller enterprises—the Mount Burr sawmill, the Terrace Inter-continental Hotel and the Collinville Stud (Parkin 1995). In Queensland the Borbidge government embarked on neoliberal reforms but never commanded a majority in Parliament and was subsequently defeated by Labor after only two years in power. Similarly the Fahey government in New South Wales (succeeding Greiner) introduced an election budget in 1994 which projected *increased* spending on education (prom-ising over 1400 extra teaching staff), health, public housing and police (Page 1995: 450).

Labor governments have adopted some of the prescriptions for liberalisation but in somewhat diluted form. In New South Wales, Bob Carr's first budget cut severely in some areas, but increased spending in others, including education, public health and the environment (Clune 1997: 385). The Carr government wanted to sell off the New South Wales electricity industry, raising funds to eliminate the state's public sector debt. The Labor Party, however, resisted. With the support of six left-wing ministers, 25 Labor backbenchers said they would vote against privatisation if the issue was not decided by the Party's Annual Conference. The government backed down. Ironically, privatisation of electricity became a major issue at the 1999 state election that Labor, on a platform of 'no privatisation', won with a landslide majority.

Liberalisation—the triple agenda of corporatisation, commercialisation and privatisation—has by no means yet been fully implemented across all states. In Victoria, the CL agenda came to an abrupt halt in late 1999 when the Kennett government was voted out of office. In other states it is the subject of political struggle both within and outside political parties. It is now in retreat in Queensland and New South Wales. As Neutze (1997: ch. 9) points out, privatisation has many variations and subtleties which produce different effects and limit choices in different ways.

The agenda has been pursued without careful and dispassionate examination of the political, technical and ecological consequences of having a city's major physical infrastructure provided by private corporations often controlled by geographically distant parent companies with no interest in or commitment to the city. City infrastructure has become vulnerable to serious breakdown, as was evidenced by several episodes during the late 1990s: the failure of Auckland's (New Zealand) electricity supply, the supposed infection of Sydney's water supply, and the explosion at Longford in Victoria which cut off the state's gas for two weeks. Following the Longford disaster, serious maintenance problems threatening worker safety were revealed at Shell's oil refinery at Corio near Geelong, (Button 1998: 2). Maintenance company director Ike Solomon commented: 'It is a standing joke in our industry that to easily get money for maintenance, you need to have some sort of failure, hopefully not catastrophic, for the bean counters to take notice' (Solomon 1998: 15).

The two other important elements of the CL model to which we now turn are greatly enhanced engagement in entrepreneurialism at state level coupled with reduced autonomy for local government.

Enhanced entrepreneurialism

Under corporate liberalism, 'place competition' between Australian cities for investment capital has replaced planning for human needs. Entrepreneurialism, already evident in SDM and in CB regimes, has been taken to new extremes. There is no serious discussion of what industries the investment should flow to. In the new policy orthodoxy, state governments solicit new capital for their cities, while municipalities are expected to act as economic 'growth machines' (Peel 1995). Here, any new urban investment—even the most trivial-seeming sporting event or office development—is hailed by state and city governments as a victory over competitors and a harbinger of 'better times' for all. Stilwell (1997) describes the new emphasis on competition between cities as a 'beggar-thy-neighbour' approach to urban policy.

Entrepreneurialism under SDM is noted in chapter 4 (Boxes 4.2 and 4.3). The theme of 'cities in competition' continued (Box 5.1). Here we can see a significant continuity between SDM and CL. 'Place competition' and 'place marketing' have become a feature of urban planning around the world and can be attributed to the pressure of fiscal restraint, the perception of 'mobile' capital that can be 'attracted' and the neoliberal orthodoxy. As a consequence, under CL, strategic and even statutory planning have been transformed into vehicles for city *promotion*, rather than city *regulation*. More broadly, the urban policy emphasis has been shifted from *managing* cities under SDM—in which certainly entrepreneurialism played a part—to *selling* cities under CL.

BOX 5.1 CITIES IN COMPETITION III: MELBOURNE GOES FOR SILVER

In 1988, after intense lobbying by the Victorian State government and Melbourne City Council, Melbourne was selected as the Australian candidate city for the 1996 Olympics. Not everyone was convinced. A community coalition, *Bread Not Circuses*, urged both governments not to waste public money on the bid and to concentrate on substantive planning issues, including the needs of under-privileged communities. The bid failed and Atlanta got the games. Sydney later won the golden 'first prize' of the 2000 Olympics.

Melbourne, led by the state government, kept trying, and won what might be described as 'silver', a second place in the realm of major sporting events. With the proposal to turn one of Melbourne's fine inner-city parks into a race track for nearly half the year, Victoria won the right to host Australia's Formula One Grand Prix. Again, this event was mightily opposed by local groups of residents living in the neighbourhood of Albert Park. But the opposition was forcefully crushed with the help of legislation denying residents access to the courts to argue for their rights.

The state government succeeded in its bid for the 2006 Commonwealth Games when the only remaining contender, the City of Wellington in New Zealand, withdrew from the contest. This bid involves a new appropriation of public land in an inner-city park for corporate sport. A new netball and hockey centre is to be built in the Royal Park 'precinct'. The Melbourne 2006 Common-wealth Games Bid Proprietary Limited [sic] claims that 'our Clean and Green

Yet, in implementation, the IP Act opens the way to weakening regulatory powers and introducing a bias in favour of development. This weakening is premised on the assumption that growth must be encouraged because of 'globalisation'. Moon (1998a: 25) comments:

> Like the RMA, the structure of the IP Act targets outcomes as the determining criterion; land use planners are to 'focus on the effects of development' (Yearbury 1997: 25). As Director-General of the Department of Local Government and Planning, Yearbury believes that because 'global capital is footloose' and regulatory structures inhibit developmental options, it is therefore preferable for each council to indicate both acceptable and unacceptable impacts.

But what is 'acceptable' and what 'unacceptable' is usually a matter of debate. It is difficult for a council with very limited resources to 'prove' that the balance of effects is negative, and without conclusive proof of such an outcome a development will proceed.

More recently, state governments have adopted *cultural* entrepreneurialism as a centrepiece of city promotion. The Victorian state government, probably realising that only Sydney can wear the 'global city' crown in Australia, seems intent now on promoting Melbourne as the premier cultural capital of Australia. Again, South Australia is a fierce competitor, but seems unwilling (or unable) to spend the vast amounts that Victoria is pouring into elite cultural facilities. Between 1994 and 1996, the Art Gallery of South Australia doubled its size, at a cost of $26 million. This considerable investment paled, however, next to the $160 million which the Victorian state government later committed to the redevelopment of the National Gallery of Victoria (Bonyhady 1999).

Subordinating local government

The CL model, if fully implemented, does not permit deviation from neoliberal norms at local level, whatever local people may desire. Most state governments stepped up pressure on local government to conform to neoliberal principles. In Sydney local government regulations have been overridden by the state in order to promote higher densities and fast-track major projects such as the Fox film studios (Murphy & Wu 1998). However, only in Victoria has the CL model been fully implemented at local level.

Mr Kennett, who had strongly opposed such restructuring of local government in opposition, turned to the task with vigour once in government. This was not a U-turn—simply that Kennett in certain respects had an opposite agenda for local government from the social democratic reforms proposed by the Labor Party. Instead of empower-ment, the aim was subordination to state priorities for development and to the neoliberal model of governance.

In May 1993 legislation was introduced to create a Local Govern-ment Board, which would have the power to remove councillors, appoint administrators and alter local government boundaries without bringing the matter before Parliament in each case, as had been necessary under the existing Local Government Act. The Local Govern-ment Board under its chair Ms Leonie Burke, a former mayor of the City of Prahran, went about the task of removing councillors and amalgamating first the municipalities of the regional towns of Geelong, Ballarat and Bendigo, and then all the metropolitan municipalities and rural towns and shires. Local opposition was simply overridden.

The Kennett government reduced the number of local councils in Victoria from 211 to 84. Over the two to three years in which this process occurred, local democracy across the state was simply suspended and councils were run by state government-appointed commissioners. These commissioners were not mere caretakers but were explicitly charged with implementing the goals of the state government for privatisation and competitive tendering. Many local assets—town halls, meeting halls, libraries—which local communities had come to regard as *their* public property were sold off. The government forced councils to put half of all their expenditure out to competitive tender. It insisted that compulsory competitive tendering (CCT) include welfare services that have not been subjected to tender anywhere else in the world.

Where a local council seemed to pose a threat to state priorities, the Kennett government intervened. One example occurred in the Shire of Nillumbik. In Victoria all municipalities are required to produce a 'Municipal Strategic Statement'. The Shire of Nillumbik in Melbourne's outer eastern fringe covers what has become known as the 'green wedge'—a sector of agricultural land between corridors of development on either side. The Nillumbik Statement is committed to preventing encroachment of urban development into this 'wedge' and to encour-aging the use of public transport (Nillumbik Shire 1997). The state government, on the other hand, wants to complete a ring freeway around Melbourne whose explicit intention is to encourage commercial, industrial and residential development on the periphery.

In 1998 the Shire of Nillumbik was the only fringe municipality to come out firmly against the ring road. The State government instigated an 'inquiry' into the council. The ostensible reasons for the inquiry involved a 'dispute' between the Shire President and the Chief Executive on matters of exceptional triviality. On the grounds that political conflicts within the council were resolved by majority vote (an 'unfortunate' feature of democracy which in this instance contradicted the plans of the Minister), the council was sacked for failing to deliver good governance. The City of Darebin, one of 10 councils in Victoria which had quickly developed a Local Agenda 21 policy process (Whittaker 1996: 4), had already been sacked by the state government. The state was not, of course, openly opposed to councils that supported Local Agenda 21. It is just that those councils with a more activist and independent frame of mind tend to antagonise a state government that desires councils to be simple agencies of state policy.

Corporate liberalism and urban governance

What then have been the effects of CL on urban governance? Here we first consider the goals of the CL agenda itself and how well they were achieved in the period of dominance of the CL program in the states. Then we consider some of the costs of CL.

Goal achievement

The CL goal was to reduce the overall size of the public sector and, by attracting private sector business investment, to reduce unemployment. What effect did the agenda have on the achievement of these goals? We get a glimpse of an answer in the figures contained in Tables 5.1 to 5.3. There is not space to enter a full analysis of these figures here, but the broad indications are clear enough.

Table 5.1 records the *dollar change* in government expenditure, and expenditure per person in the period when CL was most dominant: between 1989/90 and 1996/97. Table 5.2 records the *percentage change* in government expenditure, and expenditure per person. Of course it should be noted that levels of expenditure vary from year to year, and we are looking here at just two sample years—at the beginning and end of the period. We can see that shrinking of the public sector occurred in the period in only a few sectors of expenditure, most notably in tertiary education in most states (as responsibility for tertiary education was shifted to the Commonwealth), primary and secondary education in Victoria and public hospitals in Western Australia and Tasmania. Most states (with the exception of South Australia) substantially reduced their interest payments on public sector debt and will reduce it further in future as infrastructure privatisation shifts the burden of debt from the public to

Table 5.1 Dollar change in general government expenditure (states and territories) 1989–97

Selected sectors	NSW	Vic	Q'land	SA	WA	Tas	NT	ACT
Public order and safety	+207	+292	+247	+99	+184	+34	+31	+73
	+13	+50	+39	+58	+70	+78	+72	290
Education: primary and	+791	−174	+558	+33	+196	+8	+31	+7
secondary	+85	−76	+84	−1	+36	+33	+31	+94
Education: tertiary	−485	−583	−297	−209	−160	−48	+17	+9
	−94	−142	−119	−151	−117	−95	+53	+47
Hospitals (acute care	+231	+80	+295	+35	−60	−44	+26	+50
institutions)	−4	−10	+19	+6	−100	−77	+44	+241
Housing	+88	+17	+29	+63	+188	−10	−5	+29
	+11	+1	+7	+39	+98	−19	−5	+121
Welfare services	+238	+218	+189	+57	+32	+52	+5	+16
	+29	+40	+44	+34	−1	+113	−1	+72
Recreation and culture	+137	−10	+124	+32	+26	+14	+17	+11
	+19	−5	+33	+18	+10	+33	+50	+57
Public debt transactions	−735	−205	−205	+295	−195	−64	−39	+1
	−144	−66	−84	+188	−147	−45	−338	+20
Total current outlays	−1560	−2409	+2213	+743	+456	+72	+75	+202
	−465	−736	+297	+387	−121	+898	−608	+1034

In each box: Top figure = $ million change: 1996/97 on 1989/90.
Bottom figure = $ per-capita change: 1996/97 on 1989/90.
Source: ABS 'Total Current Outlays of General Government' (data supplied) CPI Deflator applied (ABS Consumer Price Index, 6401.0 December Quarter 1997, table 10).

the private sector. (In Victoria, for instance, in 1996/97 the impact of electricity and gas privatisations was still to come.)

But the cost of public debt was not as great as might have been imagined, considering the single-mindedness with which public debt reduction was pursued by CL governments. The cost of public ownership of the nation's infrastructure was, for example, significantly lower than the cost to the individual of a home mortgage. In 1996/97 annual public debt transactions stood at $225 per person in New South Wales, $311 in Victoria and $73 in Queensland. Privatisation, on the other hand, was an expensive option. Victoria spent $419 million in fees to private consultants for restructuring and selling its public enterprises (Myer 1999: 1).

States simply shifted their expenditure priorities and the CL agenda was successfully resisted in some states. Thus, while Victoria spent less on education over the period, Queensland began to spend more, reversing the position of a decade earlier. In 1996/97 Victoria spent $606 per person in the population on primary and secondary education. Queensland spent $648 and New South Wales $669. In the same year, while Victoria spent $469 per person on public hospitals, New South Wales spent $565 and Queensland $490.

Table 5.2 Percentage change in general government expenditure (states and territories) 1989–97

Selected sectors	NSW	Vic	Q'land	SA	WA	Tas	NT	ACT
Public order and safety	+15	+36	+46	+32	+49	+37	+31	+487
	+5	+27	+21	+27	+30	+41	+12	+539
Education: primary and secondary	+29	−7	+43	+4	+22	+3	+21	+3
	+18	−13	+18	0	+7	+6	+3	+13
Education: tertiary	−40	−53	−54	−59	−44	−45	+42	+21
	−45	−56	−62	−61	−51	−44	+21	+31
Hospitals (acute care institutions)	+8	+5	+27	+6	−7	−15	+26	+33
	−1	−2	+5	+1	−19	−13	+7	+45
Housing	+39	+10	+122	+56	+375	−29	+14	+116
	+27	+2	+84	+49	+315	−27	−2	+135
Welfare services	+39	+52	+106	+42	+14	+110	−16	+43
	+27	+42	+71	+36	−1	+117	−1	+56
Recreation and culture	+68	−5	+239	+30	+46	+32	+39	+27
	+54	−11	+181	+25	+27	+36	+19	+38
Public debt transactions	−38	−15	−49	+77	−39	−27	−27	+3
	−44	−20	−58	+70	−47	−9	−38	+12
Total current outlays	−10	−17	+39	+19	+10	+5	+7	+26
	−18	−22	+15	+14	−4	+30	−9	+37

In each box: Top figure = per cent total change: 1996/97 on 1989/90
      Bottom figure = per cent per-capita change: 1996/97 on 1989/90
Source: ABS 'Total Current Outlays of General Government' (data supplied), CPI Deflator applied (ABS Consumer Price Index, 6401.0 December Quarter 1997, table 10).

What is also noticeable is that state governments that prided them-selves on efficiency and cost-cutting started to spend much more on public order and safety, and on social welfare—that is on punishing people, and looking after people who could not support themselves. We may reasonably conclude that this was not because of a sudden generosity on the part of neoliberal governments but rather because urban life had become both less safe and more insecure and rises in spending could not be avoided. The neoliberal world, we may conclude, is both inherently less secure and more punitive.

What of unemployment? On its election in 1992, the neoliberal state government in Victoria declared (in Nicholls 1994: 24):

> The first major reality is unemployment and the need for economic development. There are many in Victoria to whom real and sustainable employment prospects are of more immediate importance than increased residential amenity.

In this aim state governments across Australia have failed, and Victoria, which has taken CL further than other states, fared no better than the others. Under a Labor government, in the period before the 1990 property crash, Victoria had almost half the unemployment rate achieved in the period of 'recovery' boasted by the conservative government in

Table 5.3 Unemployment in Australian states and territories 1989–97

Year	NSW (%)	Victoria (%)	Q'land (%)	SA (%)	WA (%)
1989	6.3	4.6	6.7	7.5	6.7
1990	6.3	5.5	8.1	7.2	8.1
1991	8.3	10.2	9.5	9.7	9.5
1992	10.4	11.8	11.0	12.3	11.0
1993	10.5	12.0	10.3	10.4	10.3
1994	9.6	10.4	9.1	10.6	9.1
1995	7.3	8.4	8.7	9.9	8.7
1996	7.5	7.9	9.2	8.5	9.2
1997	7.3	9.0	8.7	9.3	8.7

Source: ABS File 6202.0, table 8.

the later 1990s, and with the same **labour force participation rate** (the participation rate was 63.6 per cent in Victoria in 1989, when unemployment was 4.6 per cent and the same in 1997, when unemployment was 9.0 per cent; see Table 5.3).

Revised estimates from the Australian Bureau of Statistics show that in the 1990s Victoria's economy failed to keep pace with the rest of Australia: 'From 1993 to 1998 household income per head grew less in Victoria than in any other State except Tasmania, and Victoria's share of national output has fallen in almost every sector of economic activity' (Colebatch 1999: 5).

Corporate liberalism, then, tried to deliver urban governance on the cheap and failed to reduce unemployment. Australia's adoption of neoliberalism and especially its particular state form (CL) has brought costs which have made our cities less fair, less equal and less ecologically sustainable. It is impossible entirely to detach the effects of CL from that of its predecessor SDM, for both have been affected by currents of neo-liberalism. What we depict below is rather the combined effects of tendencies that have been increasingly evident and are of great importance for urban governance and planning.

Costs

Managerial policies with some claim to rationality, which were being introduced cautiously and with some thought under SDM, were rammed through quickly and with no consultation under CL. The 'casemix' funding system was introduced in Victoria at the same time as massive cuts to public hospital funding, so that it became impossible to assess whether the obvious defects in health care that followed were a result of casemix or of the cuts (Carter 1996). Professor Stephen Duckett, the architect of casemix in Victoria, remarked that 'the combined effects of casemix and a drastic reduction in the funding of hospitals has resulted in a serious deterioration in the quality of service provision' (in Tullock 1995: 455). The chief executive of the Monash Medical Centre in Melbourne said, 'The Victorian Government views casemix as a pseudo-scientific instrument to justify massive budget cuts' (Birnbauer 1994: 10). While medical care staff were reduced in public hospitals in Victoria, annual reports of the regional hospital groups show that administrative costs of the health system increased by some 22 per cent over two years 1995–96 to 1997–98 (Davidson, 1999: p. 17).

Under the CL treatment of education, schools are required to compete with one another for resources. Education, like health care, is treated as a commodity that is sold to consumers. Instead of the principle of provision by the state in accordance with need, mechanisms are introduced to allow those with more money to purchase more and better education. Schools are allowed to charge fees to provide for all facilities and activities above the bare minimum. Schools are made dependent on local businesses through 'sponsorship'. In both cases local communities with time and disposable income (i.e. rich local communities) can raise more money and pay more for the education of their children than poorer communities. Similar criticisms apply wherever social services (e.g. libraries, childcare services) are subjected to the neoliberal demands of privatisation and outsourcing. Reduced funding certainly means fewer teachers and larger class sizes. But despite various attempts by state governments to measure educational outcomes, the claim that reduced funds for schooling makes education more 'efficient' is unsustainable because, except in the trivial sense of numbers of students put through schools, there is no meaningful national measure of education outcomes: smaller dollar inputs, yes; the same or better outcomes, don't know (Steering Committee 1998: 41).

In the built environment of Australia's cities, 'urban consolidation' could have had a modest but beneficial impact on travel patterns if it meant increasing densities around public transport nodes. Instead, the policy was applied crudely and thoughtlessly, as an open invitation to developers to make private profits from communal values such as pleasant environments with good access to facilities. Troy's (1996b) extensive investigation of Australia's urban consolidation policy initiatives during the 1980s and 90s exposes how this ostensibly green reform initiative eventually produced very little in the way of ecological gains while arguably encouraging the development of environmentally deprived landscapes for working- and middle-class households (see also Peel 1995; Orchard 1995; McLoughlin 1991; Charles 1990).

On the environment more broadly, Christoff's (1998) recent

thoroughgoing review of environmental policy in Victoria shows just how vulnerable are environmental planning and protection policies in a regime whose first (some say only) priority is economic growth. According to Christoff (1998: 30), the neoliberal project caused the 'demolition of environmental institutions' in Victoria. Privatisation can lead to environmentally damaging outcomes, creating malign incentives to use more resources when conservation is urgently required (Ernst 1997: 16). An example of just such an outcome is illustrated in Box 5.2.

BOX 5.2 CONSUMING CITIES: MELBOURNE'S ELECTRICITY PRIVATISATION

Until 1996 the production and distribution of electricity was wholly in public ownership, incorporated under the State Electricity Commission of Victoria (SECV). The SECV published a discussion paper in 1989 which set out alternative strategies to balance the supply of and demand for energy to meet the target agreed at the Toronto conference on global warming: 20 per cent reduction on 1988 levels of carbon dioxide emissions by 2005.

The strategy included 'aggressive demand management' through extensive conservation and co-generation programs, and the early retirement of inefficient plant (namely the Hazelwood Power Station). The state government relinquished effective control of the supply of energy services when it privatised electricity production in 1996. Mr Dan Farell, the new company chairman of Eastern Energy (one of the new electricity production companies), said he hoped to boost profits by increasing the sale of electricity. Farell said Victoria's electricity consumption was low compared with Texas: 'Eastern Energy customers use, on average, 5,600 kilowatt-hours per year compared with 14,283 kilowatt-hours in Texas' (D. Walker 1995: 3).

The Hazelwood Power Station is working away at full steam. The plant emitted 9.45 million tonnes of CO_2 in 1995/96. By the year 2000 emissions are forecast to be 15.1 million tonnes (Greenhouse Challenge 1997). This is a real *increase* of *60 per cent* on 1995 levels. Hazelwood is by far the worst example in the LaTrobe Valley, but its emissions are not offset by real reductions in emissions by other power stations.

In California in the USA the energy companies (called public utility companies) are privately owned. But they are required by public regulation to sell not energy but 'energy services'—the qualities like home warming or cooling which energy production provides. They can do this by investing in, say, insulation of buildings (and other design features) which save energy to achieve the same level of energy services, or in investing in alternative sources of energy. If they do this they are said to produce not 'megawatts' but *'negawatts'*.

The privatisation of electricity in Victoria could have been designed along the same lines as the California system. Instead the primary consideration when

> the SECV was sold off was maximising the financial price paid. To do this required that the government encumber the companies with the *minimum* of regulation. So in effect, along with the electricity producers and distributors, the government sold the right to pollute the atmosphere.

As was well understood by earlier SDM governments (see chapter 4), the planning and environmental policy domains overlap. Environmental impact assessment procedures involve both environmental and planning legislation—subdivision controls have a similar dual constitution. The policy of removing 'unnecessary deterrents' to development has been applied in both domains. Regulatory impediments have been removed from the paths of major infrastructure works—including a set of giant new freeway and tollway projects—involving deregulatory and 'facilitating' initiatives across transport, planning and environmental portfolios. Privatisation of the public transport system is proceeding in Victoria along the lines of the British model, one which is now almost everywhere (including in Britain) acknowledged to have been a costly failure.

The Kennett government, through the Office of Major Projects, developed a raft of projects which it cynically labelled 'Agenda 21' in provocative contrast to the world program for sustainable development agreed at the Rio Earth Summit in 1992. Under the title of 'Agenda 21' it was announced: 'The Minister will fast-track projects to ensure that this Government is truly pro-business' (Victoria 1993b). The licence fees from the Casino provide funding for the projects that are designed to boost the image of Melbourne, particularly downtown Melbourne, as a 'competitive city'. Mr Kennett boasts (Victoria 1994: Foreword):

> The Government's Agenda 21 program is already helping to significantly change the appearance and character of the City by providing world-class, fully-funded cultural, commercial and entertainment facilities including Victoria's first Casino, a new $250 million State Museum and $120 million Exhibition Centre.

The neoliberal anti-planning project has not been confined to Victoria. In New South Wales, Stein (1998) records the progressive dismantling of planning and environmental policy during the 1990s by a series of administrations that have advanced a broad deregulatory agenda. In South Australia, Hamnett and Lennon (1998: 1) provide a similar

There it is my child the modern, deregulated, rational amoral, free market economy. The law of the Jungle. How awesomely BEAUTIFUL !

Law of the Jungle ?! I see no colored butterflies, no orchids or parrots. I see no great leafy canopies or gentle creatures of the wild. I see no jungle at all.

What we have here is ugly, cold concrete with rivers of rubbish and poison; suffocation, sadness and the frenzy of angry machines which nobody can stop. This is not jungle. THIS is MADNESS! Your law is COMPLETELY INAPPROPRIATE.

O.K. then CLEVER DICK. We'll change it. Who cares. We'll call it "Law of the JINGLE. We'll de-regulate the language if it's a problem. "LAW OF THE JINGLE"... How does that sound ? SOUNDS FINE

leunig

Figure 5.2 Corporate liberalism has made the funding of public works dependent on profits from gambling supplied by the most vulnerable in the community. Corporate liberalism has subjected our cities and public services to market logic—the law of the jingle!

Source: Michael Leunig, *The Age.*

account, arguing that in the past five years the conservative administration has 'presided over a litany of offences against orderly planning'.

Corporate liberalism has been accompanied by forms of secrecy which strike at the heart of democracy. The Auditor-General of Victoria, his office itself under threat of privatisation, in his final report wrote (Hannan 1999: 1):

> There appears to be a widely held belief, particularly prevalent among senior bureaucrats, that financial arrangements with the private sector should be shielded from parliamentary and taxpayer gaze . . . Unless Parliament is provided with appropriate information, its capacity to exercise its constitutional right to monitor the operations of the executive will be restricted, and accountability and good governance in Victoria may be irreparably harmed.

Corporate liberalism has made the funding of public works depend on profits from gambling supplied by the most vulnerable in the community. Corporate liberalism has sought to subject all public services to market logic. But markets meet only the needs of those who can pay.

This is no design fault or market failure, it is the essence of markets. If you can't pay, you don't get. State provision of services on the basis of equal provision for all in need is a powerful corrective to the immense inequalities that arise under a market system for reasons *outside* abstract market logic but inherent in *real* markets (bad and good luck, inherited wealth, manipulation, political deception, exploitation, corruption, crime, tax avoidance), but for which market logic has no corrective.

Most importantly, CL has placed extraordinary faith in the wisdom of the political directorate at the top. It is an autocratic doctrine that brooks no suggestion of policy alternatives. At every stage it has eliminated the possibility of counteradvice, of informed debate, of argument, of openness and transparency. Rather, CL has stamped hard on people's rights to object and offer alternatives. By handing over to private entrepreneurs not only the delivery of services but now even their planning and regulation, CL has robbed the state of its intelligence. By shedding the expertise built over many years and held for the public in the public service, CL has not only hollowed out the state but has 'dumbed it down'.

Conclusion

CL was taken furthest in Victoria under the leadership of Jeffrey Kennett. Its adoption by other states has been less far-reaching, for various reasons contingent on state politics and histories. CL remains a contested and only partially fulfilled program and, as we write, the struggle to implement CL is being waged with the help of the Commonwealth government in the hands of the coalition parties and dominated by a powerful neoliberal elite in the federal bureaucracy. Resistance to it, however, is growing as evidenced by the demise of the Kennett government in late 1999.

In the light of the experience of the failure of neoliberal governments in Australia to make a serious impact on unemployment—even at a time of surging growth in Australia—we might do well to reflect on Hugh Stretton's observation that, 'a general restraint of the public sector is rational only if it is used as a crude and easy way of maintaining unemployment in the private sector, perhaps with the idea of weakening the bargaining power of labour' (Stretton 1977: 69–70). We might also reflect on the futility and inefficiency of inter-state competition. Today we see states falling over each other in the rush to offer incentives for casinos, gambling and sporting events, which produce little in income from overseas buyers but instead impoverish large sections of society at home.

How might these events be explained and interpreted? To understand what has happened to Australia's cities (as discussed in chapter 3) and their planning and governance (here and in chapter 4), we need to look further than the events themselves: we need to understand them in the light of the theoretical critiques of planning which have developed in the past 20 years. The critique of planning from the perspective of managerialism and neoliberalism is just one such, albeit one of the most influential. But why has it been so influential when there has been a considerable body of opinion opposed to it—and it is profoundly distrusted by electorates? Perhaps it is because this critique and the prescriptions that flow from it have resonated in certain ways with other discourses, discourses of those who oppose neoliberal practices but have little to offer in their place. We turn to the first of these discourses—political economy—in chapter 6.

Part II

The forces for change

6 Cities for sale: urban political economy

In this chapter we begin our review of the theoretical perspectives and political movements that have questioned various aspects of planning theory and practice in the postwar era. Generally speaking, these forces for change in planning were international in character, taking broadly similar forms in Western (especially English-speaking) countries. For example, Marxism, environmentalism, feminism, managerialism and neoliberalism—themes we review in this part of the book—were sourced in international theoretical and social movements. 'On the ground', however, there were marked differences in how the various critical forces were interpreted theoretically and organised politically. Moreover, as we will show, there were important radical initiatives undertaken by Australian urbanists and activists—such as the 'green bans' of the 1970s (see chapter 8)—that influenced the course of overseas debates about urban governance. Our intention in Part II is to trace the origins and character of the main forms of planning critique, and then consider how they were manifested and applied in the Australian theoretical and policy contexts. We begin by considering the urban political economy critique of planning.

Urban political economy describes a set of distinct theoretical perspectives—including Marxism and anarchism—which are critical of how cities are created and organised by advanced capitalist societies. These radical perspectives on mainstream planning were originally drawn from broader critiques of the capitalist welfare state forwarded by social scientists and by grassroots political movements with increasing intensity from the 1960s. Three key contemporary political issues in the 1960s convinced many Western theorists and activists that capitalism was a fundamentally unjust and flawed form of social organisation. These issues were: the Vietnam War; the civil rights campaigns in the USA and elsewhere (in Australia, there was increasing attention given to the plight of Aborigines); and the enduring poverty experienced by many people in Western and non-Western urban ghettos and deprived rural areas. These concerns fostered a growing interest in the 1970s among theoreticians and activists in radical perspectives that argued for the replacement of capitalism with a society founded on radically different political-economic principles (e.g. socialism, anarchism). Urban political economic analysis reflected this deeply critical view of capitalism and emphasised the limits of planning within the conventional frameworks that had been established in the postwar era in Western countries, such as Australia.

This chapter briefly describes the political economic critique of planning. First we examine how urban political economy emerged from the 1960s as part of a general and growing disillusionment of many theorists and activists with the postwar welfare state and, in particular, with planning as then manifested. After this we review the impact of urban political economy on Australian theoretical debates and political practice.

Planning: 'oiling the wheels of capitalism'

Following World War II, urban planning became institutionalised in English-speaking countries. Planning became a profession in its own right, with its own academy. Initially urban and regional planning was conceived as the rational organisation of space undertaken by state institutions in concert with the key professions (architects, planners, engineers) and private development interests. This was rather a tech-nocratic view of planning, because it ascribed to the 'rational planner' a variety of bureaucratic and quasi-scientific roles. The 'science' of urban and regional planning was 'built on the premise that well-ordered and efficient cities and regions could be created through the application of uncovered laws of spatial behaviour and organization' (Johnston et al. 1994: 497). As planning became increasingly professionalised and tech-nocratic it drifted away from its roots in social democratic politics. From the 1960s, the grand social democratic vision to restrain and civilise capitalism that we describe in chapter 2 was less compelling for a new generation of technically minded planning professionals. The idea that planning was a political project was anathema to many (though not all) new professionals, who saw themselves as detached, objective experts whose main role was to improve the technical management of space and urban places.

In the later 1960s, however, more politically aware observers began to develop a pluralist theory of planning, drawing on ideas stemming from the American experience of urbanisation and from American political science (Gans 1968; Faludi 1973). Pluralists were critical of the planners' claim to objectivity and to representing the public interest. From these influences emerged a much more political view of planning, which saw it as an element in the 'play of power' that was said to characterise politics in Western liberal democracies (Lindblom 1968). The analysis of planning as a response to urban conflict stemmed from American pluralist political theory: for example, from Hunter's analysis of community power (Hunter 1953) and Dahl's more famous examination of urban development in New Haven (Dahl 1961). The tradition continued with the work of Simmie (1974) in Britain, and Rabinowitz (1969), Mollenkopf (1983) and Waste (1987) in the USA.

BOX 6.1 AMERICAN PLURALISM

Pluralism is the political theory of democracy that holds that society is composed of many different legitimate, conflicting interests and groups. Each group is entitled to define what is in its own interest and to struggle to get that interest realised by government. Indeed, government itself is made up of contending interest groups. Policy is merely the vector of pressures from many different directions. In these circumstances a general or universal 'public interest', or 'common good', is impossible to define except from the particular perspective of a particular group.

The 'tyranny of the majority' was feared by early pluralists such as John Stuart Mill and Alexis de Tocqueville (who had seen the results of the French Revolution of 1789). Different varieties of pluralist thought emphasise different attributes of liberal democracy. Arthur Bentley, at the turn of the century, proposed that government was nothing but the activity of pressure groups. Joseph Schumpeter argued that governments were formed by competing political elites, and democracy was merely the process of competition for the people's vote. Robert Dahl looked to the institutional rules of democracy which he termed 'polyarchy'—rule by many groups each of which, taken individually, represented a minority. In their later work Dahl and Charles Lindblom (sometimes called 'neo-pluralists') acknowledged that in a pluralist society business occupies a 'privileged position', in that business elites must always be consulted on policy by governments.

In the context of the **Cold War**, pluralism was used to differentiate liberal democracies from the centralised economic planning of the Eastern Bloc justified with reference to the common good. Pluralism reinforced the West's political argument that advanced capitalist states were essentially democratic and that socialist countries were essentially totalitarian. In the pluralist outlook, Western democracies were defined by the wide dispersion of power and authority (Robertson 1986: 259). Thus, 'As power was disaggregated in this way, and, according to the theory, all legitimate groups got some say in decision-making, the essentially "democratic" nature of [Western] societies was claimed to be upheld' (Robertson 1986: 259). After the Soviet empire collapsed, the need to assert value in diversity diminished and neoliberalism laid claim to a singular public interest.

Pluralists were opposed by elite theorists, such as C. Wright Mills, who held that more or less permanent elites in different political and economic spheres held the real power in American society. Acknowledgement by Dahl and Lindblom of the reality of 'business privilege' marked a major concession to elite theory, with far-reaching implications for normative democracy. Dahl (1985) suggests that so great is the power of modern business corporations that they ought to be subject to the same norms of democracy to which liberals expect states to submit.

By the mid-1960s, the social democratic vision was fading on a larger political canvas. In most Western countries, the promise of social and economic renewal laid out at the end of World War II was beginning to look hollow as problems of injustice and environmental decay mounted. In many Western countries, such as Britain, postwar reconstruction did not bring about the promised prosperity and equality. While capitalism recovered and prospered during the Long Boom, there remained large pockets of poverty, homelessness, unemployment and environmental decay, especially in the inner regions of American and British cities (e.g. Jackson 1985; Llewelyn-Davies et al. 1977). In their 1973 book *The Poverty of Planning*, Blair and his fellow authors observed with dismay the American ghetto, the South African squatter settlement, and the bitterly divided cities of Northern Ireland, in a bleak assessment of planning's postwar reform legacy.

In most urban and national contexts, class differences seemed as entrenched as ever. For many, the social democratic renewal project had failed: its main 'tools'—including economic, social and urban planning—had lost their political purpose and were now simply tech- nocratic instruments that served to reinforce a deeply unjust status quo. Thus, 'By the end of the 1960s . . . the failure of planners to resolve many of the pressing issues of the day—such as poverty, deprivation and inequality—led to a questioning of that apparently rational process' (Johnston et al. 1994: 497). A variety of political theorists and social interests were vigorously opposing the pluralist view of the state as a straightforward representative of key social interests. Radical political critiques of the capitalist state emphasised the control that social and economic elites exercised over public policy, including planning (Galbraith 1971; McConnell 1967).

Disillusionment with the effects of urban planning led urban analysts (particularly British planners and geographers) to search for critical frameworks with which to understand what had happened to the project of reconstruction, and to recover its values. Many sought explanation in Marx's theory of capitalism and the state, though other radical thought streams emerged, including Bookchin's (1974) 'libertarian municipalism', which was grounded in anarchist thinking. Some of the brightest young geographers from Britain and Australia went to North American universities and began to use Marxist theory to analyse the development and management of urban space in capitalist societies. Several highly influential essays appeared, the most famous being David Harvey's (1973) *Social Justice and the City*. Harvey's book was an early milestone on the road to a radical theoretical understanding of urban planning in capitalist societies. Among other things, the book examines 'the ghetto', an enduring problem that mainstream planning theory and practice had proved incapable of comprehending and solving. Harvey casts aside conventional planning strategies for managing cities in favour of 'revolutionary solutions' that would address the fundamental political economic causes of injustice in capitalist societies. In the revolutionary scenario, the private land market would be replaced with 'a socially controlled urban land market and socialized control of the housing sector' (Harvey 1973: 137). What Harvey had in mind was the application to urban planning of Marx's famous dictum 'From each according to their ability and to each according to their needs'.

The verdict of these critiques for planning and for planners can only be described as extremely discouraging. Clark and Dear (1981) proposed a state-centred version of Marxist analysis that acknowledged that the sphere of government was an important source of social change. Previously, some conventional Marxist accounts had focused rather exclusively on the role of business, or 'capital', in social development without giving much attention to the state. Yet even in the new accounts the democratic state was ultimately viewed as beholden to the capitalist class, which held the keys to the finance for state programs. Castells (1978) and Harvey (1978) conveyed essentially the same message. The planner is, and can only ever be, a functionary of the capitalist state apparatus. For Scott and Roweis (1977: 1118), planning theory was an 'ideology' that masked what planners really did: reinforce and legitimise 'the social and property relations of capitalist society'. Capitalism (interestingly not a term used by Marx himself, according to van der Pijl 1998: 27), was portrayed as a closed political–economic system with no space for transformation from within.

Other critiques questioned the scientific basis of planning theory and urban studies in general. In his influential book *The Urban Question* (1977), Manuel Castells dismissed urban theory as a misleading abstraction, which failed to comprehend that urban problems were in fact 'problems of societies not of particular types of places', including cities (Johnston et al. 1994: 652). Among other things, Castells was attacking the conventional planning assumption that urban problems were sourced in the arrangement and management of cities. Applying a Marxian analysis, Castells argued that such problems were not specific to cities themselves—rather, they were manifestations of deeper faults in the political economic organisation of society as a whole. In short, capitalism was inevitably beset by 'irrationalities in the allocation of urban land' (Dear & Scott 1981: 12) that no amount of 'rational planning' could correct.

BOX 6.2 MARXISM

Marxism is a theory of society derived from the political economy of Karl Marx (1818–83) and from its further development by Friedrich Engels (1820–95). In economics, Marxism is the principal alternative to neoclassical theory, which forms the basis of conventional analysis in capitalist societies. Since the time of Marx, Marxism has become a broad theoretical framework that now embraces a great variety of perspectives, though all are united by the attention given to class as a central force of social development.

In contrast to other major social theories (e.g. pluralism) that assume the existence of underlying 'social consensus', Marxism conceives capitalist society as fundamentally conflict-ridden. The principal source of conflict is the unequal distribution of property—all value-producing resources—between the capitalist and working (or 'proletarian') classes, with an unpaid proportion of labour creating the surplus which is expropriated by the capitalist class. The property-owning capitalist class controls production and has substantial social and economic power over the working class that owns little apart from its own capacity for work. By virtue of its economic power, the capitalist class also exercises considerable control over non-production realms, including the state and the domestic sphere of 'reproduction'. Political conflict inevitably arises as the working class struggles either for a share of the wealth held by capitalists (reformist politics) or seeks to overthrow the entire capitalist social system and replace it with a society based on cooperation and the social ownership of resources (revolutionary politics).

The fundamental ethical premise of Marxism is that capitalist society is unjust and based on an exploitative relationship between capitalists and workers. Wage workers carry out the production of goods and services but capitalists get to keep the profits from this labour. The abolition of private property is therefore necessary to ensure equality and an end to exploitation.

Apart from ethical deficiencies, capitalism is cast by Marxism as a profoundly irrational form of social organisation, inevitably prone to economic and social crises and ultimately unable to satisfy people's full set of material and non-material needs and desires. In more recent years, some Marxists have argued that capitalism is a fundamentally anti-ecological system whose ceaseless need for growth ('accumulation') requires an unrelenting and increasingly ruinous consumption of nature.

In the 20th century, Marxism also came to describe the political frameworks of a set of Marxist or communist societies, many of which differed substantially in their political and social constitution. For example, there were major differences between the social organisation of Soviet-Leninist states led by the USSR and the Maoist states led by China. There were differences again between these two major Marxist blocs and the types of Marxist politics and theory developed by Western scholars and parties.

FURTHER READING

Harvey (1982).

Planning practice at the 'local state' level was subjected to the bitter attack of Cynthia Cockburn (1977), a socialist councillor for Lambeth in inner London. What was the role of planning? To secure the conditions favourable to capitalist accumulation of wealth and contributing to the reproduction of unequal social relations, including the economic subordination of women. This was all that was left to planners of the high hopes of social democratic reconstruction (Cockburn 1977: 42):

> The characteristic function of the state is repression. Its main role is to keep the working class in its place and to set things up, with forceful sanctions, in such a way that capital itself, business interests as a whole, normally survive and prosper.

The only way to recover a sense of the original purpose of planning was for planners to step outside the roles capitalism prescribed for them. Scott and Roweis suggested that planners abandon their codified professional identities and become instead radical provocateurs of urban change; the 'radical planner' would undertake 'the practical development of strategies guiding human action in the search for alternative and progressive urban futures' (Scott & Roweis 1977: 1119). This call echoed other radical critiques of planning made outside the political economy framework, especially from feminists, environmentalists and various democratic activists at the grassroots level. (We turn our attention to these alternative sources of radical critique in chapters 7 and 8.)

Urban political economy in Australia

The resurgence of radical politics in Europe and North America from the late 1960s was mirrored in Australia, where concern over a variety of social justice issues—notably, urban poverty and aboriginal civil/land rights—came to the fore. A series of major studies by Professor Ronald Henderson and colleagues at the University of Melbourne during the 1960s and 70s, culminating in the landmark 1975 Poverty Report to the Commonwealth government, demonstrated the widespread existence of urban poverty in Australia (Fincher & Nieuwenhuysen 1998). Other official surveys (e.g. Little et al. 1974) also found evidence of enduring poverty in Australian cities.

As Hamnett (1997: 763) reflects, Australian planning studies at the time were 'remarkably technocratic and unselfconscious'. His characterisation is true for much of planning debate at the time, but ignores the contributions made by politically conscious urban analysts such as Stretton (e.g. 1970), Stilwell (e.g. 1974) and Troy (e.g. 1978). Their critical (sometimes scathing) analyses of planning policy and urban land development reflected an explicit commitment to social justice, and represent important early contributions to the development of urban political economy in Australia (see also Parker & Troy 1972). Another important exception was Leonie Sandercock's political-economic investigation of urban planning in Australia in her widely read book *Cities for Sale* (1977, first published 1975). At the heart of Sandercock's early exploration lay the questions (Sandercock 1977: 226):

> . . . can capitalism be civilised? Can a conscious overall strategy of redistributive social justice be achieved? Can pollution be controlled? Can the environment be protected bearing in mind the tenacious hold on power by the capitalist class, the methodological weaknesses of democracies in implementing the brightest ideas, especially bearing in mind the effect of the political preferences of the majority of Australians working

through the established political system on factors determining for example the success or failure of urban planning?

Indeed, these very same questions were at the time exercising leftist political theorists throughout the West. For Australia, Sandercock's findings were discouraging: in land use planning, at least, her analysis exposed a history of extraordinary corruption, manipulation and ineptitude that went to the core of the administrative-political system governing urban development (see also Sandercock 1979). It was hard not to draw the conclusion from this gruelling account, rich in disturbing empirical detail, that capitalism was beyond reform in any finally redeeming sense. As for planners, they did little more than oil the wheels of a deeply inequitable system.

However, as Sandercock herself pointed out—though perhaps not entirely convincingly—the question of whether capitalism could be 'civilised' was moot, at least in the West. This was because civil society itself—including the working classes—appeared to have registered a consistent preference for this social form and a deep scepticism, verging sometimes on hostility, towards any rigorous form of socialism. It seemed that all social democratic interests and allied community movements could do was maintain a constant reformist pressure on the capitalist class, and the capitalist state. The modest hope was that socioeconomic and environmental gains could be secured against the ever-present tendencies for the system to produce new forms of social and spatial inequality. Indeed, Sandercock's pessimistic outlook of 1975 seems borne out by the subsequent rise of neoliberalism and by its consequences for public policy, including planning.

Although devastatingly critical of planning and clearly in sympathy with the leftist Labor politics of the time, Sandercock's analysis was not explicitly Marxist. Nonetheless, it set the scene for the later urban political-economic work that flourished during the early 1980s, some drawing on Marxist analysis (e.g. Badcock 1984; Kilmartin et al. 1985; McLoughlin & Huxley 1986; Paris 1982; Sandercock & Berry 1983), and some not (e.g. Paris & Williams 1986; Troy 1981). By way of example, Stilwell's 1980 book *The Impact of the Current Economic Crisis on Cities and Regions* engaged both Marx's economic writings and their application to urban analysis by Harvey and Castells.

From the late 1970s Sandercock's assessment of the planning profession was reinforced by other critiques (see also Sandercock 1983). At issue was the profession's role in reproducing unequal patterns of social power and, more to the point, urban landscapes marked by inequalities of economic opportunity. An early analysis by Kilmartin and Thorns

(1978) had echoed the dismal view of the planning profession that had emerged in European and North American urban political economy. In Australia, 'the quest for professionalism . . . meant that the embryonic profession had taken conservative positions on most issues (Kilmartin & Thorns 1978: 93). Australian planners were limited by an ideological outlook characterised by paternalism and rationalism: generally, 'reformism [came] from those outside the ranks of professional planning' (Kilmartin & Thorns 1978: 96).

Using the conceptual tools of political economy, McLoughlin set out in the early 1980s to implicate Australian professional planning in the broader class affinities that characterised (and constrained) the capitalist state, winning him many enemies and a small group of admirers in the process (see McLoughlin 1984, 1987, 1994). McLoughlin argued that the planning profession was characterised by a remarkable unconsciousness, both about how cities are shaped in capitalist societies and about their own role in this 'shaping'. His 1992 study *Shaping Melbourne's Future?* elaborated this critique in an extensive examination of Melbourne's postwar growth. Here, McLoughlin sought to show that planners had, in the main, failed to achieve their own strategic goals for guiding the city's development. Instead, he concluded (Hamnett 1997: 764),

> Melbourne's growth and change over this period had been principally determined by the relative powers of various participants in the urban development process . . . Only at the local level, in the protection of environmental quality in middle-class residential areas, was evidence found of congruence between the stated aims of planning and its effects . . .

In this assessment, planners had done little other than to protect the amenity, and therefore quality of life, enjoyed by the middle and upper classes. Planning, in short, was a servant of power—planners were dupes of the capitalist class, largely unaware of the regressive distributional consequences of much of their work. In these respects, his analyses echoed the earlier work of Sandercock (1977, 1983) and many of the Marxian critiques of institutional planning made by North American and British commentators (e.g. Roweis 1981; Harvey 1978; Scott & Roweis 1977).

A group of Melbourne-based analysts associated with the Communist Party of Australia undertook the only notable policy application of Marxist thought to planning in this country. Important among these were Ruth and Maurie Crow, who were the principal authors of the Communist Party's *Plan for Melbourne*, released in three parts between 1969 and 1972 (Modern Melbourne Committee 1969; Crow & Crow 1970, 1972). This was followed a decade and a half later by *Make*

Figure 6.1 Melbourne's 'Socialist Plan', 1985

Melbourne Marvellous!, effectively an alternative socialist strategic plan for the city (Socialist Alternative Melbourne Collective 1985) (Figure 6.1). The plan received some community exposure, not to say notoriety, especially as it was publicly launched by the then Lord Mayor of the City of Melbourne, Councillor Eddie Beacham, thus enraging the local business community.

Importantly, this document—which regrettably sank quickly, leaving few political traces—embodied many of the concerns that were to register in green and sociocultural critiques of planning. Planning was to be placed under democratic control, largely through its political decentralisation. Moreover, in the shift to planning for social needs rather than economic development, there would be an expansion of moral consideration, so that the needs of non-human nature (i.e. animals, plants and landscapes) would be valued in human decision-making. Interestingly, a key feature of the plan's ecological program was support for urban consolidation; a policy that later—distorted in implementation—was to be deeply repudiated by other leftist commentators for its inequitable consequences (see chapter 5).

Overall, respect for difference, for the socially and economically subordinated 'other', was the watchword in this new socialist vision for strategic planning (Socialist Alternative Melbourne Collective 1985: 4):

> In a word, the long established socialist values of sufficiency and equity need to be supplemented with values which are anti-patriarchal, ecology respecting and committed to self-reliance and grass roots democracy based on collectives.

It is lamentable that this document, prescient in its concern for cultural and ecological respect, has been so thoroughly ignored in recent and contemporary critiques of planning.

On the one hand, then, resurgent Marxism, fed by disillusion with the results of democratic socialism in practice, provided a rigorous and convincing framework for analysis and critique. On the other, it overlooked the considerable differences within capitalist societies. Moreover, it demolished, root and branch, the core philosophy of democratic socialism, reduced its values to mere ideology, and showed the great projects of the state to be mere 'accommodations' necessary to allow capitalism to survive its crisis.

Sadly, the rare instances where Marxian thought was articulated in policy prescriptions addressed to real planning contexts were quickly extinguished due to the absence of a broad political support base. Here academic Marxism was implicated for its failure—notable in the Melbourne example—to contribute to that critically needed political base. Indeed, the separation of academic from political Marxism was a general feature of the socialist movement in Australia, which was not confined to the field of planning. Marxist disillusionment may have hastened the decline of social democratic planning and assisted the rise of managerialism (chapter 4).

The despondent view of planning cultivated by some Marxists has been criticised by various subsequent observers for its tendency to depoliticise urban policy. If planning's only possible contribution to society is to further the interests of capital, why bother with a progressive urban politics? Mees (1998), for example, has offered a different view of the efficacy of planning in Australia, rooted in a social democratic outlook that retains hope for a progressive regulation of cities that will counter the antisocial and ecologically destructive tendencies of capitalist economy. His analysis of retailing patterns in postwar Melbourne concludes that policy had a positive impact by reducing, even in some instances preventing, the development of American-style free-standing malls and the hyper-suburbanisation of commercial activity (i.e. the 'edge city' phenomenon discussed in chapter 3).

As Mees explains, a District Centre Policy was implemented, with varying degrees of enthusiasm, by the metropolitan planning authority from 1980. This policy 'sought to prevent the establishment of new regional centres and to confine major expansions to the 15 [existing] designated centres' (Mees 1998: 11). A clear instance of a socially and ecologically progressive form of planning, the policy sought to reinforce and promote retailing and other forms of development in district centres that were well integrated into the city's public transport network. This was a conscious attempt to direct new development into places that could be easily accessed by a range of community groups and not just those with recourse to private motor cars. Moreover, a city retailing pattern based on such centres would be ecologically beneficial by reducing the need for car, and indeed most non-pedestrian, forms of travel.

The policy relied largely on negative zoning—that is, the city's planning scheme 'was amended to make major developments "prohibited uses" outside the CBD and nominated centres' (Mees 1998). It was hampered by the lack of positive inducements, notably an integrated land assembly process. Nonetheless, and in spite of political opposition from major retailers, the policy was largely, if not wholly, a success. By 1997, the district centres still maintained their dominance over other retailing spaces. Mees thus concludes that during the 1980s and early 90s, 'Government policy . . . played a part in Melbourne's divergence from the American model [of urbanisation]' (Mees 1998: 17).

Importantly, Mees argues that the policy might have been more successful had it received explicit support from academic planners. Here the finger is pointed first at Marxists and second at other radical critics, including postmodernists (Mees 1998: 4):

> The 1980 policy was pilloried by academics. Logan . . . argued that planners had ignored irresistible forces of (post-)modern urbanisation, including the locational preferences and bargaining power of large retail firms, and the dominance of the car. McLoughlin . . . agreed, describing Logan's attack as 'a thorough and competent critique which amounts to nothing less than a demolition'.

Furthermore (Mees 1998: 4, original emphasis),

> The Melbourne critics' views fit neatly into the international discourse. Sudjic concludes his study with a warning that 'what the planner cannot do is to cut across the direction of events' . . . while Garreau told the Canadian Planning Association in 1994: 'I am not saying that [edge city] is the way I wish the world would work; I am saying that this is the way the world *does* work'.

Mees observes that all too often 'the world' is understood literally, eclipsing differences among cities (see also Amin & Graham 1997). Critics such as Mees certainly recognise the political-economic constraints that apply to planning in a capitalist society, but they continue to insist on the possibility of progressive urban policy. Such a position does not rule out commitment to socialism: progressive planning may be needed to check the worst abuses of the capitalist economy while the political and intellectual resources of the left are regrouped and renewed for a struggle against new forms of social inequality and environmental degradation. As evident in the work of Mees, many leftist thinkers now agree that a direct confrontation with ecological issues is a necessary part of this renewal.

Conclusion: a continuing tradition

The rise of urban political economy signalled an important radicalising impulse in planning debates across most Western countries, including Australia. There were strong criticisms of planning theory and practice made in the 1960s—especially concerning issues such as aesthetic insensitivity and professional paternalism—but it was not until the 1970s that a distinct and radical *political economic* critique was made. Urban political economy was different from the other main forms of critique that emerged (reviewed in chapters 7, 8 and 9) because it focused on planning's place in the overall constitution of capitalist society. At issue occasions when government action at federal level has had an immediate and direct effect on the urban environment. In the first instance there is the well-documented case of the Whitlam federal government's Department of Urban and Regional Development and its programs (Lloyd & Troy 1981) and the Building Better Cities program in the later Keating years 1993–96. In the second, the Commonwealth legislated to permit telecommunications carriers to erect towers for the mobile phone network and to roll out cable in city streets to carry TV channels.

The baseline for Australian urban governance is what we term *colonial bureaucracy* (CB). This was the form taken by government as the British colonies in Australia, and later the States, built the infrastructure necessary for a newly settled capitalist society: the ports and harbours, rail and tramlines, water supply and sewerage. It was based on trust in professional competence and ethics, and mobilised the expertise necessary for city-building and nation-building under the Australian Settlement (discussed in chapter 2). Laffin (1995: 73) calls it the 'professional-bureaucratic model': line departments or 'statutory authorities' dominated by professionals, and the public service as a whole regulated by public service boards.

Bureaucratic agencies were primarily accountable to Parliament and only loosely overseen by a minister, who may have had formal oversight of several departments. Politics was not fundamentally about control or steering of the bureaucracy but about the struggle for supremacy and patronage among a variety of powerful interests and factions. Only in the postwar years did this system begin to be modified by charismatic state leaders (e.g. Thomas Playford in South Australia [1938–65], Henry Bolte in Victoria [1955–72], Johannes Bjelke-Peterson in Queensland [1968–83]), who began to use certain elements of the bureaucracy as a means for achieving industrial development.

When 'town planning' was institutionalised in the state sphere at the behest of the Commonwealth in 1944 in pursuit of the government's program of reconstruction, it immediately became a specific function of state bureaucratic departments. It was natural, and suited the institutional form, to define the function in quite limited terms, as zoning 'to ensure that development can be guided or controlled to avoid conflicts between the users of land' (Butler 1982: 3). Gradually, however, pressure from community activists, developers, and the planning profession, forced a more open political debate about the function of planning and demanded that plans be more comprehensive, goal-directed and future-oriented. Eventually planning as a function of sacking of the Marrickville Council, the Minister for Local Government requested the Commission to examine and report on territorial changes to 13 metropolitan councils. Some amalgamations were proposed but were strongly opposed at local level by the Liberal Party and, following Liberal success at local council elections, the government abandoned the idea. New South Wales councils were generally larger than those of Victoria, where the matter of amalgamation was taken up more seriously.

In 1984 the Victorian Minister for Local Government, Frank Wilkes, asked the Victorian Grants Commission (VGC) to report on a possible restructuring of local government. The aim was to enlarge the range of services, particularly social services, that municipalities could offer. This was part of the government's 'social justice' strategy. It was thought that money could be saved by reducing duplication of services and cutting administration costs. These savings were to be passed on to ratepayers.

Barrister Mr Stuart Morris was appointed chair of the Local Government Commission. The approach of the government was that restructuring would be negotiated with councils. The advantages of restructuring, it was believed, would win local support. This was not to be, however, and the Municipal Association of Victoria (MAV) orchestrated a campaign of non-cooperation with the state government. Opinion polls and referenda were mounted around the state and generally showed that local people did not want their councils to merge. The then Leader of the Opposition, Mr Kennett, called for a statewide referendum on local government amalgamations (a commitment he shed when he later became Premier). Backbench Labor MPs moved within government ranks to reverse the amalgamation policy. In May 1986 several councils launched Supreme Court writs against the amalgamations. The government was seen to be losing public support and it was decided that the government would act to amalgamate only if councils voluntarily agreed to do so. Not surprisingly there were no offers. The attempt to restructure local government in Victoria came to a halt.

While Labor governments in pursuit of SDM sought a larger role for local government, they were not willing or able to force change on this sector. Respect for a consultative and voluntary process of change was coupled with the sense that local government could become a focus of opposition—egged on by the Liberal Party. Moreover, they were unable to introduce change in a 'king hit' following a claimed election mandate, for they did not control the upper houses of state parliaments (with the exception of the first Wran administration in New

Games Plan is based on minimising the impact of this major event through the world's best practice, environmental management' (Melbourne Bid 1997).

The Royal Park Protection Group thinks otherwise. A landscape plan already exists for Royal Park that has not been implemented because of lack of funding. Construction of the new facilities will require public land to be sacrificed for access roads and car parking. The group claims that 548 trees in the park will be cut down. Former Lord Mayor of Melbourne Trevor Huggard points out that public parkland around Melbourne is fast disappearing. In 1873 there were 841 hectares of park around the city. Now there are just 499 hectares. Parkland has been lost for new car parks, the new museum in Carlton Gardens (funded by gambling taxes), grandstands in Albert Park, and 'Optus Oval' (Dunstan 1998: 17). Again the state is legislating to deny residents due process of law through the courts.

The boast of the 'Clean Green Games' ('When Melbourne was named the World's Most Livable City in 1990, it scored a perfect 10 out of 10 for clean air'), is unblushingly accompanied by the boast that City Link will have been operating for about six years: 24 kilometres of high-standard freeway with the advantage of providing improved traffic conditions in the inner city—not a claim even the builders of City Link are willing to make (Melbourne Bid 1997).

Strategic planning has been redeployed, in a reduced form and with new objectives, as a central element of the 'game plan' which place competition has made indispensable to every city region. In their recent book *Surface City: Sydney at the Millennium*, Murphy and Watson (1997) describe the 'selling of Sydney', showing how state and municipal urban policies have been overshadowed during the past decade by the goal of luring investment, especially from overseas. In Melbourne's strategic plan, 'Direction 1' is to 'Provide a business environment conducive to sustainable long term economic growth'; most of the other 'Directions' have to do with supporting business, and even the 'environmental' objective is largely about promoting tourism (Victoria 1995). In South Australia, the 'Adelaide 21' strategic plan was conceived jointly by the Commonwealth, state and city governments as a means to promote the central city's 'competitive strengths' to interstate and overseas investors (Hamnett et al. 1997).

Queensland's *Integrated Planning Act 1997* (the IP Act introduced by the Borbidge government but shepherded through Parliament by the successor Beattie Labor government) combines land use planning and environmental assessment in the style of New Zealand's *Resource Management Act 1991* (RMA). This might be considered a logical strengthening of coordination of allied functions. It also contains something of the 'structure planning' idea of England's 1968 planning act.

were the ways in which planning managed the core relations of the capitalist spatial economy. For example, Marxists alleged that land use planning ensured stability in land markets, thereby maximising profits for the property-owning class. Social democratic commentators, such as Troy (e.g. 1996b: 9), countered that careful government intervention in land markets could prevent the accumulation of speculative land-holdings and thereby dampen land price inflation.

In time, urban political economy broadened to include newer variants of Marxist theory—notably regulation theory (e.g. Low 1995) and critical theory (e.g. Forester 1980)—that had emerged in analyses of contemporary Western capitalism. These variants accepted the criticism that Marxism had become too economistic and sought ways to reintroduce politics, sometimes turning to that most 'political' of neo-Marxists, the prewar Italian communist Antonio Gramsci, sometimes to the more academic German 'critical' school represented by Jürgen Habermas. While not all urban political economists drew on the Marxist critique of capitalism, there was a common view that planning was implicated in the reproduction of unjust social and economic relations.

During the 1980s, radical political economy—and especially Marxism—in the social sciences was overwhelmed by new theoretical tides, including postmodernism, environmentalism, new variants of radical feminism, and neoliberalism (itself a conservative form of political economy). Political economists themselves were subjected to criticism for allegedly giving too much significance to economic relationships in their analyses of capitalist society. Indeed, as economic analysis lost favour among social analysts, who were now attracted by cultural and environmental issues, it became rather unfashionable even to speak of 'capitalist' society.

Not all abandoned the cause, however. During the 1980s David Harvey continued to develop his application of Marx's ideas to urban and spatial theory, producing in 1982 the landmark study *The Limits to Capital*. This was followed by a set of further studies that explored the issues of culture (Harvey 1985), postmodernism (Harvey 1989) and environmentalism (Harvey 1996) within a spatial analytical framework. Harvey's work remained avowedly Marxist but began to confront and engage the important theoretical and policy issues that have been raised by feminists, postmodernists and environmentalists. In Australia, Frank Stilwell has continued through the 1980s and 90s to produce insightful political-economic analyses of urban policy issues. His *Reshaping Australia: Urban Problems and Policies* (1993a) confronts the dilemmas facing urban and regional policy in a political context dominated by ideologies—such as corporate liberalism (chapter 5)—that are hostile to planning.

Leonie Sandercock in her work in the USA and Australia during the 1980s and 90s turned to feminism and postmodernism in an effort to transcend the perceived conceptual narrowness and political impotence of urban political economy. Although never an avowed Marxist, Sandercock continues to acknowledge the fundamental contribution of urban political economy to the theoretical understanding of planning in capitalist societies. In her recent study *Towards Cosmopolis*, Sandercock (1998: 92) recognises that 'Marxist critique has demystified the idea that planning operates in the public interest, making it very clear that class interests are always the driving force'; the enduring problem for her is that by

> . . . insisting on the primacy of class interests in their counter-analysis, Marxists have either ignored, or tried to subsume into their class analysis, other forms of oppression, domination and exploitation, such as those based on gender, race, ethnicity, and sexual preference.

There was more than an element of truth in the new postmodern and cultural critiques of political economy, including its urban variants. Political economists had in some instances been dismissive of 'non-economic' issues, such as non-class differences (i.e. gender, race, disability) and the environment. Not all had been, however, and in recent years political-economic analysis has broadened to consider how cultural and environmental relations are constituted in capitalist society (e.g. Altvater 1993 and O'Connor 1994 on ecology; Gibson-Graham 1996 on feminism).

An exclusive focus on economic and class-related issues prevents urban analysis from understanding and engaging the many sociocultural concerns that lie at the core of planning in capitalist societies such as Australia. Nonetheless, planning is centrally concerned with the regulation of the capitalist land market, and is indisputably a political economic endeavour. In Australia, the case for urban political economy has probably never been stronger than at present. Just as many urban analysts were spurning the conceptual tools of political economy, a new political force was emerging in capitalist societies during the 1980s and 90s to assert a radically expanded role for the market in all spheres of social and cultural life. The reality and discourse of 'globalisation' has made its impact (chapter 3). As we discuss in chapters 4 and 5, an influential political economic ideology (shifting from managerialism to corporate liberalism) has been reshaping the Australian public sector in recent years, in the process sweeping away many of the earlier policy gains made by environmentalists and cultural progressives, including feminists and advocates of multiculturalism. In chapters 9 and 10 we show how this ideology shaped a powerful policy reform program—National Competition Policy—that is profoundly hostile to democratic, public planning, both conventional and progressive.

Before turning to consider the contemporary political-economic context of urban policy in Australia, we first review the two other theoretical-political perspectives that emerged in the 1960s to challenge conventional 'rational' planning. From radical democratic critiques and environmentalism emerged profound critiques of conventional planning and, later, Marxist urban political economy.

7

Democratising planning: radical cultural critiques

In this chapter we review another broad set of critiques that have challenged mainstream planning practice. For convenience we have grouped a large and rather diverse number of perspectives under the 'radical cultural' heading. We group them because, in spite of their theoretical and political diversity, these critiques are united by the attention they have given to the democratic shortcomings of planning and, more particularly, the tendency of state and private sector institutions to ignore the critical fact of cultural diversity. In short, the common concern of radical cultural perspectives is that social diversity is rarely reflected in planning policy and practice. Planning stands accused of 'cultural blindness', of having assumed that there are no significant sociocultural differences in 'society'. For too long, it is claimed, planning has pursued an ideal—'the public interest'—that simply does not exist in a society inevitably complicated by profound differences in cultural outlook, between individuals and groups.

Beyond these broad claims there are important differences, as we will show, between what we term 'radical cultural' perspectives. Not all, for example, entirely reject the idea of a public interest in planning. For some, recognition of social difference could become part of a reconstituted public interest—a flexible set of policy settings that would evolve over time as society itself changes. This reconstituted notion of 'the public interest' would provide a new political-ethical ideal for planning that values and nurtures the existence of different 'publics' as the basis for a healthy, cosmopolitan democracy.

The radical cultural critique of planning has been evident since at least the early 1960s, and unlike urban political economy was renewed and reinforced by theoretical developments in the late 1980s and during the 90s. As we will show, it has emerged as one of the most popular and potent critiques of contemporary planning—embracing postmodernism, feminism and a variety of other culturally focused perspectives. In Australia, political pressure by democratic interests from the 1970s helped to secure a range of reform initiatives in planning legislation and practice that sought to improve public participation mechanisms. The 1979 New South Wales *Environmental Planning and Assessment Act*, for example, enhanced the opportunities for public participation in that state's planning processes (Stein 1998). Also, as we will show, there have been more recent attempts to open up planning to new 'publics', especially Indigenous Australians.

We begin by reviewing the first radical cultural critiques that emerged from the early 1960s and which were especially directed at technocratic and authoritarian forms of planning. After this we survey the newer generation of cultural radicals, including feminists and postmodernists, who have drawn specific attention to the question of social difference and how this can be accommodated in planning theory, policy and practice.

Early critiques

Planning a 'conquering power'

The intellectual lineage for these critiques can be traced to a range of voices and movements that began from the 1960s to criticise what they saw as the antidemocratic—and, for some, the anti-humanist—tendencies of planning institutions in developed societies. As Bailey (1975: 36) noted, these emancipatory forces within (and surrounding) planning were encouraged by a broader 'international shift from representative to participatory democracy along with the radicalisation of political values in the west'. These critical strands included Jane Jacobs' (1961) famous intervention against modernist planning which, among other things, attacked the dominance of elite (usually professional) values in urban planning. Jacobs witnessed with dismay the products of modernist rational planning in America's cities: the soulless low-income-housing projects, the 'dullness and regimentation' of middle-class housing estates, the vulgar new shopping centres, and the 'Expressways that eviscerate great cities'; this was nothing less than 'the sacking of cities' (Jacobs 1961: 4). As Australian commentator Peter Beilharz (1994: 80) notes, planning for Jacobs 'is paternalistic . . . claiming to know better than the locals, and it presumes that men inhabit the outside world. Suburbia, on this account, is bad, but especially bad for women. As Jacobs herself (1961: 5) angrily remarked, the people whom planners seek to help 'are pushed about, expropriated, and uprooted much as if they were the subjects of a conquering power'.

At about the same time, Robin Boyd launched a similarly bitter attack on modernist architecture and planning in Australia. In his 1960 book *The Australian Ugliness*, he observed that 'urban technological, and mass squalor is in: ugliness au go go' (Boyd 1960: 12). Boyd's critique differed from Jacobs'—though they both abhorred modernist urban blight—because planning in Australia was never the giant urban re-development machine that it was in America during the 1950s and 60s. The flaw in Australian planning was not the desire to be a 'conquering power' but the lack of will and imagination to counter the mass vulgarism of urban free-enterprise society.

Various elements of Jacobs' outburst anticipated the later critiques of planning by feminists, postmodernists and neoliberals—in particular, her vision of the city as an evolving organic form whose purity and quality was violated by interventionist planning resonates with subsequent neoliberal critiques of urban regulation.

A decade later, Goodman repeated the charge that planning consorted with power in a larger process of oppressive socialisation that sought to erase and/or normalise 'deviant' forms of community. His denunciation of planners as the 'soft cops' of the establishment (Goodman 1972: 53) anticipated the later Marxian critiques of capitalist planning systems reviewed in chapter 6. In turn, other democratising projects emerged, such as advocacy planning (e.g. Davidoff 1965; Peattie 1968; Bernard 1970) and 'direct action' planning. In an often-cited contribution, Davidoff (1965) argued against the possibility of 'value-free planning', echoing the broader critique of positivism that was emerging in the social sciences and the groundswell of community opposition to technocratic institutional behaviour in a range of Western countries. As Healey (1997: 25) explains, Davidoff

> acknowledged that values divided people. In particular, the interests of poorer people in inner-city neighbourhoods were not the same as those of local business interests. He sought a way of planning that opened up the value diversity among the plurality of interests within a political community.

Indeed, a common thread of such critiques was the desire to liberate the plethora of community values and interests that had been either ignored or actively suppressed by rational-instrumental forms of planning. In short, the institutionalised ideals of a homogeneous public and a universal public interest were greatly eroded by new waves of grassroots protest and intellectual criticism that broke across Western planning systems during the 1960s and 70s.

Participation, an 'empty ritual'?

In time, the effect of these critical forces was to produce a new emphasis on the value of public participation in planning (see, for example, the Skeffington Report, Ministry of Housing and Local Government UK 1969). However, these discourses and practical initiatives were, with some reason, quickly dismissed as gestural by radical observers, who argued that 'participation' was really a ruse—a clever way of imposing technological and scientific thinking on communities.

Bailey argued that participation performed 'a masking function in that it appears to acknowledge and provide for participatory democracy while in fact "educating" clients towards professional views based on consensualism and physical scientism' (Bailey 1975: 39). Here 'consensualism' is the tendency of institutions to manufacture a fundamental agreement on 'basic values' that in fact reflects the particular interests of a social minority (i.e. usually elites). Echoing this criticism, Arnstein (1969) produced a 'Ladder of Citizen Participation', which was a typology of participation modes that ranged from 'citizen control', where people controlled planning, to 'manipulation', where institutions and professionals controlled people. In between, there were various 'degrees of tokenism', meaning participation strategies that had little consequence for planning or for people but which served to put a 'democratic' gloss on institutional practice. Arnstein (1969: 216) believed that her ladder 'highlights the fundamental point that participation without redistribution of power is an empty and frustrating process for the powerless'.

Nevertheless, the radical critique of professionalism and scientism in planning had the effect of establishing 'participation and consultation' firmly in the language of planning in Australia, and its use was not always just empty ritual. Sometimes there was a genuine attempt at empowerment, as in the Western Suburbs Action Plan of the Cain government of Victoria (see chapter 4). Sometimes the response was serious engagement by social democratic governments with a strong social movement, as with the 'green bans' (chapter 8). Criticism of 'consensualism' and 'scientism' has continued through the years, being taken up by postmodernists and environmentalists. The continued significance of scientism in planning systems caused many radical environmentalists to share the democrats' suspicion of participatory discourses and practices.

Recent critiques

Feminism and postmodernism

In recent years, new radical democratic critiques of planning have emerged from feminist and postmodern commentators. For feminists, planning had long been based on androcentric (male-centred) values that diminished or even ignored the needs of women (Foulsham 1992). Moreover, planning was explained as a key influence in the construction of built environments that reinforced male social patterns of dominance, partly through the production of suburban environments that 'imprisoned' many women with restrictive life patterns (Saegert 1981; Greed 1994). Planning's masculinist outlook was both a reflection of its function within a broader gendered institutional structure and a consequence of the domination of the profession by males (Leavitt 1981; Little 1994). These concerns were echoed by Australian feminists, who implicated both planning practice and planning ideologies in the creation of patriarchal cities (e.g. Allport 1986; Harman 1988). The Royal Australian Planning Institute's code of professional conduct establishes for planners a 'primary responsibility to pursue the public interest', but too often planning practice reveals 'a distorted view of the planning public' (in Jackson 1997: 226).

In 1993, a major national conference on 'Women and Planning' was held in Melbourne. A general theme to emerge from the meeting was the contention that planning theory and practice had been impoverished by the lack of attention given to women, and women's concerns, in key political and policy forums (Munro 1993). Planning by men could never produce socially fulfilling landscapes. In 1976, Wendy Sarkissian's dismal portrait of a typical postwar suburban estate ('Brown Hills') drew attention to the isolation endured by women in Australian cities (Sarkissian 1976). Despite nearly two decades of debate about more inclusive forms of planning, the Melbourne conference was told that planners were still not 'in touch with the scope and immensity of the problems which women, particularly suburban women, face in our cities in Australia' (Sarkissian & Sidhu 1993: 6).

More recently, new critiques of planning have advanced under the banner of postmodernism (Box 7.1), sometimes held aloft by commentators who had previously made feminist analyses of urban regulation.

The transition is evident, for example, in the work of Leonie Sandercock. Her thinking over the past two decades is marked by a shift from political economy to feminism (e.g. Sandercock & Forsyth 1992), and more recently by a turn to postmodernist thought (e.g. Sandercock 1998). Many feminists who had pointed to planning's oppressive ideological tendencies were doubtless attracted by the broad conceptual reach of postmodernism and the emancipatory promise of a 'politics of difference'. More generally, postmodern analysis seemed to offer a powerful framework for considering the collective implications of the confrontations between various social movements (e.g. green, preservationist, feminist, communitarian) and modernist planning that had occurred with increasing frequency since the 1960s (Gibson & Watson 1995: 8).

BOX 7.1 WHAT IS POSTMODERNISM?

'Postmodernism' has been used to describe a range of overlapping cultural, theoretical and aesthetic movements. It is therefore difficult to define with precision. At base, the postmodernists oppose 'universalism', the idea that there are universal values and uniform social practices which exist across time and space. Johnston et al. (1994: 466) summarise postmodernism as:

> A recent movement in philosophy, the arts and social sciences characterized by scepticism towards the grand claims and grand theory of the modern era, and their privileged vantage point, stressing in its place an openness to a range of voices in social enquiry, artistic experimentation and political empowerment.

Dear (1986) has identified three main dimensions of postmodernism: postmodern style, postmodern method and a postmodern time period (or 'epoch').

Postmodern style emphasises playfulness, a diversity of colour and elements ('pastiche') and, sometimes, the mixture of historical styles in a single work. Within this, postmodern architecture has sought to contrast itself with the stark universalism of modern building design. Also, postmodern film may embody an ironic mixture of cultural and aesthetic styles that aim to challenge or disrupt viewers' assumptions about social and historical conventions.

In philosophy and social theory, *postmodern method* has focused on the practice of 'deconstruction'. Deconstruction is 'a mode of critical interpretation which seeks to demonstrate how the (multiple) positioning of an author (or a reader) in terms of culture, class and gender, etc. has influenced the writing (and reading) of a text' (Johnston et al. 1994: 466). Here a 'text' can mean any form of social description or explanation, including a theory. Postmodernists reject the notion that there can be a single, overarching 'grand theory' of society, or even any social phenomenon. In short, theories and explanations are inevitably 'partial': that is to say, limited by the author's particular social position and experiences.

Some social theorists and commentators refer to a *postmodern epoch*. Here postmodern movements in culture, philosophy and style are linked to broader shifts in national and global economies and political frameworks. A key dimension is the alleged shift away from a socioeconomic system ('**Fordism**') based on the mass production of commodities towards a new globally integrated society ('flexible accumulation') based on 'production technologies, labour practices, inter-firm relations and consumption patterns characterized by the pursuit of greater flexibility' (Johnston et al. 1994: 202). Some industrial geographers, however, have questioned the scale of this supposed shift by pointing to the resilience of Fordist mass industrial production in many countries and regions. For some postmodern commentators, the rise of globally integrated information technology systems (e.g. the Internet, satellite television, global movie industry) has allowed the rapid dissemination of new cultural forms, challenging the established cultures of many regions and even nations. There is, however, debate about whether information technology has actually promoted a new postmodern diversity in culture. Many critics counter that the globalising media industry has used the new information technologies to impose cultural uniformity (largely US in character) on the world.

FURTHER READING

Harvey (1989); Sandercock (1998).

In Australia, a new and insightful fusion of feminist and postmodern work was evident by the 1990s. For example, while not expressly postmodern in character, Margo Huxley's critical examination of Australian land use regulation (e.g. Huxley 1994) has combined insight from feminist thought with Michel Foucault's analysis of institutional power in modern Western societies (e.g. Foucault 1991/1978). Watson and McGillivray (1994: 214) noted the connection between earlier feminist critiques and emergent postmodern perspectives:

> Just as feminists have illustrated the gendered/sexed nature of planning and housing in Australia, we now also need to examine the ways in which the city is modelled on particular Anglo-Australian notions of how people live.

Of course, not all postmodern analyses of planning have been sourced in feminism. In an early example, Dear (1986) applied deconstructive logic to planning theories in a wide-ranging critique of modernist planning. Here established planning is attacked on two fronts. First, urban planning's claim of undisputed authority in matters concerning the arbitration of community values has resulted in 'increased social control over everyday life' (Dear 1986: 381) for ordinary citizens. Second, public planning institutions have failed to appreciate the profound political–economic and cultural shifts that have allegedly produced new postmodern forms of urbanism. In a more ambivalent assessment, Goodchild (1990) pointed to the contradictory possibilities arising from postmodernist discourses and practices. For him, postmodernism could be read both positively and negatively. It can be regarded as a progressive critique of planning, because it has emphasised the benefits of cultural diversity and promoted democratic, localised forms of participation over hegemonic outlooks based on technical rationality. On the negative side of the ledger, however, he notes the tendency of postmodernism to conjure the image of 'a world characterised by such extreme fragmentation that collective action is no longer possible' (Goodchild 1990: 119).

A similar ambivalence about postmodernism was echoed in Australia by Freestone (1993). He noted that, while a renewed emphasis on 'local sensitivity' had emerged within planning practice, this had been coupled with a new 'ad hoc, opportunistic, political and instrumentalist' approach that had pushed planning 'further from its historic mission of social reform' (Freestone 1993: 19). Recalling our discussion in chapter 3, Mees (1998) has argued that discussions of postmodern urban phenomena (e.g. the postmodern shopping mall) have tended to depoliticise planning debates by projecting North American patterns of city change across national policy contexts, often in the absence of empirical support. Such projection has a tendency to make 'postmodern urbanisation' seem universal and inevitable.

This point exposes a paradox in postmodern debates. At the broad level, postmodernists propound an emphasis on diversity, both as an inevitable social and theoretical fact and as a desirable political value. However, the often-sweeping claims about processes of urbanisation, especially those emanating from North American critics, have the effect of erasing the empirical diversity of Western cities and their populations.

Other 'forgotten publics'

Apart from women, it is evident that planning has in the past excluded or ignored the needs and values of other 'publics' when framing notions of the public interest in policy settings. Ryan Heath, a member of the Prime Minister's National Youth Roundtable, recently drew attention to the ways in which planning, or sometimes the lack of planning, has made Australian youth feel isolated and angry (Heath 1999: 15):

> This problem starts with town planning and the privatisation of public space. For 30 years councils have welcomed large-scale private shopping centres because they reduce their responsibility to provide public space. But such centres exist to make a profit and fail to consider the needs of young people whose former playgrounds they occupy.

Kendig (1997) reminds us of the many ways in which Australia's urban built environments fail to account for the needs of older people. Other critics of planning and the development industry have shown how disabled people are systematically excluded from most built environments (see Gleeson 1999). Physical exclusion, of course, reinforces the social and economic disadvantages faced by youth, the elderly and disabled people.

In Britain and the USA, culturally informed criticism has fixed on the issue of racism in planning ideology and practice (e.g. Hoch 1993; Thomas & Krishnarayan 1994). In some instances these critiques merged with political-economic analyses (e.g. Thomas 1994) in order to highlight the culturally regressive implications of neoliberal planning agendas. Of particular concern in Australia is how the regulation of land has affected its original owners—Indigenous Australians.

Sue Jackson has studied planning's impact on Aboriginal communities in northern Australia. Her conclusions disrupt any simple assumption that planning and urban development in these regions has really been in the public interest (Jackson 1997: 221):

> Historically, the views of the urban Aboriginal community have rarely been sought by planners, governments or developers. Although contemporary planning practice now accepts a stronger role for a more expansive 'public', decision makers reveal only a token understanding of cultural difference and an unwillingness to redress the power imbalances between Aboriginal and non-Aboriginal people.

In the colonial era, planning had participated in the marginalisation and dispossession of Aboriginal peoples by assigning them to reserves on the edges of, or outside, towns such as Broome. The colonial planning practice of creating reserves for Aborigines continued in this century: as recently as the 1950s, reserves were created 'to accommodate the resident and visiting Aborigines who were not welcome members of the township' (Jackson 1997: 222). Later, as urban growth pressure mounted, another major reserve in Broome was swept aside to make way for housing development. Planning, it seems, was directed in these instances towards the cultural 'sanitisation' of urban space. Little wonder that Jackson sees planning in northern Australia as a neocolonial institution that has failed to 'take responsibility for its professional conduct in a nation characterised by vast historical and contemporary inequities between white and black' (Jackson 1997: 221).

For Wensing and Davis (1998), there is a fundamental cultural difference between orthodox planning practice and indigenous needs and values that is hardly confined to northern Australia. They write (1998: 4): 'the rational technocratic focus of much planning . . . often precludes appropriate and meaningful consultation with indigenous peoples' (see also Lane 1997). Beyond this, there is an even deeper cultural gulf separating Anglo-Australian norms, such as individual rights, exclusive property ownership, free enterprise, written law and history, and Indigenous outlooks that value social cooperation, collective land use, oral traditions and customary laws (Wensing & Davis 1998).

If planning is truly to serve the public interest, it will need to find ways of bridging these gulfs and embracing and cherishing a wider array of social values, especially values that relate to the ownership and use of land. Indeed, the recognition of Indigenous interests in property law has advanced more quickly than it has in planning law and practice in recent years. The High Court's landmark Mabo ruling in 1992 swept aside the notion of *terra nullius* (land belonging to no-one) that had framed Australian property and planning law since white settlement. The Mabo decision, and the *Native Title Act 1993* that followed, established in Australian common law recognition of indigenous law and culture, including the interests of Aboriginals and Torres Strait Islanders in land and water (Wensing & Sheehan 1997). The law, and by consequence planning, was required now to recognise that property ownership was framed by cultural values and not simply by narrow economic and legal notions of entitlement. Many planners may not yet have realised the significance of these changes, which Jackson (1997: 226) outlines:

> Following the Mabo decision, planners can no longer see the world through a colonial lens where Aboriginal lands are blank or empty landscapes devoid of cultural relationships to places and country. Nor are they lands upon which the planner can lay down land use ideals in the absence of consultation, negotiation and a willingness to compromise to accommodate cultural differences.

There is evidence that some planning authorities are recognising the need for change. Cosgrove and Kliger (1997: 216) have reported the recent attempts by Australian local governments 'to open up land use decision making processes to include Aboriginal people's understanding, links and concerns about land'. For example, Redland Shire Council in southeast Queensland has signed a 'Native Title Process Agreement' with the Quandamooka Land Council Aboriginal Corporation. This agreement establishes both a partnership approach to the development of a planning and land management strategy for North Stradbroke Island (Minjerribah) and the recognition of native title rights and interests (Australian Local Government Association 1998: 115).

If planning practice must change in response to Mabo, then why cannot planning law be similarly reshaped to accommodate Indigenous cultural values? The thoroughgoing reform of planning legislation in New Zealand that produced the *Resource Management Act 1991* established recognition of Maori cultural values as a key premise for resource management in that country. In the light of Mabo, there are compelling reasons for Australia also to recognise Indigenous values in planning and environmental law. Planners, though, should not make the culturally blind mistake of assuming that Aboriginal interests are any more homogeneous than 'European' interests. Urban Aborigines, for example, may want to be distinguished from traditional Aboriginal cultures elsewhere—which themselves are enormously diverse throughout the continent. Class and gender are inscribed in Aboriginal politics, as they are in every other dimension of human social life.

Is 'modernity' really the problem?

Not all of the newer generation of radical democratic critiques of planning identify themselves explicitly as 'postmodern'. For example, the analyses of Huxley (e.g. 1994) and Yiftachel (e.g. 1991, 1995) have shown how centralised modernist planning structures tend to discipline and control social groups and viewpoints that are considered discordant with a broader public interest. Here criticism is directed not only at planning but also obliquely at managerialism and neoliberalism, which are born of utilitarian thought. For example, Huxley's work on postwar metropolitan strategy formulation in Melbourne exposes the 'Utilitarian rhetorics of control and efficiency [as] leitmotivs of the discourse of town planning' (Huxley 1994: 149). Spatial control in this instance is explained as social control, evoking Foucault's interpretation of the modernist reformist impulse as a 'double-edged sword' which delivered improvement through rationalisation. At the local scale, planning certainly improved environmental quality, while also subjecting everyday life to new levels of rationalisation and normalisation. As Sibley (1995) argues, this rationalisation was most notably evident through zoning controls—literally, an 'enframement' of everyday life—that introduced new sociospatial boundaries of exclusion and inclusion, codified in law. As discussed above, Australian commentators such as Jackson have also drawn attention to planning's role in the 'cultural purification' of space.

In this respect, Sibley considers instructive the role played by British establishment geographers, such as J.A. Steers of Cambridge, in the development of zoning types. Both Raymond Unwin (1863–1940), the influential British planning advocate, and Steers loathed the encroachment on the English countryside by working-class housing, and Sibley implies that their motivations included class prejudice as much as a concern for the preservation of rural amenity. According to Sibley, Steers regarded one such 'spontaneous housing development' as 'an abomination . . . a town of shacks and rubbish . . . It caters for a particular class of people and, short of total destruction and a new start, little if anything can be done' (in Sibley 1995: 59).

Both men influenced the development of postwar planning in the British Commonwealth. Their prejudices are implicated in the new power given to local authorities under Britain's *Town and Country Planning Act 1947* to 'control or eradicate "disorderly development"' (Sibley 1995: 59): This facility, according to Sibley (1995: 59), 'contributed to the exclusion of working people from middle class space'. Interestingly, the measure survives in a diluted form in present-day zoning practice, both in Britain and in Australia: 'The rhetoric had an important bearing on practice, although the language of pollution was translated into less emotive terms, like non-conforming use' (Sibley 1995).

Sibley, however, neglects to mention the social and historical context of the 1947 British legislation. Later planning law may have contributed to social exclusion but the 'control' function of the 1947 legislation was coupled with a range of progressive social democratic measures (reviewed briefly in chapter 2). These measures included the construction of a welfare state, the recapture for the community of profits from speculative development, a colossal new towns program, and the devotion of massive funding to public housing in every local authority area. This new public housing was of a far better quality than the working-class 'shanty towns' that were beginning to develop around British cities before World War II—much of it occurring on 'middle-class space'. Where it did not (as in East London), it could have been because the working class did not much want to move from where it lived.

In short, criticism of modernist planning must be balanced by recognition of two key considerations. First, one needs to recall the scale and intensity of social need following World War II, both in Europe and Australia, which demanded urgent and broadscale solutions.

Second, while postwar planning may have been insensitive to individual values and aesthetic concerns, it was highly sensitive to, indeed framed by, issues of *social need*. These needs included the desperate housing situation facing many urban communities and the urgent task of repairing and renewing infrastructure that had been damaged and/or ignored during the war.

Sibley also neglects to mention the environmental externality imperative for zoning that helped produce town planning after the Industrial Revolution. Zoning was in this early manifestation as much a reformist measure as it was an exercise in sociospatial classification and control. It cannot be forgotten, as Huxley (1994) acknowledges, that zoning helped contain many environmental depredations, and doubtless improved the lives of the masses, by separating mutually exclusive land uses.

For Yiftachel (1995), these critiques do not negate the values of modernity—notably, 'reform' and 'public interest'—and modernist planning; rather, what is problematised is the tendency of planning to betray the values on which it is premised. Thus, a reformist vision need not rely upon social control; a public interest need not construct and exclude minority interests. These analyses echo the call of the German sociologist Ulrich Beck (1997), who has pointed to the urgent need for a *remodernisation of modernity*. By this Beck means a return in public policy to the Enlightenment ideals—especially the values of 'emancipation' and 'doubt'—that were erased by the development of industrial capitalism and modern bureaucratic rationality. For Yiftachel (1995: 238), the remodernisation of planning will involve 'the transition towards more appropriate forms of shaping the built environment: from planning for control, containment, exclusion and deprivation, onto [sic] planning for emancipation, inclusion, empowerment and equity'.

There are other critiques of established modernist planning that do not subscribe to postmodernism. For example, some commentators (e.g. Hoch 1993; Thomas 1994) argue for recognition of sociocultural diversity in urban regulation fixed on the rather straightforward ideal of 'cultural pluralisation' as a new value for planning. Adoption of this value would avoid many of the theoretical complexities of postmodern and poststructuralist debates that may in any case be difficult to apply to policy settings.

In Australia, as we have seen in chapter 3 (Box 3.3), there has been increasing controversy concerning the perceived cultural inflexibility of traditional planning instruments, especially zoning. Criticism has often emerged from the grassroots, from ethnic communities rather than academic postmodernists, and has fixed on the need for a broader cultural outlook in planning. Even the New South Wales Department of Urban Affairs and Planning recently admitted that 'Zoning can simply reinforce the status quo rather than allowing for diversity . . .' (DUAP 1999: 18). Recently, Australian councils have been urged to develop cultural planning frameworks that will cherish and nurture localised forms of diversity (Australia Council 1997). However, calls for greater cultural diversity in planning may unwittingly lend ammunition to the arguments of neoliberals who have campaigned for more flexibility in planning, meaning the deregulation of zoning and other land use controls. 'Diversity' is a potentially ambiguous value that can be championed by a variety of planning critics.

Recalling Goodchild's (1990) assessment, it is evident that postmodernism offers both progressive and reactionary possibilities for public policy. On the one hand, postmodernism has intensified the radical democratic critique of planning by highlighting how key values—notably, the public interest—are embedded within restrictive cultural frameworks. On the other, postmodernism has tended to promote a rather vaguely defined sense of 'diversity' as a radical new social value without always addressing the important distinction between 'good' and 'bad' social differences. Key political-ethical questions remain unanswered. Most worryingly, are the new socioeconomic divisions that have been generated by neoliberal reforms a type of diversity to be welcomed? In some postmodern analyses, unfortunately, this critical issue remains an open question.

Is difference in the 'public interest'?

In their recent work, the Australian commentators Watson and Gibson have addressed these contradictory tendencies of postmodernism (see also Gibson 1996). They search for a progressive fusion of the social democratic and postmodern perspectives, which recognises that 'Diversity and difference are intricately linked with polarization and divisions' (Watson & Gibson 1995: 256). Thus the postmodern value of 'difference' is not a simple cause for celebration—rather an ideal whose emancipatory possibilities can be realised only in the absence of oppressive power relations (Watson & Gibson 1995: 257):

> Difference implies power. Some groups have economic and social power to have their needs met in the urban system while others do not. Public participation is meaningless if only more powerful sections of the community are involved.

Moreover, the difficult issue of arbitrating between spaces of difference and their antipodes, spaces of exclusion and inequality, needs to be faced (Watson & Gibson 1995: 257):

> 'Walls'—or bounded spaces—occupied by specific groups may offer protection or places of resistance. These may be necessary for minorities to establish themselves. But even these places can quickly shift into places open to attack or abuse or lack of opportunity. Walls can, on the other hand, represent exclusion and domination—a space where those with power exclude those without. So walls or bounded spaces can have different meanings which shift all the time. Planners need to be aware of how these different meanings are constituted spatially and across time if space is to become more democratic.

Other feminist critiques seem to reflect an earlier tradition, that of American pluralism. As we note in chapter 6, the tradition has been strongly inscribed in planning thought over a long period (Low 1991: 82):

> Pluralist theory throws doubt on the traditional view of professional planning which holds that a plan demands clear, unambiguous goals to be pursued consistently over a fairly long period of time . . . Pluralist theory asserts axiomatically that planners are one among many contending groups in the political arena. Just like the rest of society, planners have their own interests, and planning is the pursuit of those interests. The goals of public policy are . . . liable to vary with the changing balance of group pressure; every group will have its own interpretation of 'the problem'; since democracy is constituted ultimately by the freedom of groups to interact there is no single authoritative line of accountability to 'the public'; accordingly planners have multiple clients . . .

While postmodern and feminist critiques have rightly pointed to the tendency of state institutions to fix rigid and exclusionary notions of the public interest, these commentators overlook important earlier thought streams in planning—notably pluralism—that recognised fundamental divergences in social values. In pluralist thought the idea of the public interest is problematic because in reality there are only groups with group interests 'pressing against one another' (in the words of Bentley 1908: 269). This perspective caused Lindblom (1959) to interpret the rational-scientific approach to government decision-making as 'disjointed incrementalism', and Davidoff and Reiner (1962) as political pressure, advocacy and public choice. Rittel and Webber (1973) posed the sort of 'wicked problems' planners faced in which no guidance could be found in consensus. Wildavsky portrayed planning as the modern religion: 'planners are men [sic] of secular faith' (Wildavsky 1973: 151); moreover, 'Planning is not so much a subject for the social scientist as for the theologian'.

More recently, the American philosopher Iris Marion Young (1990) has put a radical slant on the pluralist debate on urban culture by calling for cities of 'difference'—yet this is a 'difference' which owes more to the pluralist American tradition and its critics than to the postmodern 'différance' [sic] of Dérrida. To American pluralists difference in the outlooks, cultures and interests of social groups is to be expected in a free democratic society, but such groups may still find common cause, collaborate and form coalitions. French linguistic philosophy tends to see difference as characteristic of language itself, and especially writing, so a word has meaning only in relation to a range of other words in the language. It is not the word but the difference between and among words that is significant. Dérrida extends difference over time, thus writing is deferred communication in that a text addresses future readers and enters debates with earlier authors. If meaning is relative to language, which is an artifact of culture, then one might infer that it is difficult for people to communicate across cultural barriers. Postmodern urbanists share with the pluralists an intense dislike of comprehensive planning by the state on behalf of society. They put their trust in political process—the 'play of power'. Where they differ from pluralist antecedents is in their insistence that certain groups are habitually excluded from the political process (in Australia, see Sandercock 1998; Fincher 1998). These critiques echo earlier scepticism about the inclusiveness of actual 'pluralist' society (e.g. McConnell 1967; Mills 1956) and the demand for radical action (Alinsky 1969/1946).

However, as the analysis of Watson and Gibson (1995) admits, planning for diversity requires some larger political-ethical framework that can critically evaluate the types of different spaces which contemporary cultural and political-economic processes are creating in cities. As we explain in chapter 3, the breakdown from the 1960s of national immigration policies favouring white settlers, and its subsequent replacement by multiculturalism as an official policy orthodoxy, has unleashed powerful forces of cultural pluralisation that have produced major changes in Australian cities.

In chapter 3 we discuss the example of Sydney's Cabramatta, where cultural pluralisation has generated new culturally distinct concentrations of disadvantage: difference in many contexts equates with disadvantage, especially the concentration of economic exploitation and marginalisation. The danger of simple postmodernism—viz. the uncritical celebration of difference as a self-evident virtue—is that it collapses the critical distinction between difference and disadvantage and thereby depoliticises the production of cultural and economic inequalities.

Surely a new political-ethical framework is needed in order to arbitrate between just and unjust differences? Thus, as Watson and Gibson realise, there is a pressing need to reinstate *and reconceive* the ideal of a public interest that first animated planning. Postmodernists may well have succeeded in destabilising an 'established belief that planners can act in the "public or common good" and the "public interest"' (Watson & Gibson 1995: 258). The political importance, however, of neoliberalism, and other structural ideologies, reinstates the need for progressive 'public ideologies' that can restrain the powerful and ensure social inclusion for the marginalised. Thus, there is growing recognition now among many cultural commentators that justice requires political-ethical formulations that can be applied in real policy settings if governments are not simply to rule in the interests of economic elites (or for that matter cultural elites, including men and/or white people).

Watson and Gibson are convinced that 'indeterminacy is at the core of the social', meaning that planning must become 'action without determination'. They also, however, counterbalance this odd-sounding claim against recognition of the potentially determining power of economic elites, noting the ability of 'the market to dictate terms' of governance in neoliberal societies (Watson & Gibson 1995: 259). There can be no clearer admission, surely, of the need for a progressive ethical formulation that is robust enough to deflect the power of the market to produce spaces of oppressive difference. Gibson has argued cogently that the discourses of social justice and cultural diversity need not be in collision. She sees much potential for 'an exciting conversation between the discourses of social polarisation and theories of [cultural] difference . . .' (Gibson 1996: 11). If a monolithic conception of the public interest has been dethroned, there exists now an urgent need to identify a new democratic sense of purpose that can unify, though not homogenise, the varied cultural and social interests that planning must serve. (We return to this question in Part III.)

Conclusion

In this chapter we have grouped a rather diverse set of perspectives under the 'radical cultural' heading. While there are important distinctions between the various critiques grouped in this way, all are united by a common concern with questions of participation and cultural representation in public policy. In general, radical cultural observers of planning have expressed scepticism about the concept of the public interest which has been a guiding value for state (and some private) sector institutions in modern liberal democracies. The extent of scepticism ranges from claims that an expanded and inclusionary public interest is needed to the position adopted by some postmodernists that any attempt to frame universal values is pointless, being destined to exclude some social interests.

Agitation for democratic reform over the past few decades has produced some change to planning systems, such as the widening of public participation procedures in some state legislative frameworks (Stein 1998) and new initiatives to develop more culturally inclusive planning practices. These gains, however, have proved vulnerable to more recent and reactionary reform initiatives that have sought to reduce the influence of planning in economic and social affairs. The proponents of corporate liberalism (chapter 5) have shown little interest in the potential nuances and exclusions that may complicate a notion of 'public interest'. As we show in chapters 9 and 10, neoliberals have side-stepped the question of democracy in urban governance by reducing, sometimes radically, the mechanisms for public participation in planning and environmental legislation.

In chapter 8 we pass on to another broad set of criticisms that have been directed at planning in modern capitalist societies. While radical cultural critics have been preoccupied with fundamental human aspirations—notably, *democracy* and *liberty*—other critics have drawn attention to how planning has affected the non-human realm, nature. Again the issue of public interest is raised, only this time the argument is that non-human publics have been ignored or undervalued by traditional planning practices, with disastrous consequences for nature and for humanity itself.

8

Greening planning?
Environmental perspectives

I n this chapter we consider environmentalism and its significance for planning. Like the radical cultural critiques discussed in chapter 7, environmentalism has sought to improve and reinterpret planning rather than diminish it in modern capitalist societies. Environmentalism has also enlarged the domain of urban governance, generally by giving rise to environmental policy and regulatory systems. Many green groups and commentators share with radical democrats an attachment to progressive human-centred values such as social justice, social inclusion and participatory democracy. The effects of both movements have been registered in a progression of reforms to planning legislation and practice in most Western countries since the early 1970s.

This chapter has three main sections. We begin by tracing the origins of environmental critique and its early links to urban planning, and show how the 'green movement'—developing separately and gaining momentum from the late 1960s—mounted a substantial critique of technocratic and professionalised planning. We then show how environmentalists have sought to redirect planning towards new values: ecological sustainability, sustainable development and environmental justice. Finally we examine the relationship between environmentalism and planning in Australia. Whereas environmental planning has been widely accepted as the dominant paradigm of planning in Europe, it has far to go in Australia, although there are signs that some of its concepts are gradually being absorbed.

Early critiques

Planning the city beautiful

The ghosts of planning pioneers are no doubt surprised to see that their endeavours have been the subject in recent decades of an environmental critique by community activists and theorists. Planning was conceived in part as a form of resource stewardship that sought both to check the environmental damage caused by free markets and to preserve parts of nature for agriculture and for human enjoyment (Evans 1997). Planning in Britain and Europe was born of sanitary and housing reform movements that sought to purify and restore to health landscapes that had been poisoned by industrialisation. Some early romantics reacted to the horrors of industrial capitalism by rejecting the city itself as corrupting and a danger to human health—promoting instead 'a return to nature', meaning a return to a rural or village idyll that supposedly prevailed before the Industrial Revolution. Of course, this misty-eyed view of preindustrial society neglected to consider why many European peasants were so eager to escape village life.

Later idealists retained hope in cities but reconstituted on 'natural principles'. At the turn of the century, Britain's Ebenezer Howard (1850–1928) produced his enormously influential vision: *Tomorrow: A Peaceful Path to Real Reform* (1965/1902). At the same time a *City Beautiful* movement flourished in the USA. A common element of these was the conception of planning as a sort of sophisticated landscaping exercise. A combination of social engineering, careful landscaping and good civic design would produce the 'garden city', where town and country would be 'married' in a symbiotic rather than exploitative relationship. Although few garden cities were built, the fundamental *rus in urbe* ('the country in the city') philosophy behind them remained enormously influential in British and North American attitudes towards urban planning and civic design. In 1933 Sir Patrick Abercrombie wrote that there were two contrasting attitudes that human societies could adopt towards their environments: planning or laissez-faire (Abercrombie 1943/1933). Planning represented the higher, 'civilised' instinct that sought the creation of harmonious, cultivated and productive landscapes.

In Britain, the preservation of rural landscapes—both for their productivity and for their amenity—became a key function of planning. This ideal was not taken up with similar enthusiasm in Australia, where colonial settlement practices had established a much more hostile attitude towards the land and its original owners. As with most other

New World societies (e.g. Canada, USA, Argentina, South Africa and New Zealand), colonial Australians in the main regarded nature in starkly utilitarian terms, as a resource to be harnessed and exploited rather than conserved (Flannery 1994). Such attitudes lingered into the 20th century and are still evident in many social practices and outlooks.

There was, however, always another side of the Settlement story, revealed in many acts by public and private bodies to preserve and enhance the natural qualities of the colonised landscape. Australia's environmental movement has its origins in the non-urban sphere—the 'field naturalists', the promoters of national parks for the appreciation of Australia's unique ecology. Winston (1957: 12) notes in his history of planning for Sydney that early colonial governments quickly 'established a fine tradition of providing public parks and reserves' in cities and towns. As a result, Sydney, Melbourne, Adelaide and Perth can boast of graceful urban parks close to the city centres (see also the history of Australian planning outlined in Hamnett & Freestone 2000).

In the wake of World War II, however, it seemed evident to many observers that town planning's early conservationist instincts had been blunted by the necessities of reconstruction and by the allure of new scientific theories and techniques that prized industrial-technocratic development. As we see in chapter 2, planning during the Long Boom in Australia became fixed on growth, namely the expansion of new residential suburbs and the infrastructure required to serve them. In suburbia, 'nature' survived only in parcels—the fragments remaining in backyards, nature strips and threadbare parks. Moreover, suburbanisation facilitated and was in turn fuelled by the growth of the motor car, with serious ecological implications.

Critiques: emergent and divergent

The contemporary environmental critique of planning began with radical and utopian interventions in planning theory, embodying the upsurge of interest in the Earth's ecology in the late 1960s coupled with a revival of interest in the spiritual. Rachel Carson (1962) published *Silent Spring*, an indictment of the ecological effects of pollution from the pesticide DDT—the silencing of birdsong as bird populations absorbed DDT through the food chain and became sterile as a result. The emotional auditory impact of such a tragic image resonated with the visual one of the Earth from space viewed with wonder by the first astronauts (a development anticipated by the astrophysicist Fred Hoyle as early as 1948; see J. Young 1990: 120). A nascent green movement raised these new icons, equalling in symbolic power the red flag of socialism.

Grabow and Heskin (1973: 110) described the ecological ethic to guide planning as 'the merging of the development of the individual with the unity of the world'. That is a theme that has been much investigated and elaborated by subsequent eco-philosophers—the possibility of an ecocentric (nature-centred) rather than an anthropocentric (human-centred) perspective (Eckersley 1992). These ideas, however, were not absorbed into mainstream planning thought and practice until very recently. Jacobs' (1995) application of environmental ethics in the field of planning broke largely new ground, and drew on the advancing field of environmental ethics rather than on developments in planning theory or practice.

Environmentalism, in fact, tended to develop its own discourse about planning, independently of the professionalised field of town planning. Environmentalism, with its compelling symbols, novel goals, critical perceptions and advanced rationalities, offered a more powerful interpretation of the world than that of professional town planning. It could scarcely be resisted. In the past two decades a somewhat disparate set of discourses has flourished under the rubric of environmentalism (Eckersley 1995). Let us briefly consider just five.

Ecoanarchism

For Murray Bookchin, the ecoanarchist, action through the state is not necessary or sufficient to solve environmental problems. Rather, direct action is 'a moral principle, an ideal, indeed a sensibility' (Bookchin 1980: 47). Bookchin appeals to the idea of the citizen as a member of 'the fraternity of selves that composed the polis'. To understand current ecological and political problems, he says, we must examine their social causes and remedy them through social methods. Human society is part of the totality of the natural world: 'Social life does not necessarily face nature as a combatant in an unrelenting war. The emergence of society is a natural fact that has its origins in the biology of human socialization' (Bookchin 1990: 26). Thus, 'Social ecology tries to show how nature slowly phases into society without ignoring the differences between society and nature on the one hand, as well as the extent to which they merge with one another on the other' (Bookchin 1990: 30).

Ecosocialism

Ecosocialism's analytical premises are rooted in Marxian political economy, and therefore the capitalist mode of production is seen as the main, if not the exclusive, source of ecological crises. Ecosocialism is a transformative perspective that condemns capitalism from a 'radical, socially just, environmentally-benign—but fundamentally anthropocentric—perspective' (Pepper 1993: xi). Pepper (1993: xi–xii) says that 'Social justice . . . or the increasingly global lack of it, is the most pressing of all environmental problems'. The ecosocialist perspective was prefigured in a seminal essay by Stretton (1976) which, while recognising the seriousness of ecological problems, argued that class and social justice must be pivotal political-conceptual axes of environmentalism.

Ecorationalism

Supposing that the value society wanted to promote was 'ecological sustainability', what would be the behavioural norms required? Well, says John Dryzek (1987), that depends on the nature of ecosystems. Ecological *problems* concern the discrepancy between ideal and actual conditions stemming from interactions between human political systems and natural ecosystems. Ecosystems typically interact with one another. Ecological problems are therefore complex: they cannot be reduced to simple variables, they vary over time and space, they cannot be understood with scientific certainty, they concern collective goods such as the seas or atmosphere and therefore many human actors have a stake in them.

Ecological rationality must therefore involve two key elements. The first element is *self-regulation*—in that systems of regulation must have a built-in tendency to return to a stable state, coordination across different fields of social choice. In addition *robustness* is needed—in that the social mechanism of regulation must perform well under a wide variety of political and social conditions, and the regulatory system must possess the ability to steer human and ecological systems back to a normal operating range from severe conditions of disequilibrium. Ecological rationality demands priority over economic, social, legal and political rationality.

Ecofeminism

Ecofeminists believe that the oppression and exploitation of nature is akin to the exploitation of women by men through social structures of gender and patriarchy. Ecofeminists do not believe that animals and indeed the non-human natural world in general has any less intrinsic value, and therefore right to exist, than do humans. Whereas women are defined as 'the Other' by men—defined against a norm of masculine 'perfection'—so also non-human nature is defined by patriarchal systems of human thought. Thus nature is mostly known by what is 'lacking': intelligence, rationality, consciousness, conscience. This 'moral dualism' which privileges the human and justifies the human interest in exploitation of and domination over the natural world is objectionable in the eyes of ecofeminists. Val Plumwood (1999: 207) observes that

> in a rationalist economy which defines its hardness in opposition to the symbolic woman, as Other, and which increasingly invades every corner of our lives, we should not be surprised that care and compassion for others are increasingly inexpressible in the public 'rational context' that is defined against the domestic sphere.

Market environmentalism

Not all environmentalist discourses are directed at radical change of capitalist society. Indeed what has become known as 'market environmentalism' proposes that the neoliberal model of capitalism be extended to the environment. Hardin (1968), in a seminal essay, argued that common property, which includes all the most important environmental assets, was doomed to overuse and ultimate exhaustion. The conclusion that market environmentalists draw from such a proposition is that environments and their contents should be privately owned. Market environmentalism champions the deregulation of all direct state intervention mechanisms and the extension of market relations to all aspects of environment and society in the interests of resource conservation. In so far as neoliberalism has an ally in the environmental movement, it is in the market environmental critique.

These critiques opened up vast new territory for philosophical debate, but did not have an immediate impact on planning. What eventually gave the environmental critique real political and institutional force was the pragmatic *convergence* during the 1980s around the 'sustainability paradigm' culminating in a series of international meetings and agreements that established green values as core concerns for public policy.

Eco-sustainability and environmental planning

The recent origins of sustainability as an environmental policy objective may be traced back to the World Conservation Strategy (International Union for the Conservation of Nature and Natural Resources 1980), which was endorsed by the Australian government. After this, the principle of ecologically sustainable development (ESD) was strongly advocated in the Brundtland Report, *Our Common Future* (World Commission on Environment and Development [WCED] 1987). In 1992, the concept received further powerful endorsement at the United Nations-sponsored Earth Summit in Rio de Janeiro. This produced the Rio Declaration on Environment and Development, which was agreed to by over 170 countries, including Australia.

The WCED report defines sustainable development quite widely, as 'development that meets the needs of the present without compromising the ability of future generations to meet their own needs' (WCED 1987: 43). Thus, sustainable development seeks the achievement of justice to future generations as a key goal of public policy—intergenerational equity (Memon & Gleeson 1994: 120):

> To achieve intergenerational equity means that the actions of the current generation should not substantially limit the options available to future generations. Decision-making agencies have therefore to ensure that resources are not harnessed beyond the carrying capacity of the bio-physical systems of which they are a part. The above definition implies that development should be compatible with the continued functioning of these essential ecological processes.

Some commentators have interpreted this goal as supporting a radical program of wealth redistribution, globally and within nations and cities. Herman Daly (1996: 6) offers a correction to modern economics in which the global economy is viewed as a subsystem of the larger ecosystem and 'depends upon the environment both as a source of raw material inputs and a "sink" for waste outputs'. The economy is open and growing, but the planetary ecosystem is a relatively closed system having one input—energy from the sun, and no outlet for waste. Today this is hardly a radical perception, and does not deny the usefulness of markets, yet Daly convincingly shows that such a commonsense assumption overturns most of the current tenets of macroeconomic dogma, including the devotion to growth of GNP and free trade, and the studied neglect of national economic autonomy, human community, natural capital and grossly uneven distribution of wealth. Daly argues that economics, properly understood, has three foci, not one: not only allocation, but also distribution and scale (see Box 8.1). In the 'steady state' economy necessary for sustainability market allocations continue, but the economy is focused on development (qualitative improvement), not growth (quantitative increase). Limits are placed on the difference in wealth and income between the richest and the poorest. While information flows freely among nations, capital movement across national borders is restricted.

BOX 8.1 THREE DISTINCT ECONOMIC PROBLEMS: ALLOCATION, DISTRIBUTION AND SCALE

The economist Herman Daly argues that we must give equal weight to three problems of economics and not just to one—allocation and its efficiency—as modern economic thinking does (1996: 159–60):

> We have three economic problems to consider: allocation, distribution, and scale. *Allocation* refers to the apportioning of resources among alternative product uses— food, bicycles, cars, medical care. An allocation is efficient if it corresponds to effective demand, that is, the relative preferences of the citizens as weighted by their relative incomes, both taken as given. An inefficient allocation will use resources to produce a number of things that people will not buy, and will fail to produce other things that people would buy if only they could find them. It would be characterized by shortages of the latter and surpluses of the former. *Distribution* refers to the apportioning of the goods produced (and the resources they embody) among different people (as opposed to different commodities). Distributions are just or unjust; allocations are efficient or inefficient. There is an efficient allocation for each distribution of income. *Scale* refers to the physical size of the economy relative to the ecosystem. The economy is viewed, in its physical dimensions, as a subsystem of the larger ecosystem. Scale is measured as population times per capita resource use—in other words total resource use—the volume of the matter/energy throughout (metabolic flow) by which the ecosystem sustains the economic subsystem. Scale may be sustainable or unsustainable. An efficient allocation does not imply a just distribution. Neither an efficient allocation nor a just distribution, nor both implies a sustainable scale. The three concepts are quite distinct although relations among them exist.

From a more limited political perspective, sustainable development 'implies that during the decision-making process, the actions of a particular developer or group should not substantially limit the options available to other individuals or groups' (Memon & Gleeson 1994: 120). The principle of sustainable development has therefore tended to reinforce the values of radical cultural activists and commentators: namely, social justice and democratic governance.

The 'sustainability paradigm' has had variable influence on Western planning systems. In some countries, particularly European countries including Britain, sustainable development has become absorbed as a key goal of planning. The Netherlands and Scandinavia have perhaps taken the idea furthest into their planning systems, and in Germany and France planning has also begun to include sustainable development as a major goal. The European Union, now a political force in its own right, has promoted the idea of 'sustainable cities'. The final report of the Expert Group on the Urban Environment (1996: vi) states:

Management for sustainability is essentially a political process which requires planning and has an impact on urban governance. The process of sustainable urban management requires a range of tools addressing environmental, social and economic concerns in order to provide the necessary basis for integration. By applying these tools, urban policy making for sustainability can become broader, more powerful and more ambitious than has been generally recognised.

The EU report includes plans to limit consumption of resources, improve air and water quality, improve the quality of water returned to the ecosystem in sewage, control pollution at source, develop a 'green structure' for city parks and nearby countryside, restore and enrich soils, conserve energy, and design cities and suburbs to reduce unnecessary travel demand. Specific examples are provided from European countries (see Box 8.2).

BOX 8.2 EUROPEAN SUSTAINABLE TRANSPORT PLANNING INITIATIVES

NEIGHBOURHOODS WITHOUT CARS

The idea of a neighbourhood without cars arose from a study of the space requirements of moving and parked cars in Bremen, Germany. Almost a quarter of the entire locality can be used for other purposes when no parking space is supplied. A car-sharing scheme is planned for use by the residents. Usually 40 per cent of the road space is required for parking space. With the car-free scheme this can be reduced to about 17 per cent. The European cities forming the 'Car-Free Cities Club' work towards reductions in urban car use and possibly a complete ban on the use of the private car during working hours in inner cities. To reduce car dependence in Kuopio, Finland, a new development plan will focus on infilling previously isolated settlements with car-free neighbourhoods served by a regional bus system.

REDUCING FREIGHT TRAFFIC

Leiden in the Netherlands intends to develop a city distribution centre through which the city centre would be supplied by small delivery vans. It is estimated that 70 per cent of the goods supplied to the city could be transferred from heavy vehicles and the current 24 000 daily truck kilometres that affect the city centre would be reduced by around 80 per cent.

FAVOURING THE USE OF BICYCLES

Groningen in the Netherlands has implemented a program to favour the use of the bicycle and public transport. The idea is to institute restrictive parking policies near facilities, shopping centres and other attractive locations. As an alternative, the city provides cycle paths and public transport networks near these locations. The city has also improved its bus service through the integration of different networks, the building of separate 'bus-only' lanes, and ensuring priority for buses at traffic lights.

PARK AND RIDE

In San Sebastian, Spain, parking measures are an important element of the city's transport and environmental policy, where a number of objectives in the areas of noise and air pollution have been set. To reduce motorised traffic, priority is given to city residents, while commuters, through a combination of high fees in the centre and free parking at locations connected to the public transport network, are encouraged to use the 'park and ride' system.

(These examples are taken from *European Sustainable Cities*, Expert Group 1996.)

New Zealand in 1991 passed new planning legislation that instated sustainability as a key aim (Memon & Gleeson 1994). Japan's cities have adopted plans for ecologically sustainable development. In the USA the treatment of ESD is very variable, with quite advanced legislation in some areas (e.g. California), and a few institutions carrying out groundbreaking research (e.g. the Rocky Mountain Institute) against a background of widespread antipathy. In the world's largest and most populous countries such as China, India and Indonesia, sustainability does not rate highly (if at all) in urban governance.

The sustainability ideal, and the cluster of concepts derived from it ('urban sustainability', 'ecologically sustainable development'), has had enormous indirect significance for planning. The relationship between ecology and humanity, particularly human social and economic endeavour, has been boldly underscored, leading to a new questioning of economic growth, a value that postwar Western planning has supported. Development—including urban development—can occur only within a new ethical-political framework that safeguards the interest of nature while also protecting the interests of human society (intra/intergenerational equity) from the actions of human beings and agencies.

Recent years have seen the growth of a literature of 'sustainable cities', drawing strongly on the exploration of ecologically sustainable development with a lineage in the Brundtland Report and the Stockholm and Rio conferences (e.g. Haughton & Hunter 1994; Nijkamp & Perrels 1994). The rubric 'sustainable planning' has been coined to describe forms of urban and spatial regulation that attempt to place the goals of sustainable development at the core of urban and spatial regulation (e.g. Blowers 1993; Breheny & Rookwood 1993). The main assumption of this new planning formulation is captured in the subtitle of a recent essay by some its advocates (Newman 1997): *The Ecological and Human Dimensions of the City Can Be Part of Town Planning.* (Indeed, as Evans [1997] argues, these considerations *must* be part of planning.)

In Britain, town planning 'ran out of steam' (1997: 4). The values that drove town planning were based around an environmental problem, the unhealthy and impoverished environments of old industrial cities, which by the 1970s had radically changed. The emergent environmental problem was no longer confined to cities, to buildings, to lack of physical infrastructure, or even to nation-states. The new environmental problem is of greater scope, concerning the atmosphere, soil, water and overuse of the Earth's resources. To address this problem town planning becomes 'environmental planning' or 'environmental governance' (Low et al. 1999: ch. 14).

Australian interpretations

The rise of environmentalism

The Australian environmental critique of planning emerged with the rise of the green movement itself. The Commonwealth government in 1992 produced a *Draft National Strategy for Ecologically Sustainable Development.* The government's Ecologically Sustainable Development (ESD) steering committee turned its attention to the planning system, recognising 'the need to improve land-use planning and to incorporate the principles of sustainable development in environmental impact assessment' (Beder 1993: 90). With the election of the new Commonwealth government in 1996, however, official commitment to the strategies produced by the ESD steering committee quickly waned (Christoff & Low 1999). The new government deliberately downgraded the policy significance of sustainability and re-established economic growth as a key political value. The 'de-greening' of Commonwealth policy followed the familiar (CL) course set by conservative state governments during the early and mid-1990s (chapter 5).

Concern for urban issues has fluctuated in the green movement. Christoff (1999) outlines three waves of urban environmental governance (see also Christoff & Low 1999). From the early 1970s, there was an upsurge of interest in Australian urban and natural heritage. As a result, membership of the Australian Conservation Foundation grew fivefold between 1967 and 1971 (Papadakis 1993). Since this time there has been a shifting alliance between urban activists and the green movement. In the early 1970s there were conflicts over urban environments. Popular movements to protect inner-suburban areas from invasive development were supported by the building unions, which imposed bans on construction—the 'green bans' (see Box 8.3; also Manning & Hardman 1975; Jakubowicz 1984; Burgmann & Burgmann 1998). The world's first 'green bans' were imposed on the construction or destruction of buildings which a union—the New South Wales branch of the Builders' Labourers Federation—regarded as socially and environmentally irresponsible. This was a powerful movement informed both by a Marxist analysis of the role of labour and a radical democratic critique of planning (chapters 6 and 7). The legacy of the green bans has been uneven, however. During the 1990s, construction and forestry unions have often placed themselves in direct opposition to the green movement by supporting the continuance of employment-generating projects, such as woodchipping and freeway/motorway construction.

BOX 8.3 THE GREEN BANS

During the 1970s the New South Wales branch of the Builders' Labourers Federation, under the leadership of Mr Jack Mundey, imposed bans on 'development' (demolition and construction) which the union had decided was irresponsible: 'The union's guiding principle, which aroused such strong emotions and which underpinned environmental activism, was the concept of the social responsibility of labour: that workers had a right to insist that their labour not be used in harmful ways' (Burgmann & Burgmann 1998: 3). The union also insisted on the rights of women to work on equal conditions with men, and helped groups such as prisoners, homosexuals, Aborigines, students, the women's movement, and poorer home buyers. By October 1973, the green bans (Burgmann & Burgmann 1988: 4)

> had halted projects worth easily $3000 million (at mid 1970s prices) according to the Master Builders Association (MBA). By 1975 bans had halted $5000 million of development, saving New South Wales from much of the cultural and environmental destruction it would otherwise have suffered. The bans were a deliberate confrontation with the power of capital. In the absence of sufficiently sensitive planning and conservation regulations, the builders labourers took it upon themselves to dispute employers' rights to build what they liked where they liked, and they were prepared to defend their bans on picket lines and at demonstrations.

The bans are a continuation of a wider struggle for the enlargement of democracy that has been going on for centuries. Jack Mundey explained how the union's ultrademocratic principles led inexorably to green bans (Burgmann & Burgmann 1998: 53)

> It is not good enough in a modern society to say that the only right an individual has is to vote once in every three years in an election. I believe in everyday democracy. If a decision is incorrect, any individual or organisation has the right to do all that's necessary to change that decision. Otherwise, how can decisions be altered? All such matters should be subjected to public scrutiny. All laws are changed, not by the 'great' thinking of legislators, but by the extra-parliamentary activity of ordinary men and women who want to see wrongs righted (Mundey quoted in the *Sydney Morning Herald* 1 August 1973).

Green bans were imposed and destructive development stopped at Kelly's Bush, an area of pristine bushland on the Sydney waterfront (June 1971). Numerous other bans on development projects in Sydney and Newcastle followed during the next few years. The union also campaigned against the building of freeways in the interests of ecological responsibility, and halted the Northwestern Expressway that would have destroyed houses and local environments in Glebe, Ultimo, Balmain, Annandale and Summer Hill.

FURTHER READING

Burgmann & Burgmann (1998).

'Motorcar madness'

At the same time, popular opposition to modernist transport planning was emerging as a powerful critical force, especially in cities such as Sydney and Melbourne that had been threatened with the construction of major North American-style freeway networks. In time, this critique of car-focused development was absorbed by the environmental movement as a general objection to modernist planning. Much of the initial criticism of car-focused planning emerged from the grassroots and thus centred on the *localised* impacts of freeway building, emphasising the social, aesthetic and environmental stresses that such developments placed on communities.

The most vocal opponents emerged in gentrifying inner-city neighbourhoods, such as Melbourne's Carlton. Here well-organised and well-resourced communities were able to mount successful campaigns against road-building schemes, such as the infamous 1969 Melbourne Transport Plan (MTP), though these critical forces never managed to broaden their political bases—at least not for long—to form an enduring social movement opposing modernist transport planning. While grass-roots resistance to the MTP caused the Victorian government to reduce the scale of freeway plans, there was little evidence that transport planners changed their thinking (Beed 1981). Thus, at present the anti-freeway battles in Melbourne are being fought all over again as the state of Victoria maintains a huge new road-building scheme that revives the modernist vision of car-dominated development.

In an early broadening of the transport critique, Beed (1981) argued that policies stressing spatial consolidation and greater reliance on public transport were needed to reduce the social, economic and environmental costs of urbanisation. His thesis anticipated the arguments for urban consolidation that environmentalists and urban analysts were to promote during the 1980s and 90s. New intellectual critiques emerged in Australia, reflecting a broader ecological perspective that linked transport planning to issues such as urban morphology, energy use and climate change (e.g. Moriarty & Beed 1991; Public Transport Users' Association 1995). A common feature of these environmental critiques of planning approaches was strong advocacy for a shift away from motor-car-based development towards a greater reliance on integrated, multimodal public transport systems. Moreover, these Australian critiques reflected and contributed to a broader international criticism of 'car dependency' in planning ideology and practice (e.g. Hass-Klau 1990; Vuchic 1981). Reflecting an increasingly prevalent view among environmentalists and some urbanists, Alexander and McManus argued that Australia's cities had been 'seduced by the automobile' (1992: 6) and that planning had been the principal agent of seduction. In short, planning was cast as little more than a 'pimp' for the motor car lobby.

The most famous contribution to the ecological critique of modernist transport planning was made by Newman and Kenworthy, in a series of controversial analyses (e.g. 1980, 1989, 1992) that claimed to find a causal relationship between urban form and energy use. Much of Beed's (1981) earlier findings were echoed though this time in bolder exhortatory tones. In particular, Newman and Kenworthy assembled evidence which purported to show that the low-density urban forms endemic to North America and Australasia encouraged, even demanded, much greater energy consumption levels than did the more compact cities of Europe. The claims were sweeping and were used to indict not only the morphology of Australian and other low-density cities, but also the cultural frameworks that had engendered societies marked by 'automobile dependence' (Newman & Kenworthy 1989: 2):

Australian cities are all basically Automobile cities . . . in the new post-war suburbs all Australian cities [seem] to have much the same kind of transport patterns, set firmly in place by a structured low density suburbia and a car-oriented culture.

Their work did much to strengthen political, if not always intellectual, support for the policies of urban consolidation that were finding favour among Australian governments in the 1980s and early 90s. Among urbanists, however, Newman's and Kenworthy's arguments had a rather more mixed reception that included a significant chorus of angry criticism.

Kirwan (1992), for example, questioned the methodological premises of Newman's and Kenworthy's analysis, especially their decision not to use traditional multivariate analysis. Importantly, a multivariate analysis would suggest that Australian cities could reduce their levels of energy consumption by various policy means without resorting to consolidation strategies (Kirwan 1992). These and other criticisms of Newman and Kenworthy were made more forcefully by a range of other urbanists, such as Troy (1996b) and Orchard (1995). In the main, these critics objected to the 'green' compact city ideal, on the grounds that it threatened the established egalitarian values of Australian planning which had distributed—if not always successfully—good-quality housing and generous living space to the working classes.

Urban agendas

The national government withdrew from involvement in urban planning from 1975 under the conservative parties. Campaigns to save wilderness areas (e.g. the Franklin River in the early 1980s) reinvigorated the green movement but redirected public attention away from the cities. Urban and non-urban environmental movements became widely separated. Urban issues (the 'brown' agenda), with the exception of toxic waste disposal which was always a preoccupation of Greenpeace, were largely neglected by green 'environmentalists' (see Christoff & Low 1999).

One critical urban environmental issue, heritage buildings and landscapes, received little attention from mainstream greens. Nonetheless, in time, an appreciable urban heritage movement emerged, and its successes were registered in new development controls to protect and enhance the historic built environment (particularly under SDM governance, see chapter 4). Heritage protection has, however, proved to be a flimsy defence for historic places and environments, many of which have been ravaged by both public and private sector developers. Moreover, in a recent critique, Buxton has questioned the object of established heritage protection, arguing that it has tended to value highly select and often isolated environments, condemning 'most of a city—the interrelated and varied streetscapes, the lanes and even the drains and the parks—to the wrecker' (Buxton 1998: 7).

Recent currents

In the 1990s the environment movement has focused attention on global issues (such as climate change, global and transboundary pollution, and biodiversity) in which the distinction between 'green' and 'brown' recedes in importance. The contribution of cities to the consumption of environmental resources and the use of the environment as a sink for waste products have come to prominence in planning theory and practice, both in Australia and overseas (see Low et al. 1999). There is a growing awareness in Western town planning professions of problems of water supply, waste disposal, and the impact of urban growth on habitat and energy use.

Even though there is a common failure to appreciate the contradictions between economic and ecological imperatives, some elements of the Australian planning profession have begun to accept the need for ecologically sustainable urban development. Schemes for 'ecocities' have begun to appear (e.g. the Halifax project in Adelaide, and a competition for ecological sustainability in the Jerrabomberra Valley on the fringe of Canberra). Serious consideration was given to issues of ecological sustainability in planning at two conferences held in 1997: the 'Pathways to Sustainability' conference in the City of Newcastle, and the state conference of the Victorian Division of the Royal Australian Planning Institute. In Newcastle sustainable development projects include renewable energy power generation, including wind turbines and photovoltaic generators, and the use of methane from waste landfill. Newcastle's Local Agenda 21 management plan includes energy savings, transport planning to reduce car dependency and encourage bicycle use, measures to restrain water consumption and protection of local biodiversity.

Among the states, the New South Wales government issues guidelines for ecologically sustainable development to all local councils (NSW Government 1998). Under the *Local Government Amendment (Ecologically Sustainable Development) Act 1997*, 'councils are now expected to adopt a strategic "whole of council" approach toward the recognition of ecologically sustainable development and to respond positively to environmental problems in their area' (NSW Government 1997: 1). Local councils are required to include the goal of ESD in their local management plans and in considering any applications—under planning legislation—for development. The state government itself, however, is not required to monitor its own activities on a 'whole of state' basis, and the more difficult issues involving conflict between economic development and ecological goals (such as reducing greenhouse emissions from industry, domestic heating and transport) have not been fully confronted (Christoff & Low 1999).

South Australia has produced a cooperative policy with the City of Adelaide for ecologically sustainable development in that city. Queensland's *Integrated Planning Act 1997* has as its purpose 'to achieve ecological sustainability by co-ordinating and integrating planning at the local, regional and State levels', by managing the process by which development occurs, and by 'managing the effects of development on the environment' (section 1.2.1). The core of the Act (following the principle of the New Zealand *Resource Management Act 1991*) is based on bringing together all the approvals that are required before a development proposal can proceed. If the Act's purpose is to be achieved, much depends, of course, on the way 'ecological sustainability' is to be assessed. Undoubtedly it can be assessed rigorously—but will it be? The Act seems mainly designed to smooth out development application procedures. Especially at issue is the strength and independence of environmental impact assessment.

Local government in Australia has begun to adopt and implement Local Agenda 21 policies. A local government environment network, 'Environs Australia', is promoting and disseminating the concept of ecologically sustainable development. A recent survey of the nation's 770 councils conducted for Environs Australia showed that 34 councils were actually subjecting their policy processes to Agenda 21 criteria (Whittaker 1996, 1997). Although this represents only 4 per cent of councils, many are large urban councils and together they account for about 18 per cent of Australia's total population. In 1996, 119 councils (about 15 per cent) were showing an active interest in ESD. The cities of Sydney, Melbourne and Adelaide have recently joined the International Consortium on Local Environmental Initiatives (ICLEI).

Reflecting overseas shifts, especially in Europe, Australian planning systems have resounded in recent years with renewed demands for participation and renewed local urban environmental activism. These demands have redirected attention from recycling, traffic calming and the protection of remnant habitat, to consultative planning, environmental performance monitoring and state of the environment reporting by the Commonwealth and state governments. Information about disparities between regions, cities and suburbs is provoking calls for environmental justice. Pressures are building to generate nationally coordinated and, where possible, uniform air and water emission standards.

Conclusion

Environmentalism is by no means a unified set of principles, beliefs and arguments. But, as we have seen with the upsurge of the green bans in Sydney, the discourse can inspire social movements to have a direct effect on city development. Environmentalism is linked to ideas of democracy and citizenship. The green bans resonate with Bookchin's ideas about the value of direct, non-violent action as well as with the political values endorsed by ecosocialists and ecofeminists.

The concept of ecological sustainability is one that must be at the core of all urban planning policy and practice in the 21st century. European nations have fully adopted ideas of ecological modernisation which Australia cannot afford to ignore. Australian society has shown itself on numerous occasions to be open and responsive to environmentalism when it has been shown that environmental initiatives can achieve beneficial aims. Political leaders in some Australian states have engaged with this public concern and begun to insist on strong regulation of development for ecological ends.

In the city the potential tension between ecological responsibility and social justice emerges. Yet it is a false dilemma created when the only alternative to increasing employment is understood to be the neoliberal model of growth and the corporate-liberal mode of urban governance. In chapter 9 we turn to this final and influential critique of planning: managerialism and neoliberalism.

9

Let the market decide! From managerialism to neoliberalism

Among the various reform agendas, it is neoliberalism that has had the greatest effect on the institutions of planning in the past 10 years. As we have made clear, the impact of neoliberalism is a major stimulus for writing this book. The tide of movement to embrace the market in everything threatens both planning and democracy. We have seen the results of this tide on both cities (chapter 3) and their governance (chapters 4 and 5). Advocates of neoliberalism want to go much further. Unless the tide turns, all meaningful planned intervention in the land economy will be abolished.

In this chapter we first review in more theoretical terms the shift from a social democratic form of managerialism to full-blown neoliberalism. We then outline some of the threats to planning that neoliberalism is now vigorously pursuing. We consider such threats pursued under the framework of National Competition Policy, arising from the development industry, and within the planning profession itself.

Managerialism and neoliberalism

From the moment that government planning began to be seriously considered, opposition to it started to form. All through the 1950s and 60s Friedrich von Hayek—like Mannheim, an Austrian exiled to Britain in the war years—turned out book after book denouncing government 'collectivist' planning. Hayek argued for individualism (individual freedom from the constraint of community, society or state), the rule of law, the virtue of the automatic coordinating effect of the market, consumer sovereignty, private property rights, and a minimal state to see that the law is observed. Building on Hayek's work, Robert Nozick developed his theory of entitlement (essentially property entitlement) in explicit refutation of Rawls' theory of justice (Nozick 1974). Public choice theorists (e.g. Arrow 1951; Buchanan 1977) argued for the principles of the market to prevail over political deliberation. Rothbard (1973) even proposed that there was no field of government activity that could not ultimately be performed better by 'the private sector': indeed, the very existence of public and private sectors in a market society was to Rothbard anomalous. Even the existence of monopolies is acceptable, provided that they are private monopolies and that at some point firms have competed to own them (Lal 1998).

These ideas were powerfully promoted by well-endowed 'think tanks' in the 1970s and 80s (Self 1993: 64–7; Cockett 1995). The neoliberal critique suggested that economic instruments provided the best solutions to problems of allocation, distribution and coordination, even in the sphere of politics. The critique was readily digested by the economics academy throughout the English-speaking world, including Australia, promoted by private think tanks (Institute of Public Affairs, Institute for Private Enterprise, H.R. Nicholls Society, Tasman Institute, Centre for Independent Studies, Centre for International Economics) and adopted by politicians. Thus, in a speech to the Victorian Parliament, Alan Stockdale (later Treasurer in the Kennett Government) says (*Victorian Parliamentary Debates*, 29 August 1991: 314):

> As F.A. Hayek has pointed out in his book *Constitution of Liberty* and other writings, the free market has a superior ability to transmit information between businesses and their customers. The socialist view of the workings of free markets is wrong and has been rejected throughout the world.

In the sphere of urban development there has always been political and intellectual opposition to planning from conservative interests, which regard it as an unwarranted intervention in the land economy. The conservative critique ranges from deep antipathy to any form of planning to a variety of positions that accept some form of intervention within certain contexts and carefully circumscribed limits. The intellectual case against urban planning rests essentially on the proposition that planning both distorts land markets and raises the transaction costs of development through bureaucratisation of the urban economy (e.g. Maser et al. 1977; Pennington 1999; Stull 1975). It is argued that these 'diseconomies' reduce employment growth and stifle the ability of the land market to satisfy consumers' needs for housing and transport. The general prescription of conservative critics is for the removal of public regulations (e.g. zoning) from land markets on the assumption that private coordinating mechanisms (e.g. covenants) will produce more efficient resource allocations. These critiques were absorbed by managerialists in Australia, who became influential in the urban governance of the 1990s.

As we see in chapters 4 and 5, urban governance moved from a form of managerialism connected with the project of social democracy ('social democratic managerialism') to a type of neoliberalism that we called 'corporate liberalism'. The shift to the latter model indicated that state governments wanted to retain control of key elements of metropolitan systems while moving large areas of social service provision into the market. On the face of it, this was a massive shift. Social democracy applauds planning and seeks to find better ways of directing the state apparatus to achieve its ends. Neoliberalism abhors planning and seeks to withdraw the state apparatus from intervention in the market. So how did this happen, and why?

Directing the public service to achieve a variety of social democratic goals for the city encountered two major problems: coordination, and 'overload'. Social democratic urban governance demands that the full range of urban social services be supplied equitably to all within the spatial jurisdiction (territory) of the government at the time required. This means, for instance, that schools, health care facilities, public libraries and public transport must be provided at the same time as new housing, roads and water services. In addition, the timely arrival of shops and entertainment facilities is needed.

One of the criticisms of planning practice in the 1970s was that zones (pilloried by managerialists as mere 'lines on maps') were provided for housing which could be built and sold quickly, but that little else in the way of services was provided in areas of urban growth. Also, it was said that zoning produced a uniform and restricted range of housing types (Paterson et al. 1976). Urban services might eventually come along five, 10 or 20 years later but that was of little comfort to the new residents at the time. It was certainly not good planning or good governance. Somehow public sector services (e.g. schools) had to be coordinated with private sector services (e.g. shopping and entertainment), and a wider range of housing types better fitted to demand profiles had to be encouraged by relaxing zoning.

Ministerial control and rationalisation of departments was only the first step towards the coordination required. The budgetary process had to be arranged so that funds for urban services were available in time. Key departmental chiefs had to coordinate their day-to-day activities for, however rationally structured, there had to be a division of labour and expertise within the public service. One giant department could not handle everything. Coordination at the best of times requires a more or less united Cabinet. If there are rivalries between ministers, or if ministers want to use their departmental responsibilities to build 'empires' and promote their political careers, then coordination is in serious jeopardy. In addition, a range of entirely new issues emerged: heritage protection, environmental protection, childcare, aged care, services for Aboriginal people, services for migrants, services for people with learning difficulties, and many more. Internationally, pluralist theorists began to talk about 'government overload' (Rose 1979).

For a time managerialism was closely associated with the social democratic project advanced by the Australian Labor Party. But in the same period neoliberalism was growing as a discursive force, and the worldwide institutional movement away from the Fordist international order was taking place. It was only a short step from the idea of managing the public sector—to *mimic* the private sector—to simply *replacing* the public sector. There were those who argued that the market would produce fairer as well as more efficient distributive outcomes (e.g. Paterson 1988). These voices became louder and more insistent in Australia with the advance of neoliberalism on the world stage (Pusey 1991). Bureaucrats at state as well as federal level changed their minds. As global material realities and ideas in good currency changed, the link between managerialism and social democracy began to decay during the later 1980s and was finally torn apart by the financial crisis that occurred between 1989 and 1991.

Considine and Painter (1997: 4–6) describe the transformation. The early reformers—Coombs, Wilenski and other social democrats—had been interested in 'social and political aspects of public service reform: equal opportunity, representative and participative bureaucracy, and open government' (Considine & Painter 1997: 4). The first wave of managerialist reforms had been built on an alliance between social democrats and 'advocates of a tightly run, hierarchical, and thoroughly modern form of organisation typified by the large private corporation' (Considine & Painter 1997: 5):

> There was a gender bias in these images of efficient organisation. The new managers were identified by supporters and critics alike as 'lean and mean', less interested in virtues such as loyalty, duty of service, and more apt to define themselves as 'fixers' and 'guns for hire'.

By the later 1980s it was clear that economic pressures to contract government expenditure had not been deflected by corporatisation and commercialisation: 'the binding faith in corporate management soon gave way to commitment to a small business logic of entrepreneurial management' (Considine & Painter 1997: 5). The public service 'was imagined as an elite core of centralised 'principals' managing service contracts with a host of independent 'agents': the contract state.

According to Considine and Painter (1997: 6), this new image (associated with corporate liberalism) represented a sharp break from the earlier form of managerialism: 'The intellectual justification for the amended managerialist vision is provided by "agency theory" and "public choice theories" which between them undercut the legitimacy of the management role itself' (see also Donaldson 1995). Thus, instead of trying to solve public sector management problems (coordination and coping with multiplicity) within the framework of government, the leading managerialists moved towards the 'market solution', in which public services are removed from the governmental sphere. At the same time neoliberal politics was embraced by conservative political parties swept to power following the economic crisis of 1990. A new and powerful coalition was formed between managerialists and politicians of the right.

Economists provided answers to the problems of coordination and overload, answers which planners schooled in the tradition of the blueprint plan could not offer. Paterson, an economist, a planner, and one of Australia's leading managerialists, attributes the lack of coordination to the failure of planning education to equip practitioners with intellectually rigorous analytical tools. The planner was naked, he wrote, in the company of economists, engineers and administrators, who employed methods with: 'the axiomatic rigour of mathematics, economics, and psychology, or the practical potency of engineering and administration' (Paterson 1976: 40). There is some truth in this observation. But there was another item lacking in the planner's education, an understanding of politics and political ethics, something not found in the managerialist's toolbox either. Without it planners and managers, however rigorous, become mere instruments of power, unable to comprehend the use to which they are being put.

Neoliberalism has gone a long way towards reshaping urban governance and planning, but the agenda goes much further. In what follows we identify and discuss some of the reform programs that are currently working to reshape Australian planning.

National Competition Policy

The federal Labor government, in conjunction with the states, established the framework for a National Competition Policy (NCP) in the early 1990s. The members of the Council of Australian Governments in 1995 enshrined the NCP in a set of written agreements. NCP has already had far-reaching effects in many areas of public sector activity in Australia and, as we will show, its impact is now being felt in the planning arena. It is therefore worth considering in a little detail its underlying assumptions and values. These are set out in a report which set in motion the process of 'reform', that of the inquiry conducted by F.G. Hilmer—the 'Hilmer Report', as it became known (Hilmer 1993).

The legitimacy of a market depends on the principle of 'consumer sovereignty': firms compete to serve 'consumers' of goods and services. The legitimacy of the state depends on democratic choice through the political processes. In keeping with the thrust of public choice theory, the Hilmer panel sought to change these long-established assumptions by applying the value of consumer sovereignty to the activity of the state. The Hilmer Report proposes nothing less than a major revision of Australian democracy. The principles of the market are to govern the activities of the state.

Fundamentally at issue is the process which defines that notoriously slippery but indispensable political concept, the 'public interest'. The elites of authoritarian societies of every political colour have justified their acts—both benign and nefarious—in the name of the public interest. In utilitarian economics the public interest is invoked to justify ignoring or overriding the political demands of minority pressure groups. In a pluralist democracy, however, the public interest is defined by being publicly *contested* through a variety of democratic processes: parliamentary and local government deliberations, legal processes, pressure group activity, and lobbying, all under the uneven public scrutiny of a competitive press. It is in fact a strength of pluralist democracy that within it the public interest sheds its foundationalist, elitist and totalitarian garb and submits to the rough wear and tear of free political debate.

For many neoliberals, social consensus is unobtainable, and the logic of the market provides the only public interest (Pennington 1999: 45):

> At the core of the Austrian [Hayekian] account is the insight that in a liberal society there is typically no social consensus about values and thus the way in which resources should be collectively disposed. One of the key advantages of markets, therefore, is that they allow individuals with disparate and inconsistent plans to coordinate their activities through a process of mutual adjustment, as market prices indicate the relative value placed on goods and services by other members of society.

Thus neoliberals appear to find themselves in common cause with the other major contemporary foes of social consensus, postmodernists (see chapter 7). Breaking this uncomfortable political connection is surely crucial to postmodernism if it is to avoid being dismissed as the cultural logic of neoliberalism.

Under the Hilmer proposals the public interest is put back on its authoritarian and bureaucratic pedestal. The underlying definition of the public interest with which Hilmer works is consumer sovereignty (though it is not mentioned), achieved via 'efficiency and economic growth' (Hilmer 1993: xvi). Observing the NCP process, Dore believes that 'Planning in the public interest may become defined in terms of contribution to competitiveness as much as to social, heritage or environmental factors' (Dore 1997: 162). The problematic nature of this public interest ideal in conditions of financial inequality of consumers (often now extreme inequality) is not addressed by Hilmer. The idea of ecological sustainability is nowhere mentioned in the report. Economic growth is presumably to be defined as growth of gross domestic (or national) product, itself a problematic indicator of public welfare (Argy 1998: 15–20; Waring 1988: 55).

Hilmer seeks to apply this faulty and restricted concept of the public interest universally, including within government. It is admitted that there may be exceptions to the econocrat's notion of the public interest. Reference is made throughout to 'other social objectives', an apparently residual category (Hilmer 1993: xvi). According to Hilmer, these other objectives may sometimes justify departure from the above public interest norm. Whether they do so or not, however, is to be determined through 'an appropriate and transparent process' (Hilmer 1993: xxix).

So what is this process? One might think that the deliberative processes of a working pluralist democracy (parliamentary committee processes, for example) might have much to offer by way of transparency. But no, Parliament is not to be trusted. Instead 'the committee concludes that the primary basis for permitting exemptions from the rules should be an authorization process of the kind currently administered by the Trade Practices Commission' (Hilmer 1993: xxiv). The exceptions are thus to be determined by a committee of bureaucrats meeting in a far-from-public forum and not in any way subject to the cut and thrust of open debate. Moreover, these bureaucrats (the proposed successor to the Trade Practices Commission, namely the Australian Competition and Consumer Commission—ACCC) 'should be directed to give primacy to economic efficiency in determining questions of public benefit' (Hilmer 1993).

The Hilmer Committee thus ensures that the public interest (or public benefit) against which all public regulation is to be tested is narrowly circumscribed and ultimately determined by bureaucratic fiat. The ACCC, with the powers proposed for it by the Hilmer Report, was created by Parliament and is supported by the present Commonwealth and state governments, which thus voted to deprive themselves of the power to determine what is in the public interest and to restrict democracy. Australian citizens, should they become aware of what has been done, might well feel aggrieved. No other pluralist democracy in the developed world has given away such political power to a committee of bureaucrats.

The political potency of the NCP derives in large measure from the extent of its political-economic aims, which include reform of both public services and public regulation. Critically, the reforms aim at 'removing legislation that restricts competition in particular markets' at state and Commonwealth levels (Industry Commission 1995: 4). This, of course, reflects the agenda promoted at global level by GATT and the World Trade Organization. To date, implementation of the NCP has spurred the privatisation of public assets, especially state instrumentalities, and also the shift to market pricing in government business enterprises (Hood 1997). The formulation and implementation of NCP reforms have largely been undertaken without significant public consultation. In late 1997, an independent member of the Australian Capital Territory Legislative Assembly publicly claimed that, 'The Council of Australian Governments was ruling Australia by executive decree and ramming [national competition] policies down the throats of state and territory parliaments' (*Canberra Times*, 23 October 1997: 5). Moreover, the NCP framework was forced on local government without consultation: 'The principles set out in this Agreement will apply to *local* government, *even though local governments are not parties to the Agreement*. Each State and Territory party is responsible for applying those principles to local government' (in Neilson 1997: 9n, emphasis added).

Of central interest here is that the reform process has been extended to planning. By 1999, several state and territory governments had embarked on NCP reviews of their development control systems. One key effect of NCP and other federal reform pressures on the planning systems of New South Wales and Victoria has been the introduction of competition for development approval (Mahony 1997; McInerney 1998). Under the new system, private practitioners can be accredited as approval authorities for certain categories of development. The idea is that an applicant seeking planning approval will be able to choose between private and public bodies for the assessment of the proposal. Presumably this will encourage competition between accredited approval bodies, leading to greater regulatory efficiencies and, in turn, lower transaction costs for applicants. The privatisation of development control follows earlier similar reforms to building approval systems in several states.

However, as Mahony (1997) points out, the effective privatisation of development control in local government threatens to reduce public participation and accountability in planning, while also increasing the risk of decisions that contradict local community interests. In terms of participation and accountability, several objections arise. First, the reforms pass a vital aspect of public decision-making from elected to non-elected bodies. Second, the changes will also free private certifiers from the public accountability procedures that bind local government activities, including plan making and development approval. They will also 'circumvent the use of freedom of information legislation or administrative law remedies' in respect of planning decisions (Mahony 1997: 11). In sum, the NCP reforms will 'reduce public rights of participation which government made so much of in the 1970s but which are now decidedly out of fashion across the country' (Bonyhady 1997: 1).

On the issue of quality, Mahony (1997) points out that private certification systems in other areas of governance—notably building control—have led to a decline in regulatory standards, sometimes threatening public safety. In late 1997 the Australian Council of Professions voiced concern about 'state reviews of competition policy [that] could lead to unqualified people passing themselves off as experts' (ABC News, 17 November 1997). The Council noted that privatisation of regulatory approval processes raised the spectre of poor and incompetent servicing in key professional areas that affect public safety, such as building control and engineering.

Perhaps most importantly, Mahony observes that the NCP changes in New South Wales will increase regulatory uncertainty in the planning system and thereby actually contradict the aims of the reform agenda itself (Mahony 1997: 18):

> even from a purely economic perspective, there is a strong argument that the certainty of land use and land value provided by land use planning are matters of public benefit. Such certainty is a necessary precondition for business confidence, let alone competition.

The Victorian government has also embarked on an NCP review. The consultant brief released for the first stage of this review requires a study that would, among other things (Department of Infrastructure 1997: 4),

- identify the nature of the restrictions on competition arising from the Victorian planning system;
- analyse the likely effects of the restrictions on competition and on the economy in general;
- consider alternative means of achieving the same results as restrictions on competition, including non-legislative means, and the costs and benefits associated with those alternative options.

In this document, 'restrictions on competition' can include 'the administration of the planning scheme *and* the actual regulation of land use and development by means of . . . planning schemes' (p. 5, emphasis added). Thus the brief intimates that the NCP principles can be used to question not only the basis of *how* public planning 'services' are supplied but also the rationale for the development controls themselves. The review might therefore conceivably recommend both the privatisation of planning approval and the reduction of development controls. This view is further justified by the prescription that the consultant study will examine the 'relevance' of 'government intervention through the planning process' in the land economy (p. 4). One senior Victorian planner has reflected that 'In planning there may be very little business left following the legislative review against competition principles . . . the future of planning could be at stake' (Dore 1997: 162).

The thrust of the NCP reforms has another important effect. The NCP attitude is that planning is a discrete function—a 'service', just like providing a road or a housing lot. In this perspective the service that planners provide is delivering a plan. According to neoliberal ideology such services are more efficiently delivered by private companies competing in a market. This view of the planning 'service' fails to recognise that part of the service is coordinating the services provided by other government and private sector actors. If planning becomes a discrete, privatised function outsourced to private firms, the coordination function of planning becomes impossible. A private firm cannot intervene effectively and continuously in the various activities that need to be coordinated if a government is to provide for the various needs of the people within its territory at the right time and in the right place. The underlying assumption of neoliberalism is that any coordination that occurs will be carried out by the market. But it is precisely because of the failure of markets to coordinate service delivery effectively for desirable ends that planning is needed at all. Governments, like private firms, make plans because they want to perform better across all their activities. Planning is a core aspect of the thinking and acting of good, publicly accountable government.

These 'reforms' have seemingly been accepted by the planning profession as natural and inevitable. Indeed, some professionals are now complicit in the neoliberal anti-planning agenda.

Planners and developers

Performance reviews

In 1997, Australia's national Planning Officials Group (POG) conducted a 'performance review' of state and territory planning systems. The POG has functioned in recent years as a national forum for senior planning officials from the state, territory and Commonwealth governments. While the POG has no direct role in NCP, recent evidence suggests that it has itself pursued a neoliberal reform agenda. In 1996, the POG employed a consulting firm to undertake a 'Planning Systems Performance Review (PSPR) Project'. The aim of the PSPR project was to derive 'objective' measures of how various land use planning systems 'perform'. The consultants attempted to identify these measures through a consultation process that has involved a range of 'stakeholder representatives' in each of the states and territories. During 1997, three discussion papers were produced and publicly released for comment (Maximiles Consulting 1997a, b, c).

What do the papers reveal about the project and its implications for public planning? First, they evince a very poor conceptual grasp of both the nature of planning and the reasons for its existence. There is little evidence in the papers of the 'expert planning advice' the consultants claim to have received. There is little appreciation of the administrative structure of Australian planning systems—for example, the basic distinction between statutory and strategic processes. In these papers the 'planning system' is presented as a permit-issuing framework for 'customers' in the property market. The third paper reflects a supposedly broader view of the planning process, by focusing on the role of 'suppliers' among the group of system 'stakeholders'.

Overall, the project papers released thus far reveal a partial, and ideologically conditioned, view of public planning. There is both a weak conceptual grasp of how planning frameworks are actually constituted and, of more concern, no real appreciation of the reason for the public regulation of urban change. Instead, planning is conceived as simply another 'service' within the land economy, a sort of 'quality check' on the development process that ensures its maintenance through the imposition of certain longer-term considerations (environmental and social). By focusing on 'system outputs', and by adopting managerial consumerist language to describe the planning process and the socio-political interests within it, the consultants have simply served the brief given to them. The project aims presuppose a managerialist view of planning, as something like a processing system whose inputs and outputs can be objectively quantified and measured with all the certainty enjoyed by the manager of a factory production line.

Such assessments of planning by management consultants are now commonplace. The talk is of consultation and 'clients, customers and stakeholders'. One might expect a wide range of citizen and community groups to be considered as having a 'stake' in a city's development. But no, 'stakeholders' are professional and business groups. Consider one recent competition review of planning. The stakeholders interviewed to comment on the Planning and Land Management Group (PALM) in Canberra are business groups such as the Housing Industry Associ-ation (HIA), and professional groups such as the Royal Australian Institute of Architects, the Royal Australian Planning Institute and the Real Estate Institute. 'Focus groups' were also used but without description of the process of focusing or of which groups were included: so much for transparency (Ernst & Young 1999: 115). The *Canberra Times* comments: 'The tone of the report is to get PALM to bang out development applications as quickly as possible with as little fuss as possible and with as few people and as little expenditure of money as possible' (Editorial, *Canberra Times*, 16 January 1999: C2).

Management consultants' approaches to planning such as that of the PSPR and the review of PALM might be said to follow in the path of the Hilmer Report in their bureaucratisation of the public interest. In fact, however, they erase any sense of the public interest in planning by fragmenting a broad and democratic sense of purpose into the numerous outputs that can apparently be measured, indeed predicted, with certainty by 'system managers'. The broader shift desired by the positivist view is to replace the public interest with a diverse set of 'stakeholder interests' which can be monitored through proxy output measures (for example, the system's ability to satisfy developers' interests might be gauged through indexes of permit turnover times and permit refusal rates). If 'customer satisfaction' is to supplant the public interest as the new performance measure for planning, then it must surely follow that economic and sociopolitical power will be the new arbiters of who wins and who loses in the land economy.

It must be asked why the POG is setting out to measure 'planning systems' in this peculiar way? The answer is that POG seems to desire a set of measurable performance criteria that could form the basis of a service contract. Put differently, the end result of the project might be to permit the 'outsourcing' of public planning services to, presumably, the most cost-effective supplier. The idea is hardly new—it is one consequence of the new local government legislation in Victoria (which requires that at least 50 per cent of all council services be contracted out)—but its apparent support at the national level suggests that the practice may become more widespread.

By mid-1998, it appeared that the POG reform agenda had made little institutional progress. At this time we were informed by one senior public sector planner that the review had been 'shelved', and had been overtaken by the other two main neoliberal reform agendas for planning, NCP and the proposals forwarded by the Property Council of Australia. We turn now to considering the latter reform initiative whose aim, ostensibly, is to standardise Australia's state-based development control regimes. This proposal is embodied in a joint submission to Australia's planning, housing and local government ministers by various development lobby and professional interests, and coordinated by the Property Council of Australia (Property Council of Australia 1997). Revealingly, the title, *Unfinished Business*, is the same as that of a recent tract by Sir Roger Douglas, the former Finance Minister of New Zealand who helped to engineer and implement much of the neoliberal reforms that have transformed that country since 1984 (see Douglas 1993).

'Unfinished business'

The development sector interests that have endorsed the draft report include such bodies as the Housing Industry Association and the Real Estate Institute of Australia which, together with the Property Council of Australia (and its predecessor, the Building Owners' and Managers' Association) have been critics of various aspects of planning regulation in the past. (According to McInerney [1998: 144], 'The Property Council of Australia now virtually sets the agenda for conservative government discussions on property issues'.) What is perhaps most surprising about the draft report is its seeming endorsement by a number of professional bodies that are more usually associated with advocacy for planning, such as the Royal Australian Planning Institute (RAPI) and the Royal Australian Institute of Architects. The RAPI's support for the draft report was surprising, given the Institute's critical regard (see RAPI 1997) for the earlier (and similar) reform proposals pursued in 1996 by the Property Council of Australia at a national forum ('Leaders' Roundtable on Planning Control Reform') and through two discussion papers (Property Council of Australia 1996a, b).

The Property Council report notes that, while Australia's state-based building controls were harmonised within a new national system (Australian Model Code for Residential Development) in 1995, there has been no attempt yet to apply 'the same discipline to our development control laws' (Property Council of Australia 1997: i). The document announces that its vision of a uniform national development control regime will deliver better planning outcomes, offer business and the community greater certainty, and lower business and community costs. It might well be argued that a national system of development control would realise community benefits by reducing or even removing the pressure on state and city governments to employ continuous planning deregulation in the competition for development capital. However, that is plainly not what the Property Council intends.

In recent years, 'place competition' between state governments has unleashed powerful deregulatory pressures within the various planning regimes and has also encouraged governments to employ significant public resources in efforts to attract various forms of mobile capital. Several observers (including the Industry Commission 1996) have criticised the wastefulness of this scramble for capital that is, in part, encouraged by the diversity of planning regimes in Australia (also Murphy & Watson 1997). But this sort of benefit is not explicitly mentioned in the Property Council report, which instead foregrounds the fiscal advantages of national integration. Indeed, the central focus of the analysis is economic efficiency, with social and environmental values relegated to second-order considerations (Property Council of Australia 1997: 5).

Although there is a vague reference to 'community benefit', the major emphasis is on the efficiencies to be gained for the business sector from a standardised planning system. This view is supported by the document's many references (e.g. 'red tape', 'too prescriptive', 'anti-competitive administrative practices', 'impediments to investments', 'unnecessary inconsistencies' and 'duplication') to the inefficiencies and rigidities that are allegedly the most pressing shortcomings of the present arrangements.

The report also opposes any exclusive public control of regulatory approval processes as an 'artificial monopoly' that is, by nature, 'inefficient and anti-competitive', and explicitly endorses the application of NCP to planning. By contrast, little is made of the environmental and social failings (or strengths) of the current regimes, and how these might be addressed. Only one of the 20 recommendations made by the report touches on social and environmental objectives—even here the rhetoric of efficiency is invoked, with the report arguing that a 'tight focus on defined outcomes will help governments rationalise land use' (Property Council of Australia 1997: 15).

The report explicitly lauds the reforms to planning controls that have been undertaken by the government of Victoria in recent years. The reduction in the number of zoning categories in the state planning regime from 2871 to just 25 wins warm praise from development lobby interests while also, however, drawing criticism from community and environmental groups. Thousands of zones may certainly have been excessive, but there is a strong case that flexibility in zoning definitions is warranted to enable localities characterised by great social and ecological diversity to make their own regulatory choices. While developers may demand administrative efficiency and regulatory simplicity, it is equally true that democracy requires regulation that is sensitive to social and ecological difference.

Finally, the experience of reform to Australia's state-based system of building codes may reveal what the Property Council has in mind for planning. Troy (1998: 6) believes that the standardisation of state building regulations within the national AMCORD framework 'was part of the campaign to reshape the attitudes of Australians to their cities and to get them to accept lower standards'. He argues that the shift to uniformity in building law lowered the general standard of such controls as state codes were standardised around a lowest regulatory common denominator. Troy (1998: 7) remarks that 'the private sector wants to use a highly centralised institutional structure behind which it can hide in achieving the deregulation of planning and development'. In the words of another observer, 'If the PCA has its way, land use planning will become a process to support the market needs of the development industry' (Moon 1998b: 19).

Unlike the POG reform initiative, the Property Council's proposals seem to have gained a powerful momentum in institutional settings. Although by mid-1998 the RAPI had withdrawn its official support, the Property Council's agenda secured endorsement from a national meeting in Adelaide of an elite forum of powerful planning interests, made up of planning officials, development industry lobbyists and the representatives of various professional groups. This forum met to discuss the *Unfinished Business* document, and concluded with an agreement on a draft outline for a proposed national development assessment system. From the minutes of this meeting, it is obvious that the proposed development assessment system mirrors very closely the framework suggested by the Property Council.

It is doubtful that many in the broader Australian planning community are yet aware of the forum, and what was agreed to at the

Adelaide meeting. But there is every likelihood that this initiative will profoundly influence the course of planning reform in Australia in the near future. The forum proposed the constitution of a national Development Assessment Forum (DAF), comprising representatives from industry, government and the professions. Funding was sought from the Commonwealth for a permanent secretariat to resource the DAF (which seemingly would supplant the role of the POG). There is no suggestion of a broader community representation; nor is there any apparent support for a wide-ranging public debate on the objects of the proposed DAF. In August 1999, the HIA conducted a national planning conference in Sydney whose theme was 'Planning a National Approach to Development'. In particular, the conference considered the prospects for a 'harmonised national planning system', focusing on the work undertaken by the DAF since 1998. As the conference brochure itself put it, the meeting brought 'together *high level* industry and government representatives to discuss the future of planning and development in Australia' (Housing Industry Association 1999, emphasis added). The Adelaide and Sydney meetings both cultivated elite, 'high-level' opinions on planning and its future. It seems difficult to reconcile the constitution and conduct of the meetings, and the DAF itself, with any recognisably democratic vision for planning.

Conclusion

Neoliberalism has not yet been fully accepted by Australian citizens. It has never been welcomed. Indeed the reforms have been foisted on the nation by bureaucrats and governments that have been either compliant (Labor) or enthusiastic (Liberal, Coalition). The agenda has been pursued in stealth and behind closed doors. It has been treated by the media as an inevitable process of change under the supposedly compelling force of globalisation. No-one has bothered to ask how much of the logic of 'globalisation' is in truth compelled by world events and how much is a conventional wisdom soaked up by a state sector in the grip of ideologically driven econocrats.

As we see in chapter 5, the urban governance model of 'corporate liberalism' has enjoyed a measure of popular support, but it has by no means been universally adopted in all Australian states, and the agenda of neoliberalism is still unfolding. It seeks to return Australian cities to a disastrous 'government by the market', in Self's phrase (Self 1993). Any hint of 're-regulation' for public purposes is condemned as 'a new metamorphosis of the dirigiste beast' (Lal 1998: 1). 'Dirigiste', correctly translated, here merely means steering the economy. Is the economy the only sector of social policy where government 'steering' is not allowed? If so we must ask why, when it is the economy as currently structured that is causing environmental and social ills.

As van der Pijl (1998: 165) observes, 'Only through the cumulative momentum of a series of particular, largely contingent episodes can we hope that the forces capable of imposing limits on the capitalist exploitation of people and nature can prevail, and the suicidal drive of neoliberalism reversed'. The movement against neoliberalism is gaining force worldwide. But the difficulty, and danger, for the opponents of neoliberalism is that a decisive new model of governance has not yet emerged; until it does, governments (such as that of Blair in Britain and the Red–Green alliance in Germany) may be forced to cling to the discredited neoliberal orthodoxies. In chapter 10 we draw together the main elements of the four major critiques discussed in this and chapters 6, 7 and 8, and begin to sketch the outlines of a new agenda.

10 The impacts on planning thought and practice

W hat can we learn about planning from the critical strands of thought discussed in the previous four chapters? What indicators do they give us about the future of planning as we reflect on the experience of cities and planning? How do these indicators square with the human values of justice and freedom discussed in chapter 2? In this chapter we pause to take stock, but also to move on towards a 'revaluing' of planning. We discuss what the four critiques are telling us about the content of planning and about the nature of planning—what should be planned and how, and also what sort of activity planning is. We do so with the help of some contemporary literature on the themes that emerge from the critiques: professionalism, democracy, the environment, and economic growth.

Planning and professionalism

From urban political economy we learn of the essentially political nature of planning. Where pluralists acknowledge that planning is implicated in political struggle, viewed as 'pressure', Marxists say that it is *class* struggle. Radical cultural critiques add *gender* and *ethnicity* to the political sphere. These are not mutually exclusive arguments. The political sphere is imbued with class, gender and ethnic tensions whose dimensions and impacts vary across nations. In attempting to define itself as above and beyond politics, planning adopted the professional stance. Planning, however, never actually possessed the real source of professional legitimacy: knowledge and technique.

Medicine has techniques of treatment based on a theoretical understanding of the body, *engineering* has techniques of construction based on the behaviour of materials under stress, and *law* has techniques of advocacy and judgement based on theories of jurisprudence. Town planning has no such techniques based on a theoretical understanding of cities. It must necessarily be such a comprehensive exercise that the professional stance becomes impossible. Whereas the useful fiction can be maintained that a human body, a physical structure, a legal case or even a market can be treated as a natural object, a 'thing', which the professional stands outside of and can thus operate on, this cannot be so with a city. Both the Marxist (chapter 6) and radical critiques (chapter 7) of democracy remind us of that.

If *urban and regional* planning cannot properly be considered a profession, the same is also true of *environmental* planning (chapter 8): 'Environmental planning . . . is conceived as an integrated and holistic approach to the environment that transcends traditional departmental and professional boundaries, and is directed towards the long term goal of environmental sustainability' (Evans 1997: 5). Environmental planning is even more demanding and even more encompassing than town planning.

Rather than denying the validity of professionalism we need to rethink our ideas about the role of professions. Professional knowledge, inadequate and incomplete as it invariably is, is useful, but it is not the only sort of knowledge that is useful, and it is not apolitical (as Lindblom & Cohen [1979] and Innes [1995] point out). Knowledge developed within different professional and academic spheres that sometimes conflict is useful. We do not deny for a moment that microeconomics is useful, but it is one among many methods of analysis, and without particular privilege over others. Ordinary knowledge held by 'non-professional' people is also useful. Does it make sense, then, to abandon professions and hand over the steering of cities to a cabal of politicians, as the corporate liberal model proposes?

Elected politicians have an important and responsible role as final arbiter; they are ordinary people with ordinary knowledge and are elected to represent ordinary people. In short, they are a reflection of ourselves. We should expect no more of them than we expect of ourselves. They depend on advice from others. But today the advice they receive has been increasingly filtered, reduced and censored to let through only that which conforms to neoliberal orthodoxy (Argy 1998: 238). Politicians represent a guarantee of democracy that happens to provide a remarkable avenue to non-violent social change. But the wisdom of political practice depends on many and alternative sources of professional and bureaucratic advice—and dissent as much as consent.

Wise environmental planning, like wise city planning, is a matter of wise governance. That requires the abandonment of stereotypical roles of professionals and politicians (and stereotypes of valid knowledge), and the creation of political institutions that maximise the knowledge entering the system (urban, environmental) and influencing its development. The corporate tasks of making mobile phones or computer software is less complex by many orders of magnitude than delivering wellbeing, justice and ecological sustainability. The wisdom of the Scandinavian and Dutch models of governance is just this capacity to bring a vast range of knowledge into the policy-making process. The application of knowledge is often a slow and expensive matter, but the long-term consequences of *not* applying knowledge to the maximum are likely to be ecologically and socially as well as economically disastrous.

Democracy is a requisite for good governance. Environmentalists and radical critics of planning demand that planning encompass an enlargement of democracy. Both managerialism and neoliberalism, however, envisage its shrinking to the mere formalism of government by elected political elites.

Friends and foes of democracy

The demand for the enlargement of democracy (discussed in chapters 7 and 8) has attempted to resolve two central (and interrelated) crises that overtook Western planning from the 1960s: one of sociopolitical legitimacy, and one of ecological sustainability. Each has, in different ways, sought to show that democracy in industrial society rests on the fictional objectivity of technical rationality—the professional stance discussed above (Beck 1997: 41). For Beck (1997: 41), democracy does not begin and end with elections, majority rule and the secret ballot—supposedly technical decisions are no exception. Democracy should be a continuous process of discussion between people and their government at every level. As feminists have repeatedly stressed, good planning is not so much a matter of identifying an overriding 'public interest' as encouraging many and diverse publics to have input into the planning process.

In Australia and in other Western countries, such as Britain, the social and environmental enlargement of democracy has made some progress, with new emphasis being given to consultation and public participation in urban environmental planning (Evans 1997; Healey 1997). The partial absorption of these reform tendencies in planning has marked the transition of planning from an instrument of 'simple', industrial modernisation to a much more ideologically open, and uncertain, process. In turn, this shift reflects a new *reflexive* form of modernity (in which society *learns* from its own behaviour) marked by a greatly heightened critical awareness of the *limits* of technical rationality within institutions and especially within civil society.

Contemporary neoliberalism, in its various institutional and political guises, has set out to reduce democracy in the domain of planning. Although portrayed as an inevitable and necessary response to globalisation, neoliberalism (chapter 9) is not in the *public* interest but in the interest of the 'corporate public': the plutarchy of transnational corporations, the market prophets working from lavishly funded right-wing think tanks, and the mercenary army of consultants and managers who earn their fees from the promotion and management of markets (McDermott 1991). The echo of past class struggles resounds in the contemporary calls for efficient and standardised planning regulation. This has always been the aim of business interests. What is new is the conceptual and political reach of these demands: neoliberals desire both to contract the domain of public planning (deregulation) *and* then to remove segments of the residual sphere of regulation from public control (outsourcing). In both instances, the *raison d'être* of planning as a political and public tool for correcting and avoiding market failure is brushed aside in favour of a new minimalist form of spatial regulation, whose chief purpose is to facilitate development.

As Orchard (1995: 76) notes, much of the environmental and cultural reform rhetoric that was directed at planning by both governments and social movements during the 1980s has given way to a new vision of urbanism—the 'productive city'—that derives from an increasingly unrestrained neoliberalism. In this new vision, planning is reduced to 'urban design' which is necessary to international competitiveness. This simple nostrum resonates with a certain conventional wisdom: 'nice places' are needed to attract 'nice (i.e. wealthy) people'. Good urban design (i.e. democratic, functional, aesthetically pleasing) is a vital element of urban governance, but it in no way substitutes for urban planning. The new design fetish is evident in recent policy documents, such as *Designing Competitive Places* (Australian Local Government Association 1997) and *Urban Design in Australia* (Prime Minister's Urban Design Task Force 1994). The recent trumpeting of design signals more than a simple resurgence of environmental determinism—the proposition that the appearance of built environments determines the quality of social life and the nature of human urban experience. What is both novel and worrying about the policy rhetoric of such documents is the implied reduction of planning to a 'politics of surfaces'. By this we mean the reduction of substantive socioeconomic, cultural and environmental programmatic objectives to nothing more than representations, images and 'visions'. In a real sense, the triumph of the productive city signals an end to the long antagonism between the market and planning in neoliberal Western societies—with the triumph of government by the market (Self 1993).

The productive city seeks not a new accommodation of the market to planning—*it seeks to reconstruct and redeploy planning as a market dynamic in itself.* Thus, 'in an increasingly competitive market-place, the right outcomes cannot be left to the chance success of a regulatory approach; they need to be included in the design from the start' (Australian Local Government Association 1997: 4). There must be a new accommodation to the 'verities' of the market. Public planning must be subordinated to—indeed, supervised by—the market.

In the Hobbesian 'war of all against all' that corporate liberalism has declared, emergency powers are invoked, normal civil institutions are suspended, and planning is enfolded within a process (the market) it had once sought to contain and civilise. Thus, in the new politics of place generated by neoliberal governance and built around the grotesque stereotype of competitive masculinity—economic globalisation—planning re-emerges from reform camp now as a conscript in the interurban battle for investment capital. 'Competitive places', we are told, are what win wars, and they have four main qualities: they are 'livable'; 'ecologically sustainable', 'aesthetically attractive' and 'economically vital' (Australian Local Government Association 1997: 4). The strategic mission of planning is to secure these qualities for places, though generally speaking there is only one weapon issued for the purpose: propaganda, meaning the valorisation of surfaces by whatever means (physical and rhetorical redecoration, 'hearts and minds' campaigns, the cultivation of major events).

As is evident from the *Designing Competitive Places* example, the signifiers of green and cultural politics are absorbed within the productive city's own bright rhetoric, though the real substance of these critiques is carefully discarded in the process. In 'place competition', democratic processes are requisitioned by the state, often through residual planning mechanisms, such as ministerial call in powers, and sometimes through a wholesale seizure of rights, such as the constitutional changes to civil and political rights undertaken by the Victorian government in the 1990s (Webber & Crooks 1996).

And what is all this for? It is for 'growth'. It is to lift the magical numbers produced monthly on which all eyes in Parliament are fixed.

Cities have truly now become 'growth machines' (Molotch 1976)—growth, that is, of business activity, which is measured by GDP.

Planning, the growth model and urban governance

Planning is connected to the model of growth and the model of urban governance. Globalisation does not presuppose the mechanical inter-locking of levels of politics like cogs in clockwork. Indeed we have learned, from the feminist critique in particular, that such a singular logic when institutionalised becomes oppressive and obliterates the real differences among people in society. Nations still have the capacity to choose the model of growth, to negotiate their conditions of engage-ment with the global economy. As we see in chapters 4 and 5, the adoption of a certain growth model at national level does not *per se* restrict the freedom of states to choose their own model of urban governance. There *are* alternatives.

Alternatives to the neoliberal growth model

In their recent work, the Australian economists Fred Argy (1998) and Peter Brain (1999) outline alternatives to the neoliberal growth model. Both point to the dangers and deficiencies of the growth path on which Australia has embarked. Neither have much to say about the environ-ment, though Argy (1998: 29) observes that 'we do not seem to be doing enough to protect future generations against, or making adequate income provision to compensate them for, the exploitation of depletable natural resources'. Argy (1998: 176) also notes the degraded urban environ-ments of high-growth Asian cities. Brain is silent on such matters.

Both Argy and Brain, however, offer critiques of neoliberalism and alternative growth models. Argy (1998: 80) points out that Australia has no need of 'smaller government' because the government sector in Australia is already small by international standards. Smaller government will not increase incentives to work or improve quality of life. There is nothing to be said for privatising infrastructure without a 'full and detailed comparison of the relative community benefits' of private versus public provision in each case (Argy 1998: 85). Argy refers to Gregory's research, which shows that wage flexibility does not deliver increased employment, and indeed cuts to the public sector have not been matched by employment growth in the private sector (Argy 1998: 100, citing Gregory 1996: 100, 207; refer also to this volume, chapter 5). Microeconomic reform must be tempered by careful compensation for its damaging consequences for equity, employment and stability (Argy 1998: 104–5). In place of 'hard liberalism', Argy offers 'progressive liberalism'.

Progressive liberalism places no more weight on increasing GDP per head than on other dimensions of welfare—work security, work availability, quality of life, distributional equity (Argy 1998: 109). The 'progressive liberal' policy agenda is made up of three broad elements: 'a more consensual social and quality of life agenda, a macro-economic policy framework which gives higher priority to employment and makes greater use of short term demand and incomes management, and a program of structural reform focused as much on employment growth as on efficiency' (Argy 1998: 111). Progressive liberalism would help to produce a more balanced geographical distribution of jobs, rather than emphasising only coercive approaches to 'labour mobility' (Argy 1998: 154). The progressive liberal agenda, Argy contends, is not a substitute for growth but a precondition of continued growth and prosperity.

Brain argues that Australia's neoliberal growth model, focused on maximum exploitation of 'comparative advantage' (see Box 3.1), is mainly designed to help commodity production. He posits three main reasons why the neoliberal growth model is flawed. First, the dominant economy, the USA, will not allow industries in which it lacks comparative advantage to run down, because maintenance of such industries is required to keep poverty within tolerable levels (the same is true of all the world's core economies). Second, the neoliberal model assumes that, in a world of free capital flows, capital will automatically flow to the industries that will enable the country to exploit its comparative advantage, so as to export its way out of a balance of payments crisis. This, Brain says, is 'nonsense' (Brain 1999: 69). The enormous flows in the late 1980s into what were seen at the time as easy money ventures with high and quick returns (typically, property investments of various sorts) left Australia without the capacity to overcome its balance of payments problems and with a massive and growing private sector debt. Third, the prices of commodities for export tend to decline compared with innovation-intensive products resulting from adaptation to new technologies. A manufacturing sector supporting high levels of research is necessary to long-term economic growth, but this is a high-risk sector requiring 'a mutually supportive program of manufacturing investments' in which government takes an active role (Brain 1999: 70).

Australia, Brain argues, cannot in fact hope to base its future prosperity on the neoliberal model of comparative advantage. Rather, this country should actively seek to create the conditions for the growth of the *leading* industry sector, the knowledge industry. Creating the conditions for the incubation of the knowledge industries requires much more than competition. In fact, it requires careful public planning of infrastructure and the existence of a large common pool of knowledge to which all participants are willing to contribute and which they share. The knowledge industry model is based not on the experience of factory discipline (like corporate liberalism) but on the American collegiate world of the 1970s supported by universities and research institutes: 'The knowledge economy concentrates innovation-intensive industries in places where people who are highly skilled in the technology of each industry can form and maintain these loose, quasi-business, quasi-social networks' (Brain 1999: 122). What Brain constantly stresses is the social and communal character of knowledge production on the basis of which fruitful competition can occur.

If the competitive market is appropriate for industry, *it does not follow* that this is also the appropriate model for the institutional support and public planning required for the knowledge industry model to work. Brain (1999: 231) observes:

> Governments will need to repair the damaged integrity of public admin-istration. For at least twenty years, short-term politicisation has corrupted previously inviolable standards of public service. To see what we have lost, we need to look elsewhere. In Taiwan, the role of a public servant is to act in the public interest through his or her working life, avoiding conflicts of interest.

Brain insists that government must maintain its traditional role of provider of community assets, though a more creative approach is required: government needs to provide whole city precincts with 'best-practice integrated infrastructure to encourage the development of industry clusters' (Brain 1999: 236). Melbourne's Docklands is a case in point, and is 'the best hope of establishing a global city status independent of Sydney' (Brain 1999). But 'if the government insists that the private sector provide the bulk of the infrastructure, the precinct will become a largely residential, entertainment, and commercial complex' (Brain 1999).

Planning is necessary to *sustain* the environmental quality that attracts growth in the first place. For instance, years of freewheeling development on Queensland's Gold Coast have degraded the region's environment: the built landscape is blighted by 'tacky' buildings and the beaches have been spoiled by shadowing from high-rise towers that were allowed to proliferate along foreshores. A recent study has shown that the Gold Coast's economy is now suffering the consequences of environmental blight: 'The coast is losing market share to other Australian destinations because it is seen as too expensive, too commercialised and unsafe' (Roberts 1999: 15). Even a modest degree of environmental planning would have contributed towards the development of a more sustainable regional economy.

If we accept aspects of the above critiques of the neoliberal growth model it is evident that providing the conditions of growth requires not mimicry of the market but good governance.

Alternatives to the neoliberal model of urban governance

Recent work by Capling et al. (1998) and by Self (1999) seeks to reinstate a more complete idea of the public interest, to revive political choice, and to present a democratic model of urban governance.

Capling et al. (1998, 94–100) argue that the neoliberal model of governance has four major disadvantages: it is biased against the poor, it represents a threat to democracy, it denies the benefits of democratic and consultative process in service delivery, and it entails a loss of public control over key elements of development and hence a loss of the public *planning* capacity. (These points are also contained in Self's broader critical analysis of neoliberalism.) Let us consider each point in turn.

First, under the neoliberal model, there is a major incentive for private contractors to avoid the most costly cases. When social services are handed over to private contractors, governments thus lose control over the micro-level allocations. Whenever there is a public concern for the internal distribution of services in the interests of social justice, contractors have powerful incentives to do only what will enhance profits: in housing excluding poorer tenants, in education excluding students from poorer or otherwise disadvantaged homes, in health excluding the more difficult and unprofitable cases.

Second, if private contracting becomes the norm, information tends to become closed: 'commercial in confidence'. Information about service delivery could benefit potential competitors. But this also excludes the public and Parliament from knowing what is going on. Paradoxically greater freedom *from* scrutiny by the public will be provided to politicians by putting a service out to a private contractor: 'Such contracts may serve to shield senior officials from political scrutiny, from pressures from the electorate and from other contractors' (Capling et al. 1998: 97).

Third, the value of the *process* of provision of a service may be lost (Capling et al. 1998: 97):

> The provision of new housing, for example, is often directly linked to the creation of safe and self-reliant communities among otherwise vulnerable

populations. Consequently, policy makers will wish to involve local neighbourhoods in plans to re-zone land, accommodate building plans to local heritage priorities, and to situate houses in proximity to transport and childcare.

In short, a government that values democracy will want to facilitate public participation in planning but will be unable to do so if the provision of services and housing is solely a matter for the private sector. The timely provision of services subject to government coordination becomes impossible. Another example of process benefit is the ability of a government to run the service in such a way as to encourage consumers to reduce their demand (for water or electricity, for example). The achievement of such benefits by regulation is much more complex and difficult.

Fourth, shifting the majority of services to the private sector reduces the public sector's competence in managing such activities. The best operators leave public employment, forcing policy-makers to rely on advice from outside (advice whose quality cannot be assured) about future needs and the best available technologies. The 'steering' of a health or education system requires skills developed in the course of its detailed management. Likewise, planning skill needs to be developed 'in house' (Capling et al. 1998: 99, citing Foster & Plowden 1996: 2–10):

> The development of a planning capacity within government imposes special burdens upon public servants which do not fall to private firms. Public planning requires democratic consultation about the preferred future of citizens and their standard of living. Planning requires consideration of the impacts which any given service may have on other public values and public costs which may be shifted to other parts of the public sector. This necessitates sharing of information between those who deliver the service, those who pay for it, and those in other affected public organisations.

What, then, is proposed in place of the neoliberal model of urban governance? Australia's political institutions must be directed at forging public purpose from the multiple, varying and often conflicting purposes of the many legitimate interest and pressure groups in society. Difference and disagreement are healthy for any society, but ultimately good governance is about resolving differences and turning the collectively agreed direction into action. Thus the authors say that public institutions must embody ways of resolving conflict over (a) the 'agreed path to economic prosperity', (b) 'distribution of the benefits of prosperity to all' (a and b together form the 'growth model'), (c) 'the promotion of civic values', and (d) 'support for innovation and learning' (Capling et al. 1998). None of these key issues can be resolved by abdication from the difficult political task and handing the resolution of conflict over to the market (Capling et al. 1998: 106):

> without new forms of collaboration between key social interests such as unions, welfare associations, environmental groups and employers, the state will lack sufficient authority to fashion new interventions . . . Mediation, conflict resolution and planning structures which are brokered by government and authorised by parliament may hold the key to forms of 'new governance' which allow public purposes to drive energetic intervention once more.

For Self (1999), the new model of governance must be about the revival of political choice. The nation-state must have a bigger, stronger role in the global economy because it is the *only* power that we citizens control through our democracy which is capable of solving the sort of social and environmental problems we face today. The state must demonstrate the virtues of *cooperative* working in the delivery of its own services instead of slavishly copying *competitive* corporate behaviour (more strongly reiterating the point made by Capling et al. above). Social services must be kept within a democratic political framework rather than allowing their erosion by privatisation until only an inferior public system remains (Self 1999: 225). The form of service provision does not entail tight central control; 'rather the state is better seen as orchestrating the operation of a variety of service providers', but 'the framework still needs to combine the case for diversity with a reasonable degree of equality in access to services' (Self 1999: 226).

While arguing for an enlarged role for the state in 'orchestrating' service provision, Self also applauds the communitarian analysis, which argues for greater power to be given to local communities in controlling service delivery. Practically, this might involve the transfer of responsibility for the management of public housing to tenant cooperatives (successfully demonstrated in Victoria in the 1970s), the management of schools to elected school boards, and social service delivery to volunteer bodies. In 'localisation', much depends on the institutional conditions under which it occurs. In a restrictive and competitive context dictated by the State in which localities are forced to compete against one another for resources, or raise funds locally, localisation can only sharpen already existing spatial inequalities. In the USA much service delivery is locally governed *and* funded with the corresponding tendency for rich places to get better services and poorer places worse ones (see Wolch 1990). In Sweden, at least until recent years, services were governed and organised at local level, but the central state was always present to equalise funding and guarantee a common standard throughout the country. Self favoured the latter kind of localisation.

Self notes the increasingly acrimonious politics of 'territorial defence'. True, he says, some of this is mere NIMBYism (not in my backyard)—the protection of narrow territorial interests against the wider public interest. But much of it is also the community's reaction in defence of threatened common amenities and facilities: public transport, parks and open space, safe streets, pleasant unpolluted environments. Local defence is often the only defence against encroachment by more powerful economic and political forces that have no special claim to represent the public interest. The appropriate response to such politics is not to denounce it or forcibly repress the energy released but to give local communities greater power to plan their areas, and control unwanted developments. This is not just a matter of negative regulation; communities also need to be able to promote *desirable* developments to improve their environments and establish the services they need. In order to be able to engage in positive development, however, municipal councils need the backing of land legislation (such as exists in Holland or Sweden), enabling local councils to acquire land at prices that exclude potential development value (Self 1999: 230).

Widespread involvement by individuals in their local communities is the best way to create the shared value systems that keep a society from breaking apart. To paraphrase Self (1999: 231)—and the philosopher of liberalism J.S. Mill—one learns about democracy by participating constantly in the governance of one's public institutions, services and environment. Self points out that, contrary to the assumptions of the CL governance model (chapter 5), democratic decentralisation does not place limits on economic growth. In fact, following Putnam's (1993) studies of Italy, strong civic traditions with active collaboration between local businesses and workers are associated with enhanced economic development.

These models of urban governance demand more and better public planning—more sensitive, more consultative, subtler, better coordinated public planning capable of learning from local communities in all their diversity. To give up public planning does not produce better services, better environments, more freedom, more consumer sensitivity, stronger and more sustainable economic growth with better outcomes for the environment, but *less and worse* of all these things. It is time to stop pretending that the market is better, and to start learning about planning again.

Conclusion

Australian public policy in 1999 is lagging the world by at least 10 years. Australia is one of the very few countries where public policy is still marching to the neoliberal drum. In Europe neoliberalism has been all but abandoned. America, Japan and the Asian tigers never followed the pure neoliberal model. The one nation that tried it was New Zealand, and its social cohesion was destroyed in the process; its economy is in a mess and in the 1999 general election neoliberal reform was decisively rejected. While Australia pursues the agenda of the 1980s, the world's core economies are gearing up to adapt to the imperative of ecological sustainability.

The more thoughtful Australian economists acknowledge the limits of their discipline. Thus Gittens (1999: 15) writes that 'making our economy more ruthlessly efficient, and many activities more overtly commercial' risks breaking down the glue that holds society and the economy together. And when that happens, says Gittens, 'no-one will be more amazed than the economists—it's not in their model'. Nor, as Gittens writes, is the natural environment.

We absolutely reject the view that 'growth' according to the neoliberal model will provide for Australia and for the world a socially fair, environmentally sustainable future. The model of growth and the model of urban governance, as we suggest at the beginning of this chapter, should not be regarded as determining the model of planning. It is clear that, regardless of assertions to the contrary, there are alternatives to neoliberalism in both growth and governance. Our purpose in this book is not to build new models of growth or of governance but to propose a new model of urban planning. We hope that our model of planning will in turn feed into debates on both growth and governance. We argue for a new and better approach to public urban planning, and defining this new model is the task of the next and final part of the book.

Part III

New agendas for planning

Revaluing planning

Justice . . . is the great pillar that upholds the whole edifice. If it is removed, the great, the immense fabric of human society . . . must in a moment crumble into atoms.

Adam Smith, *The Theory of Moral Sentiments* 1759 (1976 edn: 86)

Injustice anywhere is a threat to justice everywhere. We are caught in an inescapable network of mutuality, tied in a single garment of destiny. Whatever affects one directly affects all indirectly.

Martin Luther King, letter from Birmingham Jail 1963

This book has analysed Australian planning and its many critics. As we state in the introduction, our work has been coloured by a strong sense of crisis that has beset Australian planning as it has struggled to deal with its progressive critics—Marxists, radical democrats and environmentalists—as well as the fundamental challenge to its existence posed by neoliberalism. Our review reflects the values that we have strongly espoused—justice, freedom, democracy and ecological sustainability. Earlier, we went to considerable lengths to recover the historical justification for postwar planning in Australia, so that its strengths and defects might be clearly appraised. Now it is time to look forward, towards the type of values and practices that we think are necessary if planning—reflecting a revitalised democracy—is to be renewed in Australia. Part III presents our vision for planning.

We have pointed out that there always have been, and still are, alternatives to the neoliberal vision—a vision that includes planning but subordinates democracy to the market, the antithesis of the values we espouse. In contemporary Australia, 'globalisation' appears as the 'destiny machine'—the producer of dreams and futures, of riches for all. In the dream there is no place for politics, just obedience to the market rule. History, of course, tells us that fulfilment of this fantasy is constantly deferred for most; and even for those who achieve it there is a sense of emptiness because of what has been lost. The 'dream machine' as we have shown in this book is threatening our cities and regions with a nightmare destiny of social division, environmental degradation and democratic exhaustion.

The alternative is a democratically constructed future through a careful process of deliberative politics. This requires planning, because planning at base is simply the fair and open deliberation about alternative social and environmental futures resulting in decision and action widely supported. *Good* urban planning is an essential feature of democracy, not its antithesis as neoliberals claim. What form then should a renewed planning take? How will it avoid the mistakes of the past that produced the sorts of problems that we survey in Part II of this book? We answer these questions here by outlining a set of values that we think would produce good planning.

In what follows we argue first for the revaluation of planning. By this we mean renewing popular support for planning. Then we outline a new value base for planning, framed around four key principles. We begin by arguing, first, that planning should be ethically driven: that is, founded on a particular vision of freedom, justice and democracy, and humane values. Second, planning must, we suggest, be conceived as environmental governance, to which conception the tools of planning (survey, spatial analysis, zoning, market regulation, architectural design etc.) must be subject. Third, planning should be conceived as 'dialogic': that is, framed by public deliberation at every level. Fourth, planning must be regarded as multi-tiered: that is, the structure of environmental governance must be seen to extend from the local to the global with policies and powers appropriate to each level. In conclusion, we argue that planning as environmental governance should be regarded as open-ended. Deliberation must extend to the underlying values and institutional structures on which planning is based.

The need to revalue planning

Given what we have surveyed in Parts I and II, it is not surprising that, throughout Australia, some professional planners have expressed dismay at the corrosive effects of neoliberal reforms on established public planning systems. Thus Wensing (1998: 2):

We are at an important turning point for planning in this country. If we as planners in the broader sense of the word, do not unite and become more vocal with our concerns, then we are in danger of seeing planning being reduced to a rubber stamping exercise, if this has not already occurred in some jurisdictions.

The Commonwealth government has washed its hands of any involvement with cities and their planning. The capacity for thoughtful, well-researched and consultative planning has been much reduced in most states. There now seems little public appreciation of the need for spatial regulation in Australian cities (see Fincher 1998). However, alarm about these changes in the 'planning community' has not, it seems, found much voice or sympathy within the profession's established advocacy body, the Royal Australian Planning Institute (RAPI). On the contrary, it appears that the RAPI has, in at least one instance, actually thrown its weight behind the forces that are trying to dissolve planning: initially endorsing the reform proposals forwarded by the Property Council of Australia (PCA) before later withdrawing its support (see chapter 9). It seems that the national leadership's support for the draft PCA document contradicted the opinions of many members (see Wensing 1998: 2). This raises the issue of whether the RAPI has identified in recent times rather too closely with the development industry and its political interests, leaving the values of planning largely without the support of professional advocacy. McLoughlin, it may be recalled, argued that (McLoughlin 1992: 131):

> lack of interest in the development of theory, in the clearer conceptualisation of what social purposes town planning should serve, has rendered the town planners, both in the forum of a professional Institute and, more importantly, as an element in the public service bureaucracies, almost impotent in the debate on the subject.

Lamentably, the RAPI has failed to lead planning debates within key policy realms and in the broader community. Many people remain unclear about why planning is necessary and what benefits it brings to society.

Nonetheless, many in the profession have begun to speak out against the neoliberal reform agenda. Debate and protest have been registered within the RAPI's most important ongoing discussion forum, the *Australian Planner* journal (e.g. Dawkins 1996), and also in the newsletters of the state divisions (e.g. Moon 1998b). Some of the strongest voices of protest, however, have been raised outside the main discussion forums of professional planning. In 1998, the Urban Research Program at the Australian National University hosted a national forum to consider the many dilemmas facing Australian planning (see Gleeson & Hanley 1998). Individual commentators have also recorded their alarm at the erosion of Australian planning. Pat Troy, a long-serving champion of egalitarian values in Australian planning, has written (Troy 1998: 9):

> Part of the story of the high standard of living attained by urban Australians lies in the long . . . efforts by a host of activists and reformers responding to and leading political campaigns to improve living conditions for the lower income members of society. The flag they flew was one of progress and equity. The recent history of the introduction of national standard building codes is one of striking the colours, of lowering the standard. It is no less a departure from the commitment to an egalitarian society than capitulation to the demands of those who seek deregulation of the labour market and the introduction of market led provision of educational and health services.

Thus, as Troy argues, the use of regulatory standardisation to cloak the agenda of deregulation marks a profound shift away from the values that have animated postwar planning in Australia and other Western countries. Moreover, as we have shown, the same broad agenda threatens the environmental and democratic gains that have been won in planning spheres over the past two decades.

Subsequent reform movements and discourses have shown that the established values of planning, of which Troy reminds us, were insufficient for a variety of ecological and sociocultural reasons. Nonetheless, most reformers within both radical streams would agree that egalitarian values were a necessary, if insufficient, condition for humane and ecologically sustainable planning. As we have argued, new strands of critique sought an enlargement of egalitarian values and not their erasure—principally through the extension of cultural respect and moral worth to a larger range of human and natural communities. Although the various traditional and radical reform perspectives have contested the ideal of 'progressive planning', they have been united, at least at a broad sociopolitical level, by a common concern to democratise both planning values and the benefits of spatial regulation. It is precisely this 'meta-concern' of progressive planning that is directly imperilled by the neoliberal project. Thus, both established and 'radical' progressive interests find themselves—perhaps unexpectedly, and perhaps in some cases unconsciously—in a common cause that must justify and defend planning's continued existence.

What then can traditional advocates and sympathetic reformers do to restore the ideological and institutional bases for planning? Indeed, can these two groupings identify a common political-conceptual ground, given the potential that exists for disagreement over what constitutes an equitable and effective form for planning? Put differently, can the various advocates for planning agree on a common set of values for the reregulation of space? As Davison and Fincher (1998: 189) have observed, 'it is easier to demonstrate the flaws of orthodox planning practice than to reconstitute the planning profession along new lines'.

We think that it is possible to distil a new set of values for planning that would provide a basis for its renewal in the new millennium. We do not discard the ideals of the past; on the contrary, we seek renewed commitment among policy-makers and planners to equitable and orderly development. But this value base needs enlargement, to accommodate a greater focus on democracy, respect for difference and ecological wellbeing than was evident in postwar planning. In what follows, we outline in broad-brush strokes a new value set for planning. In the next and final chapter we will turn our attention to specific policy issues that should form part of the agenda of a revitalised planning regime in Australia.

Planning for freedom, justice and democracy

As McLoughlin (1994) argued so persuasively, town planning has to be reconnected with the mainstream of debates in philosophy and the social sciences if it is to restore itself to political relevance. Planners have to be able to justify their practice, and to know when and why the various tools of planning are applicable. This is the core of their discipline, not some optional extra into which students may be allowed to delve as an indulgence. Of course, the philosophy of political economy is contested. But planners must themselves be able to take an active part in the contest, to know where they stand, know what the arguments for and against planning are, to know who are their intellectual 'allies' and 'enemies'.

Planners must be capable of defending their discipline, not in a bigoted way, merely exhibiting prejudices, but by virtue of the better argument. They must be able to connect and compare new ideas with the traditions of thought from which they came—and tell the difference between new ideas and old ones dressed up in new language.

A new planning is about the pursuit of freedom, justice and democracy. These terms are not unchanging universals so much as part of a code in which 'being human' has come to be defined. There are other parts of the code of common humanity that are not in any way subsidiary: values of cultural identity, of 'difference', of care and compassion, of citizenship, of community, of spirituality (Eckersley 1992).

All of these terms, as with freedom, justice and democracy, have to do with enabling humans to live materially replete and spiritually satisfying lives.

It is not enough simply to say this. Planners must know the meanings of the words as they appear in and are connected to a web of argument—a web whose ramifications can be understood only through the classical and modern literature of political economy. They must understand how the ideas at the core of planning have been connected historically to political and social reality—the material reality of how ordinary people have lived, and the horrors and satisfactions of their lives. What use is a discussion of freedom, for example, without knowledge of the unfreedom of the factory workers of the 19th century and the wage slaves of today's new 'flexible' economies? The reality of power in capitalist societies in the 21st century is no less infused with class and gender than it was in the 19th and 20th. But 'violent revolution', substituting one ruling class for another, is no more the answer today than it was in 1944 or, for that matter, in 1898. Feminists have never favoured this option for confronting patriarchy.

A new Australian planning must identify the absolute limits of the tolerable within a city. For example, no Australian city should contain such poverty as to render people homeless. Homelessness is a complex process involving vulnerable people. But blaming the victim is not a just strategy. Poverty is almost always part of it. How is the poverty of the vulnerable in society to be relieved—and in such a way as to preserve for them a space of freedom and dignity?

At a different scale, no city should impoverish its own public urban fabric: both in the social (e.g. education, health, housing and community services) and the physical (e.g. sewerage, roads, public transport) domains. The maintenance of our urban fabric is not something that should be sacrificed in the name of economic success (or 'competition'). Down that road lies social breakdown. Widespread and fairly distributed environmental quality is a condition of economic success. A new planning should identify a lexical order of social need: the need for survival and health, for example, comes before the need for entertainment and cultural diversity.

Planning as environmental governance

Planning has always been concerned with the urban environment (Evans 1997). Plans and strategies have addressed local variations in environmental quality within cities, such as those arising from chemical pollution as well as from inadequate infrastructure and dilapidation of the built fabric. Today, as a result of the rise of environmentalism, we know that planning must do more. Planning must also consider the contribution cities make to global resource consumption. Cities are ravenous consumers of nature: they use the atmosphere as a sink for CO_2 and its equivalents; they consume land, water and non-renewable resources; and they often reduce biological diversity (Low et al. 1999).

The postwar paradigm of town planning stressed coercive regulation—typically land use zoning—to limit the negative effects of markets. The subsequent rise of neoliberalism stressed the virtue of unfettered markets. As the market paradigm loses its authority, what is emerging is a third paradigm of 'environmental governance' in which it is understood that, far from being natural, markets are designed through political processes (Hempel 1996). Incentive systems can be built into markets to produce benign results in terms of the political values planners seek. There is no such thing as a free market. Every market is structured by certain regulations that have specific effects. *Regulation* invariably precedes markets. Just as regulation can create markets that deliver short-term profit, social polarisations and ecological destruction, so can regulation create markets that work, for instance, for social justice and ecological (and economic) security, yet preserve a sphere of individual freedom.

Environmental governance is about the design of the institutional structures and incentives that produce the built environment (Healey 1997). We must not allow this design to be either undermined or monopolised by economistic ideologies (e.g. CL) whose creed is the naturalness of the market. For example, improving the transport service, modal interchange and coordination is not a physical planning solution but it is an 'environmental governance' solution (discussed further in chapter 12).

In urban planning there has to be a reasonable balance between the prescription of some kind of blueprint for land use and the creation of space for personal freedom and cultural diversity. Most European nations find that balance in a system in which the limits of development are clearly prescribed and consistently applied—usually with the force of law. The purpose is to protect the value of land, which everyone recognises is derived from the environmental context—what Germans term the 'Umwelt' (literally: the surrounding world)—in which a plot of land is situated.

There is room for change of land use plans by political processes, but not such as to render meaningless the purpose of planning. In Australia planning processes have been tolerated which increasingly reflect either the current state of the market or the current state of political play. What is needed is environmental governance which reflects a process of public deliberation, under the specific understanding that the end result will be a certain mixture of incentives and regulation—a plan—that will be stable until the next scheduled process of deliberation. Within the plan there still has to be flexibility to respond to changed circumstances, but total flexibility negates the plan, and makes nonsense of the process of deliberation. Why would anyone waste their time in deliberation if the decision arrived at after hard work today were overturned tomorrow? In such a system much depends on two factors: the strength of the process of public deliberation, and the principle of subsidiarity. Let us now explain these terms.

Planning as dialogue

The old paradigm of planning relied heavily on the model of representative democracy, where all responsibility and accountability and all decision-making power lies with an elected committee, a Parliament or council, which in turn elected an executive or Cabinet. Accountability is assured via the hierarchy in which the leaders control the bureaucrats and the non-leaders control the leaders through elections (Dahl 1961). In this model, 'democracy' is reduced in effect to a single act of election on a single day every three to five years. It has been well recognised that this model does not adequately represent public desires, nor make the best use of the knowledge held in the community. Taken to the extreme, as it is in the model of corporate liberalism (chapter 5), it becomes a recipe merely for quick and stupid decision-making. The representative model is a necessary minimum, not an optimum model of democracy.

At a global level, Hempel (1996: 5) defines environmental governance as 'the people, political institutions, regimes, and non-governmental organisations (NGOs) at all levels of public and private policy making that are collectively responsible for managing world affairs'. The further away from the most local level, the greater the use made of informal deliberative networks. But in practice that means just about every level above the parish. Deliberative democracy, which has grown of necessity, should now be recognised formally as essential to good environmental governance.

Healey (1997: 244) says of deliberative planning:

> The articulation of strategies requires those involved to stand back from
> their particular situation, to re-think problems and challenges, to work

out opportunities and constraints, to think through courses of action which might be better than current practices and to commit themselves to changing things.

This is no small task. The aim for planning is to open up to the maximum the range of values, ideas, and options for action that the political community, however defined, is able to create, and then to come to agreement about the best course of action. Recognising an absence of discussion in Australia about planning values, the Town and Country Planning Association of Victoria released in 1997 a *Charter for Planning* that sought to reinstate several key values, with an emphasis on the need for open, deliberative modes of governance. The Charter states that, 'Individuals or groups must not be prevented by technical, administrative or financial barriers from exercising their legitimate roles in the planning process' (Town and Country Planning Association 1997: 3).

Of course, extension of democracy is difficult and complex. There are four major questions that a prescriptive model of deliberative planning must always seek to answer:

1. Who in the relevant political community should be included and how are they to be included?
2. How are artificial situations of equal power (no power) to be created so that argument develops fairly and openly?
3. How is deliberative planning to be connected with representative systems of accountability?
4. How is discussion to be concluded?

First, deliberative planning assumes that there are many configurations of interest that should be included in the planning process. But how those configurations are to be found is problematic, and the question can be answered only in practical situations. Inevitably it is a matter for judgement. The underlying principle, however, is to make sure that those voices that are normally silent are heard; moreover, that hearing them leads to including their perspective in whatever decisions ensue (Sandercock 1998).

Second, (unequal) power cannot be eliminated. The 'play of power' surrounds every planning decision (Forester 1989). But there are moments in decision-making when the play of power is suspended and when deliberation can take place on the basis of equality of voice. Traditional forums—the council, the court, the Parliament, the community meeting—sometimes provide such moments that create the opportunity for arguments to develop, for minds to be changed. But these traditional forums are often exclusive 'clubs' that limit social participation in both explicit and subtle ways.

The world of everyday planning practice revolves around public discussions—information nights, feedback sessions, and consultation forums—where the quieter voices of the lonely, the disempowered, the afraid and the angry can be heard. For the rational, the technocratic, the powerful—those with little time and large responsibilities—these voices seem infuriating and distracting. But if justice and democracy really mean anything, then these voices must be listened to and acknowledged in deliberations about alternative futures. It will not do for planners to dismiss or belittle the quieter voices. If planners do this, they mock their own values. Democracy is hard work. Justice is a demanding taskmaster.

Third, those who advocate deliberative planning do not want to abandon, but rather to augment, existing structures of accountability. The aim should be, in Friedmann's terms, to develop the political community of everyday life in such a way that institutional structures of accountability are obliged to respond. The democratic aim of existing representative institutions is to create a rich tissue connecting the people with their government. In reality the connection has become increasingly thin, and Western governments in recent decades have listened to a narrow range of constantly mobilised economic powers. If a participatory culture is to develop, Healey (1997: 293) notes, 'the machinery of government must be surrounded by requirements which encourage inclusionary responsiveness to the diverse ways of living, ways of doing business, and systems of meaning of the relevant political communities'. Healey (1997: 292), drawing on Friedmann (1987, 1992), writes:

> In discussing the political forms of such an enterprise, the significant dimensions of institutional design emerge as rights (of access, of challenge to the exercise of power), resources (of time, space, knowledge, skill, relational links, social capacities), policy principles or criteria (which encourage critical thinking, which stress quality), and distribution of competencies (among levels of territorial life, which cultivate self-reliance).

Fourth, opening up decision-making to the diversity of political communities evokes the fear that no decision will ever be reached, no conclusion to the debates and discussion will be achieved at any point. Certainly, deliberative decision-making and participatory practice involves a great deal of time and effort. Decisions will be deferred until there is broad agreement. They will not come quickly. Yet they *will* be more enduring. The present system may well react quickly to demands made by those with maximum power, yet we are fooling ourselves if we regard the Australian planning system today as 'decisive' in the sense of delivering good decisions that will be maintained and provide a sense of stability and continuity. On the contrary, the system is chronically flexible. Decisions are either never really made—always leaving open the option for developers to change their minds later—or they can be changed at will when new, powerful actors enter the game.

Existing procedures have to be acknowledged to be unsatisfactory. Leaving decisions to 'the market' means entrenching class and gender inequities, and is a surrogate for enhancing power differentials. Decision by a hierarchical, corporate state can easily lead to the same result unless government leaders consciously adopt a participative model. In both cases informal decision-making will inevitably develop 'behind the scenes' to enrich governmental knowledge ('governance without government') (Rhodes 1996). As governmental capacities and competencies are eroded by neoliberal government-shrinking policies, the importance of these informal channels grows. These channels must be opened to a much wider range of political communities, a process that will expand organisational needs of planning agencies as they absorb greater information flows. To meet this challenge, the competence, skills and knowledge capacity of government needs to be restored.

Multi-tiered planning

The principle of subsidiarity demands that a higher level of government should not undertake what a lower level of government can do for itself. This principle has been used to underscore an emergent European spatial planning system that has, it seems, thus far enjoyed wide-ranging political support (Gleeson 1998). Thus the entire structure of government from the national to the most local should be involved in urban planning, but only under the condition that the most detailed planning is left to the most local level. In Australia we need a fully integrated system of spatial and land use plan-making in which the three levels of government (local, state and Commonwealth) participate in appropriate ways.

There is a particular need for the Commonwealth government to take on the task of spatial planning, identifying areas of environmental vulnerability and social need throughout the whole nation, areas for action to which funding will be applied. In recent years, the blanket application of neoliberal policies to economic restructuring and public service provision has devastated Australia's regional communities and fuelled the explosive growth of reactionary politics (Fincher 1998). We support the calls of Stilwell (1993a) and Self (1995) for a new regime of national and regional spatial policy in Australia that would correct the tendency of markets to produce uneven sociospatial development. As part of this, we identify the need for a national audit of environmental quality and of the infrastructure required for national economic advancement. Within this national framework the states must be recognised as the first tier of local government—regional government (Self 1995).

We might prefer regions that better reflect patterns of settlement or labour markets or some such (as does Stilwell 1999). However, our history (and the Australian Constitution) has determined the existence of the states and their boundaries, and there is little point in trying to change them (even the British unitary system of government has lately become more 'federal', with the introduction of parliaments for Scotland and Wales). States are, in any case, entirely workable city-regional administrative units. What is needed much more is *constitutional* recognition of local—municipal—government. The British model arguably gives too much power to Westminster to determine the very existence of local government, and the Australian states have inherited Westminster's power. In continental Europe local government cannot be dictated to in this way. There are strong central powers of course, but these must negotiate with local government, not overpower it.

If this sort of planning is anathema to our present mainstream of economic thinking, then it must be observed that such a system does not appear to have done any economic harm to the European nations. In Asian countries the absence of proper planning has contributed to the decline of their cities (as well as to major reverses to their economies) through unbridled speculation. Getting the fundamentals right means more than producing a budget surplus. We do not now see capital in flight from the Netherlands, Germany or France, where integrated planning systems have been working for most of the postwar period. Indeed these nations are now the core of a united European economy of immense power.

Of course, the limits of governance do not today stop at the frontiers of the nation-state. It is widely agreed that the nation-state has lost some of its power. Corporations have gone beyond the rule of the nation-state, and they demand governance (see Dahl 1985). So there have to be ground rules for the operation of a global market responsive to the pressing demands of ecological responsibility and justice. As Tawney (1981/1944) observes, someone must make the rules, and if it is not public power then it will be private, unaccountable, power. The growth of global governance, we believe, will continue in the 21st century. So we expect also the growth of global institutions. The burning question today is not whether global governance is a good idea, but how to make global institutions democratically accountable. Planning systems today must be prepared to encompass an expansion upwards to the supranational level as much as downwards to the local.

Opening up planning

Finally, the new planning cannot, we believe, be about building a society according to a predetermined model. In this we agree with Beilharz (1994: 113): 'To be a socialist, in this context, is less a matter of striving towards the light on the hill than of seeking to interpret and change modernity in accordance with such core values as freedom and dignity'. We cannot here provide definitive answers to the questions we pose above. Indeed, we resist simple universal principles that can be used to decide all cases. This is not to deny the importance of universal ethical principles (justice, compassion), merely to insist that their application is a matter for judgement in each case on the basis of an enlightened and principled praxis (Low & Gleeson 1998).

The developed world has seen a shrinking of the sphere of government in the past two decades, and with it a withering of the sphere of politics, a narrowing of the parameters of political debate, a focus on simple uniform standards, and their authoritarian application through bureaucratic fiat. Thus society is socialised to accept the market as the final arbiter of everything—thus everything is reduced to commodity form, supplanting all other values. This is social engineering on a scale never seen before. As we have shown, this model of politics is seeping through the whole institutional fabric of Australian planning. Politics, and with it what used to be called 'public planning', has been engulfed by microeconomics. Democratic society has regressed from the principle of planning which Mannheim thought it would grow into. Our world has become a world for makers only (*homo faber*) to the detriment of each person's need for solidarity—the company of feeling and thinking fellow beings (*homo communitatis*: a person of the community). We want to restore a planning which embodies enlarged thought, moulds an inclusive public sphere, and recaptures the spirit of democracy.

Conclusion

Clearly, planning needs revaluation if it is to survive in any meaningful form in the new millennium. This means both renewing political and institutional support for planning, while also broadening its value base to accommodate the criticisms of modernist governance that have been made by radical democratic interests and by environmentalists. We have outlined in this chapter the basis for a new value framework. Our ideas are merely a suggestion, a contribution to a broader discussion about the future of planning that must inevitably emerge as neoliberalism gives way to a renewed yearning for humane governance, already evident in Australia and overseas.

As we mentioned earlier, there is an urgent need for specific ideas about how to renew Australia's cities and their governance. We will need more than value statements to guide us if unrestrained markets are to be replaced by democratic institutions and policy settings. In chapter 12 we turn our attention to the question of what needs to be done to restore and renew the badly eroded foundations of urban planning.

12 Better planning: from policy to action

> *Planning is a* public *function. Its purpose is to promote a more convenient, attractive and equitable pattern of development than the kind of development produced through unregulated markets.*

Peter Self (1998: 45, original emphasis)

Values are the basis of action. But they do not directly tell us how to act, how to plan for a democratic and sustainable society. We must compare what we value against what we have, and make decisions—often involving difficult trade-offs—about what actions are necessary to get us nearer to where we want to be. In this chapter, we outline some policy priorities that emerge from the value framework elaborated in chapter 11.

As Frank Stilwell reminds us, 'A commitment to social progress requires the identification of appropriate prescriptions' (Stilwell 1993a: 130). And yet no-one has complete knowledge—not even within the confines of a specific policy sphere such as Australian planning. The all-knowing analyst is as much a figure of fiction as the consumer with perfect knowledge of market information. We acknowledge the limits to what we know about planning issues and therefore the particularity of our priorities. We do not claim novelty. If planners read something in what follows that they are already doing or trying to do, or arguing for, that does not surprise us at all. We simply say 'more strength to your arm'.

As we say in chapter 1, these proposals are intended not as a complete program for action but as a starting point for discussion. We would welcome their refinement and enlargement through deliberation and argument. This reflects the value we have already placed on planning as dialogue in chapter 11. In what follows we briefly explain our policy priorities. We begin with what we see as the most general and the most urgent priority—reinstating public planning—and then proceed to more specific proposals for action.

Reinstating the government of space

We have shown that Australian planning has been overtaken by political reform, largely sourced in neoliberalism. Planners have been left side-lined and demoralised by the new priority given to economic development. As Self (1999: 244) remarks, 'planning is increasingly *perverted* by market pressures and dogmas' (our emphasis).

There are many reasons why neoliberalism should be rejected. If the primary task is ecological sustainability (ultimately, survival of humankind), then the regulation of the economy *must* discriminate between those industries and processes which are ecologically efficient (i.e. contribute to sustainability) and those which are not. Socially, the disastrous polarising effects of neoliberalism simply have to be counteracted. There is patently something radically wrong and mon-strously unjust about an *American* growth model in which the net wealth of one billionaire is equivalent to that of the poorest hundred million (Nader 1999), in which 2 per cent of the adult population languishes in gaols, and blacks are seven times more likely to be imprisoned than whites (Gray 1998: 117). Contrary to the moral vision of classic liberals, the arid prelacy of neoliberalism today sees nothing wrong in such vast inequality, indeed applauds it (see Demsetz 1995). Neoliberals denounce the attempt to direct the market to serve the public interest as 'dirigisme', which they say failed with the collapse of the Soviet imperium (Lal 1998). But 'dirigisme' also created the New Deal and the welfare state that paralleled unprecedented economic growth in the USA and Europe. Today we need an *Australian* growth model that is both inclusive, compassionate and sensitive to ecological limits.

One of the strongest features of the structure of governance in Australia is that each major metropolis has a government (two in the case of Brisbane: state and city) with the functional scope, power and authority to deliver in a coordinated way and on an equal basis to its citizens all the social and physical services that a population requires. Such a performance is in principle entailed by democratic governance on the basis of one vote, one value. Yet in none of the cities is this performance anywhere near fully achieved and, as we have seen in chapter 3, social and spatial inequality is getting worse. In its most extreme form poverty means homelessness.

Part of the problem of unequal service delivery was undoubtedly the fragmentation inherent in colonial bureaucracy. The social democrat project sought to address this problem but was outflanked by the rise of neoliberalism (as we have seen in chapters 4 and 5). Just *because* democratic government with comprehensive power entails equal distribution, neoliberals seek to transfer as much as possible of the distributive task *out* of the sphere of the state. In doing so they return urban governance to a more fragmented condition than that of colonial bureaucracy, and make thoughtful and consultative metropolitan planning impossible.

Our analysis has drawn attention to the negative social and environmental consequences of planning deregulation. Yet planning is actually indispensable to the long-term functioning of market economies—for planning is everywhere, from the corporation to the World Trade Organization. Yet the role of planning is effaced in market dogma. Unrestrained markets inevitably threaten their own existence: tending to despoil their habitats, even consume themselves. The socialisation of markets accomplished in *The Great Transformation* (Polanyi 1975/1944) of *laissez-faire* capitalism is once more in acute failure. On what basis, then, can markets be constrained to behave responsibly and in the public interest? We suggest that the government of space demands a reassertion of citizenship, renewal and strengthening of public planning agencies at both state and Commonwealth levels, the restoration of metropolitan planning, and the real inscription of ecological sustainability into planning practice.

Towards 'spatial citizenship'

In chapter 11 we call for the revaluation of planning, meaning the renewal of political and institutional support for spatial regulation in Australia. What does this renewal require? First, it requires that governments commit to 'spatial citizenship'. By this we mean a framework in law and policy that guarantees the right of all citizens and communities to a minimum level of social and physical infrastructure, economic opportunities, environmental quality and political participation. The implementation of these rights must be measured—through appropriate spatial analysis and standards—and their realisation monitored by the Commonwealth and by the states at a range of spatial scales, including local, metropolitan-regional and statewide.

Evident disparities and inequities should be corrected through a comprehensive planning effort, involving redistributive public investment and other social and cultural initiatives that would prevent the exclusion of any community from the mainstreams of national life. There are precedents—past and contemporary—that could be built on. For example, since 1933 the Commonwealth Grants Commission has addressed the issue of interregional equity in Australia by advising on the interstate distribution of public funds (Stilwell 1993a). The Commission's role and powers could be extended so that it can ensure a minimum uniform level of service provision within and between the states and territories.

We do not accept the argument that globalisation makes uneven social and environmental development inevitable. No social process lies outside the realm of political control; no human phenomenon is unstoppable. It is entirely within the power of Australian governments to mitigate, even rectify, the new forms of economic polarisation described in chapter 3. After decades of market liberalisation, there is no question that 'trickle-down' economics has failed. Governments must now act to restore the rights of all citizens—wherever they reside—to a minimum level of material welfare and access to culturally valued goods and services. For example, if access to the Internet is increasingly necessary for participation in the mainstreams of social and economic life, then governments must secure such access—through planning—for those citizens with limited market power.

We applaud the insistence of feminist theorists on diversity and difference (see Sandercock 1998: 187–9). We acknowledge that citizenship must never become a straitjacket of conformity. On the contrary, citizenship entails the right to assert difference and struggle against conformity. Yet the culture of the group can sometimes demand *individual* conformity, and we also uphold the right of the individual to struggle against group pressure. Most importantly, we must not mistake difference for poverty. If cultural difference can only be sustained by poverty, and if this difference diminishes when poverty is alleviated, then, we say, so be it. The citizenship we are talking about here is the right to the most basic conditions of life that make freely chosen difference possible.

As we mention in chapter 3, many people feel abandoned and disenfranchised by the changes that globalisation has wrought in Australia's cities and regions. The renewal of public sector planning in Australia is vital to the renewal of citizenship. Planning must be re-equipped with the skills and institutional capacities necessary to counter the exclusionary tendencies of globalisation. There is no place for National Competition Policy (NCP) in planning. NCP is anti-democratic (see chapter 9), and we call for the abandonment of reviews that have been carried out under this framework.

Renewing public planning

In order that skilled, politically sensitive and consultative planning can be carried out, the skills, resources and morale of public planning agencies must be rebuilt. In almost all cases, that will require more staff in public agencies. The trend to wholesale outsourcing of urban analysis and policy development that has flourished under neoliberalism must be reversed. The research capacities of major state, metropolitan and local planning agencies will have to be rebuilt. There is no compelling reason why private consultants should be the preferred source of policy analysis and advice for state and local policy-makers. There is every reason to believe that a properly resourced and reskilled public sector could provide independent and cost-effective advice to policy-makers. This cannot be done on the cheap. Skills and time cost money. As we have already argued, rebuilding the public sector will require a re-allocation of resources from private to public purposes.

Fundamental to the cause of planning renewal is the restoration of a metropolitan planning focus that is based on in-depth, published social analysis. Australians are entitled to much more and better than the current mixture of jargon-ridden, secret (commercial-in-confidence) reports from private consultants, and the promotional brochures advertising metropolitan plans for wide public consumption. What is lacking is the full supporting argument for metropolitan plans, with the logic exposed and supported with credible evidence. We should expect at least the same degree of intellectual rigour from metropolitan plans that the courts expect from evidence and the academic community expects from published research.

Creating environmental governance

If planning is about environmental governance (chapter 11), then eco-sustainability must be advanced at all policy levels. This strengthens the hand of strategic planning: sustainability requires a concern with intra- and intergenerational equity, as well as the integrity of ecological systems now and in the future. A strategic view in turn foregrounds the issue of justice and spatial citizenship. The current fad for 'benchmarking' the qualities of cities and regions needs to be recast. Benchmarking means comparison with other cities with a view to economic competition. Monitoring must go much further and measure progress towards social justice, spatial citizenship and ecological sustainability (exposing any conflicts between these goals where they occur), not just competitive performance against targets that reduce to economic positionality.

Environmental governance also requires the rigorous application of ecologically sustainable development (ESD) principles at all policy levels. Australian local governments have been gradually adopting Agenda 21 planning frameworks (Christoff & Low 1999). But local government needs help from the Commonwealth and states. In this respect the demise of the national ESD framework since 1996 has been a backward step. Some state governments have given ESD a central place in their planning legislation. Queensland's new *Integrated Planning Act 1997* establishes ecological sustainability as its leading purpose, though critics have questioned its ability to realise this aim (chapter 5). Sustainability is a key aim of *Shaping Our Cities*, the new metropolitan strategy for New South Wales' greater metropolitan region, encompassing Sydney, Newcastle, Wollongong and the Central Coast (Department of Urban Affairs and Planning 1998). The important thing now is to see that the ESD goal really *changes* the nature of urban development. This is an uncomfortable political task, for any constraint on development will be noisily resisted by the development industry—until the industry sees that the political will is strong enough to prevail and to be maintained. However, mere rhetorical use of ESD to conceal a reality of 'business as usual' will rapidly bring the ESD project into disrepute. Commonwealth involvement here is essential to prevent competitive watering down of ESD regulation by the states in order to gain temporary investment advantages.

Ecological sustainability *can* be measured, but planners must spend much more time exploring its measurement. Crude measures such as gross density are worse than useless. Planners need to look for innovative regulatory means to achieve ecological sustainability. One important approach is to encourage the use of 'slow transport' in cities (on foot and on bicycle), and to find ways of patterning density to encourage slow transport and public transport. Effective metropolitan planning arguably requires the power deriving from public ownership of land for future development. There have been quite successful efforts in the past to build up land banks (though these were sometimes rorted by unscrupulous officials). These initiatives must be revisited and some power restored to the community to capture the development value created by rezoning decisions at the metropolitan fringe.

A new approach to growth

Planning as 'growth management' will never achieve ecological sustainability if current economic dynamics are not rethought and reformulated. Progress is being made to shift the ideals of planning towards the ESD goal. But the evidence is that planning policy and practice remain fixed on the task of facilitating urban growth. The sustainability of standard models of economic and physical growth is rarely questioned in any profound sense. Nevertheless, the weight of evidence from environmental analysis suggests that entrenched patterns of economic growth are utterly unsustainable (chapter 8).

Economic growth in its present form is not an end in itself. Growth can take many forms—material and non-material—which are more or less sustainable. We conceive and measure growth in crude terms—as the expansion of commodities (products and monetised services)—but there are other things that can grow and be valued if we choose to do so. We might choose to value environmental quality and seek to enhance this through an 'ecological growth model'. We must look beyond simple material production in two ways: towards an economy of repair and towards the dematerialistion of growth. Planners must insist that economic models show how the economy is performing with respect to ecological sustainability.

To achieve 'ecological growth' we may need to move from an economy of *production* to an economy of *repair*—of our damaged society, of our damaged environment, even of our used products. The Swedes call this the 'ecocyclic society'. The economy of repair may well grow more rapidly in the 21st century than the economy of production. Economic growth need not be diminished by making it subordinate to ecological sustainability. Indeed an economy of repair is as much a growth economy as an economy of production. An economy of repair can create new jobs, and offers many and various opportunities for business and private enterprise. The economy of production will not cease, but it will become more innovative. Ecological innovations are even now being developed by our own inventors and by our economic competitors in the sphere of production. The hybrid-fuel car is one example, also fuel cell technology for making electricity. An ecological economy is already in the making. It will be brought into being by ecological regulation. Our production systems must respond to fit this developing global economy of the 21st century.

The physical growth of cities is based not just on rising need (growth in population and households) but also on the ceaseless expansion of wants and preferences encouraged by the progressive freeing up of markets in recent decades. The market by its nature seeks ways to expand itself by inflaming our passion for things. In cities, we are persuaded to want larger housing, more cars, bigger roads, more holiday travel, more household commodities from exotic locations, more shopping centres and more space for work: all the products that the existing production system can, without short-term risk, readily supply—no matter what the cost to future generations!

There is now broad recognition that this ceaseless expansion of the built environment has reached the limits of the 'environmental spaces' of many of the major cities (see Wackernagel & Rees 1996). Emergency policies—new growth management strategies, such as urban consolidation—are rushed into the breach. Consolidation may contain the net use of land (though even this is questionable—see McLoughlin 1991), but the gross consumption of nature continues unchecked. The economy and planning remain geared to the construction of new dwellings, other buildings and urban infrastructure. New home construction and alterations currently account for almost 30 per cent of private domestic investment in Australia. Could not this investment pool flow towards more sustainable patterns of built environment enhancement? The same question could be asked about other forms of investment.

We ask: can this expansion of preferences be contained or redirected into non-material forms—such as more leisure or new forms of social service—thus reducing the economy's relentless consumption of the natural environment? There is work to be done. There are unemployed people to do it. If the market cannot put the two together, then government must. But the work requires training, fair pay and a future, not just 'work for the dole'. (A more demeaning and stigmatising name for a public program is hard to imagine.) Enhancing wellbeing may not require major physical growth and a greater consumption of resources. Planning *can* play a role by guiding the production of built environments that address needs while encouraging and satisfying new forms of non-material desires. We cannot enlarge on such a complex matter here, but we call for a thoroughgoing debate among planners, economists, ecologists and the community itself on this issue.

Importantly, this debate cannot even occur until planning disengages itself from the economic development role that it has been forced to assume by neoliberal reform. As we have shown in this book, planning's role in many domains has been redefined from growth manager (under SDM, see chapter 4) to growth promoter (under CL, see chapter 5). This reduces planning's ability to secure sustainable forms of urban development. In all public policy domains, including local government, planning should be strictly separated from those agencies promoting economic development. Finally, as we argue in chapter 11, the Commonwealth must be brought back into planning. It is the Commonwealth that has principal responsibility for citizenship, and it *must* involve itself in promotion of spatial citizenship.

Sustainable urban development

Planning for balance and self-containment

Where growth—outward (traditional) and vertical (consolidation)—occurs, sustainability requires that its qualitative components be balanced. New development must aim to maximise in-situ satisfaction of needs, and even desires. If left to itself, the urban land market often produces environments that satisfy a narrow range of needs and desires, forcing people to travel great distances to reach what they need to make a fulfilling life. Think of the 'dormitory' suburbs that have characterised much postwar suburban development in Australia. This is not an attack on low-density development *per se* but a critique of what has been produced: often long distances for workers and social isolation for child-carers.

Sometimes balance has been a question of timing. We refer here to the long-acknowledged problem of infrastructure and housing coordination in new residential developments. Progress has been made—there has been far more attention in recent years by state and local governments to the problem. There have been improvements to the coordination of infrastructure and service delivery by government agencies, though this has been reversed in some contexts and also complicated by the privatisation of utilities and decentralisation of social service provision.

Programs such as ILAP (Integrated Local Area Planning) helped to reinforce the need for coordination of planning and delivery of services and infrastructure across a range of local government functions. Also, in most states, developers may now be charged levies by local governments and state utilities to help ensure balanced residential development. (South Australia is a notable exception, due to the land banking activities of the South Australian Urban Land Trust.) The shift towards greater use of developer charges (and hence user-pays financing), however, has been accompanied by new restrictions on state and local governments to raise infrastructure finance independently (Neutze 1997). This raises the possibility of new inequities of infrastructure provision, as poorer and/or harder-pressed local governments are forced to pass on considerable user charges to new (and perhaps existing) residents (Troy 1996b). We believe that the shift towards developer charges, and user-pays financing, cannot provide what is needed. The states should raise infrastructure investment funds that can be distributed to local governments on the basis of demonstrated social and economic need. We believe that good arguments exist for uniform land taxation—

necessarily a Commonwealth initiative to prevent competitive tax-cutting by the states—throughout Australia for the purpose of financing urban infrastructure (Stilwell 1999).

Restoring a metropolitan focus

At the broader metropolitan scale, there is a need to restore balance to increasingly asymmetrical patterns of employment creation, retail expansion, residential development and service provision. Unfettered land markets produce what Marxist geographers have termed 'uneven development': that is, sociospatial inequities that include spatial polarisation, locational disadvantage and environmental variation (chapter 3). These are not anticipated by abstract market logic, and therefore are ignored or unconvincingly explained away by neoliberal economists. But they occur in real markets, in actual institutional and cultural settings, working through distributions in practice. In the USA, these patterns are revealed in a variety of ways: 'gated' residential communities; edge cities that service the privileged; enclosed shopping malls that exclude the young and the 'deviant'; a progressive withering of public space; and dying strip centres and downtowns. These dysfunctional sociospatial patterns also threaten ecological sustainability: the separation of employment and housing encourage car use, poor areas suffer environmental degradation, and fringe residential growth is driven by the inability and/or unwillingness of private land markets to renew blighted areas.

Most Australians live outside the inner city and should properly be the focus of planning thinking and policy making on the state and metropolitan scales. Planning must renew living spaces before it renews showplaces. We believe that there are strong arguments for a managed dispersion of key social and economic activities, towards a polynucleated urban form characterised by a healthy CBD and thriving district centres functioning as nodes in properly integrated public transport systems. This may seem a radical aim but it is no more than counterpart cities in Europe, Asia and America will be trying to achieve in the 21st century—and are indeed aiming at today.

This model of metropolitan structure requires careful and *consistent* planning that can direct private and public sector activity. We see considerable merit in the growth management strategies adopted by Californian planning agencies during the 1980s and 90s. For example, the Southern Californian Association of Governments' (SCAG) 1988 draft *Growth Management Plan* aimed to improve regional ecological and social sustainability by fostering a balanced share of jobs and housing in new and existing urban development. This plan was itself a component of a broader strategic plan for Southern California that encompassed mobility, environmental and housing needs plans. The SCAG concern with balanced development was, of course, driven by a sense of environmental crisis in the region, especially rapidly deteriorating air quality, that had been produced by decades of freewheeling, market-driven urban development. In time, the planning effort broadened to include rigorous state-specific environmental standards for new motor cars that shook the entire US auto industry. Australian cities are *much better placed* than American cities to achieve similar goals: they have much more extensive fixed-rail infrastructure (as good as many European cities!) and patterns of urban development better adapted to its use.

Enhancing public transport

Both ecological and economic considerations demand the greatly increased use of public transport in Australian cities. Australian state governments, however, have failed to plan and resource the public transport service effectively. As has long been understood, the transport system is the single most important infrastructural element shaping the metropolis and determining its pattern of growth. Transport systems must be planned as a whole. That means that the impact of public transport on road use must be considered in roads planning. *Road use saving* is as important for good transport planning as *road space-making*. The pricing of road use must equate with the pricing of public transport use to remove perverse incentives. Transport planning must be taken out of the hands of professional road engineers, whose skills in road-building are not an appropriate basis for transport planning for ecological sustainability and social justice.

Instead of applying coercive regulations to increase urban density (hoping to replicate European cities, which have higher public transport use), planners should act first on the incentive systems which cause people to use their cars for most journeys. The pricing system needs to be altered to ensure that the full monetary costs of a journey are paid at the time of the journey (road pricing, or the much simpler method of paying the full cost of insurance and registration at the fuel pump). Only then might some form of zoning be tried, incorporating density gradients around public transport access points—and then only after local public consultation. It should be obvious that increasing residential densities in places where there is no viable alternative to the use of the car will have no effect on transport behaviour.

Fixed rail, light rail (trams) and bus routes must be fully coordinated to reinforce and support one another, so that it becomes possible for people to move effortlessly, swiftly, comfortably and safely between modes and destinations on a single ticket. Privatisation makes this difficult, in most cases impossible. The management of public transport must be taken back into public hands. The impact of the transport system on urban development must be planned to generate the pattern most consistent with spatial citizenship (a right to public transport access for every household) and ecological sustainability.

Regenerating public space

In recent decades, a withering of public space has accompanied, and expressed, the declining commitments of Australian governments to a democratic public interest. Privatisation of state agencies, such as utilities, has reduced the physical public domain. New retail development has focused on privately operated and controlled shopping malls. The management of other public domains, including universities, schools, recreation facilities, has been reorganised along market lines. In the new privatised community spheres, 'unruly' behaviour is codified and prohibited, discussion is limited by market priorities, dissent is discouraged, and narrow, acquisitive values are celebrated.

We urge planners and policy-makers to roll back the privatisation of space and to establish new and inclusive public domains that will nurture non-market human values. The revitalisation of public space should be an explicit planning policy priority. We applaud the current metropolitan strategy for New South Wales for its commitment to enhance the 'public domain'. Both state and local governments need to find ways to assert public values within, and public controls over, the new private communal spaces, such as shopping malls, that have proliferated in recent years. This is not to urge a return to the past. Recognition also needs to be given to the fact that public space has long functioned in ways that have excluded or devalued many publics, including disabled people, youth and women.

Iveson (1998: 29) urges us to think about the creation of 'multi-public public spaces', where cultural and social group differences—including specific forms of expression and behaviour—might be acknowledged and nurtured. For example, privately controlled shopping malls might be opened up to 'non-consumer' publics, such as young people, through new access rights and the provision of recreation spaces that nurture particular forms of expression, such as street art, music and even the simple, satisfying practice of 'hanging out'

(Iveson 1998). Planning agencies could help to open up and democratise private communal spaces by using them as nodes for public and community activities and land uses.

We have suggested some fairly specific policies for urban planning. At least as important is the governmental process through which these policies may be discussed, modified or rejected and new proposals made and shaped. Planning must, if it is to gain and retain wide public support, enhance democracy.

Democratising planning

An inclusive public interest

Postmodernists and other radical democrats are right to oppose narrow conceptions of the public interest that enslave planning to the will of professional and economic elites. As we have shown, the 'public interest' in planning has too often in the past masked the interests of the powerful or the views of technocrats.

The alternative suggested by relativists is, however, no less problematical for planning. As we have remarked (chapter 9), entrenched opposition by some postmodernists to the notion of social consensus echoes, and in some political contexts (e.g. academic debates) actually reinforces, the neoliberal critique of a democratic public interest. Australia is a *society*, not a mere ensemble of individuals or communities, and there are interests that connect all of its citizens, such as universal wellbeing, environmental quality and social harmony. Planning must concern itself with the welfare of all, though that often requires the unequal treatment of groups and places in the interests of equity. Therefore, planning must ultimately serve a broader public interest. The broad value framework that we outline in chapter 11, we believe, defines the public's interest in planning. We suggest that this framework is sufficiently inclusive of the variety of social outlooks that occur in society to constitute a broad and democratic statement of purpose for planning.

It must also be remembered that when democratic notions of the public interest are undermined or even swept aside, *power* decides whose interests policy will serve—today the power of a new managerial class. Neoliberals have sought to install the market as the arbiter of public interest, claiming that the pursuit of profit neatly coincides with the collective view. The long historical record of capitalism shows us how particular are the market's social interests. The market is no substitute for democracy in defining the public interest.

Beyond the broad principles that we suggest in chapter 11, the task of governments—local, regional and national—is to articulate what the public's interest is in any particular policy setting. This does *not* mean that the public interest is just whatever Cabinet says it is or whatever the minister says it is. Social, economic and ecological circumstances differ widely across policy domains, requiring from planning sensitivity to local context as well as a commitment to diversity where it meets the test of justice. Cultural pluralisation may be entirely consistent with justice and democracy. But here consistency with the broader democratic framework of a public interest is necessary to prevent negative forms of cultural diversity—ethnic segregation of the forced kind, segregation of poverty—from emerging. By contrast, economic diversity is rarely consistent with the test provided by a public interest. Indeed, a central role for planning as we have defined it in this book—and as others have defined it historically—is the prevention and/or mitigation of economic polarisation. As we note above, we must not mistake difference for poverty.

Maintaining openness

A plan is a collection of policies for a city, not made lightly and not to be changed on the whim of a minister or a developer. Planning means sticking to public policy in the face of development pressure. That needs to be clearly registered. It will be difficult, because the culture of planning in Australia is quite the reverse: the first sign of developer pressure often results in capitulation. Planning is about making and expressing an inclusive public interest. But the process of finding that public interest is complex. If one party wants a change of plan, many others may not. Democracy, as stated in chapter 11, is hard and highly skilled work, requiring a commitment from policy-makers and leaders to constant discussion about social and environmental change. Policy discussion must maintain a radical awareness of its potential limitations and exclusions. This means that policy analysts, such as planners, must actively seek to broaden policy discussions—hearings, forums, debates—beyond the confines of vocal and accessible interest groups. The silent, the marginalised, the 'difficult' may be hard to find, hard to understand, hard to include sensibly in policy discussions, but democracy demands that their voices be heard and that their needs be addressed.

Planners must counter the always-present—and perhaps under-standable—desire of policy-makers to close and neatly enframe discussions. Rationality can serve the cause of democracy where it improves the organisation of debate and the rigour of analysis. But planning is irreducibly political—a process, as we have defined it, of constant negotiation of environmental alternatives. Planning is about balancing in actual policy contexts the science of rational analysis with the art of political negotiation. The expectation that a policy will be consistently maintained over time is a fundamental part of effective planning. But in its continual making and remaking, democracy requires extensive and intensive policy discussions to balance the all too self-evident need for certainty and action against the necessity for openness to alternatives. Doubt is a democratic virtue.

Openness requires of planners a willingness to change when democratic negotiation demands it. This means that planners must surrender during policy discussion some of the authority and privilege that their professional status confers on them. Negotiation is only democratic when power is shared. After nearly three decades, Arnstein's (1969) 'Ladder of Citizen Participation' remains as relevant as ever. 'Participation' can mask and therefore protect the power of elites, including professional experts. Democratic participation, by definition, is a process that radically exposes decision-making to 'scrutiny from below' and ultimately to compromise and change.

Finally, the principles of democracy and cultural respect demand that Australian planning accommodate the values and the social priorities of Indigenous Australians. There are already precedents for opening up planning in this way at the local level (chapter 7). These schemes should be learned from and replicated in other settings. Moreover, Australia should follow New Zealand's example and inscribe recognition of indigenous cultural and ecological values in planning and environmental legislation.

A new framework for planning education

If it seems that what we have proposed requires the knowledge and wisdom of a sage, that is no underestimate. If there is to be public planning, we will also need public servants with considerable range and depth of education: not 'philosopher kings', but at least philosophers (*pace* Paterson 1976). The traditional Oxbridge education for the British civil service was 'politics, philosophy and economics'. That is very much the educational grounding which good planning demands. But of course it needs one further discipline: geography, which today nearly always includes 'environmental studies'.

Professional planners need a broad education that combines philosophical understanding contextualised by time and space. Essential to the economics of planning is an understanding of time, place and culture to frame the working through of abstract principles. Planners must have a broad grasp of the principles of economics. This must not, however, be the sort of narrow indoctrination of the precepts of neoliberalism that seems to come with most of today's economics courses. An education in economics must include institutional economics, economic history, Marxian economics and urban economics along with neoclassical microeconomics. Understanding the political and cultural dimensions of globalisation is also essential today.

This broad grounding must be tempered by an understanding of political philosophy and ethics. An urban planner cannot go far along the path we lay out above without an understanding of the principles of democracy—where democracy came from and under what circumstances—and justice in different political systems. The basis of law and 'the rule of law' also needs to be included here, and the nature of 'property' and 'class'. Public policy is a field in which the planner must be skilled and have a broad understanding. This is especially important if the links between policy domains are to be understood. Public sector management should be a part of the public policy course. Planners need skills in facilitating public consultation and participation, and this should begin at undergraduate level, and be further refined at postgraduate level. Finally, and perhaps most centrally, planners need human geography to provide the spatial dimension to their thinking. Of course *urban* geography is critically important, but so also is the new awareness of global ecological conditions and limits. Both social theory and history are obviously going to be elements of such a course, but these are properly subsumed within the core disciplines of politics, philosophy, geography and economics (PPEG).

The basis of planning education should, thus, be a four-year PPEG university honours course. Such a course should be tailored to the specific needs of a public servant in planning. Although no such course probably exists at present in our university systems, if planning were to gain ground as a public activity the universities could very easily respond. Such a basic grounding is indispensable for all planners in order to counteract the tendency to restricted vision, for example of economic or design determinism.

This is of course a generalist education, not a professional training. The professional part of planning education should come in a postgraduate specialisation in any one of a number of fields: design, law, environment, housing, transport, recreation, information systems, and perhaps commercial development. Part of all such professional training should be a core course in planning theory and practice. Public participation practice must be included in this core. In postgraduate education—which could be provided by technical colleges as well as universities (specialising in different skills)—the generalist planner would acquire a specialist skill. Skills education could be expected to vary widely over time and to be engaged in from time to time during the working life of a planner, either updating an existing skill or adding a new one. The basic undergraduate education would not need to be so finely attuned to change.

The education of planners depends on the sort of jobs we expect them to do. In a planning organisation it is possible to envisage a career path which leads a specialist from any domain to a leadership position in the organisation. Meanwhile, the specialist planner could be expected to practise in a department of planning at local, state or federal levels, or in private consultancies. Planning education in Australia is not organised at present to prepare for such a career path. But this is what is needed if the job is to be done properly.

Conclusion

As we look ahead to the 21st century, there are ideas we must leave behind in the 20th. To these ideas we say 'No'. We say 'No' to government by autocracy and 'No' to government by the market. We rephrase Keynes' words for today:

> It is *not* true that a society organised along market lines alone will deliver sustained growth. It is *not* true that growth measured by Gross Domestic Product will deliver widespread wellbeing, satisfying employment or social justice. The world is *not* so governed from above that short term profit, fair distribution and conservation of the Earth's resources coincide. It is *not* so managed here below that in practice they coincide. It is *not* a correct deduction from the Principles of Economics that national 'enlightened self interest' always operates in the global interest of ecological sustainability. Nor is it true that national self interest generally *is* enlightened.

Bill Clinton, in his election campaign, allegedly said 'It's the economy, stupid!'. It's not. It's the stupid economy. The economy fixated by short-term profit. The economy of the 'bottom line'. The economy of social breakdown and ecological disaster. The economy which consumes itself. That economy we must leave behind. But we must also awake from the political stupor which comes with the belief that if we leave distribution to the market, all will be for the best in the best of all possible worlds.

Are we then 'dirigistes' and collectivists? Do we want to 'steer' aspects of economy and society? Are we in fact planners? Yes, of course we are. The question is not whether the economy, society, our cities, the use of our lands are to be steered; but by whom, in what way, and in whose interests. Is the steering to be by the corporate class or is it to come from the collective wisdom of the many groups, associations and cultures that always form in a healthy democratic society? The latter is surely the Australian way. How to mobilise that collective wisdom, how to facilitate convergence on public action, is an extraordinarily difficult political task, but it is one we must, as planners, undertake.

Bibliography

Abercrombie, P. 1943/1933 *Town and Country Planning*, 2nd edn, Oxford University Press, Oxford

Alexander, I. & McManus, P. 1992 'A new direction for Perth transport?' *Urban Policy and Research*, 10(4), pp 6–13

Alinsky, S.D. 1969/1946 *Reveille for Radicals*, Vintage Books, New York

Allan, A. 1998 'Marion: a study of a super-regional centre and its impacts on Adelaide' *Urban Policy and Research*, 16(2), pp 117–30

Allport, C. 1986 'Women and suburban housing: post-war planning in Sydney, 1943–61' *Urban Planning in Australia: critical readings*, eds J.B. McLoughlin & M. Huxley, Longman Cheshire, Melbourne

Altvater, E. 1993 *The Future of the Market: an essay on the regulation of money and nature after the collapse of 'actually existing socialism'*, Verso, London

Amin, A. & Graham, S. 1997 'The ordinary city' *Transactions, Institute of British Geographers*, 22, pp 411–29

Argy, F. 1998 *Australia at the Crossroads: radical free market or a progressive liberalism?*, Allen & Unwin, Sydney

Arnstein, S. 1969 'A ladder of citizen participation' *Journal of the American Institute of Planners*, 35(4), pp 216–24

Arrow, K. 1951 *Social Choice and Individual Values*, Yale University Press, New Haven, CN

Australia Council 1997 *Better Places, Richer Communities*, Australia Council, Sydney

Australian Bureau of Statistics (ABS) 1971 *1971, Census of Population and Housing: characteristics of the population and dwellings, local government areas*, ABS, Canberra

——1993 *1991 Census of Population and Housing: census characteristics of Australia*, Australian Government Publishing Service, Canberra

——1997a *Year Book Australia 1997*, Australian Government Publishing Service, Canberra

——1997b *1996 Census of Population and Housing: selected social and housing characteristics for statistical local areas*, ABS, Canberra

——1998a *1996 Census of Population and Housing: population growth and distribution, Australia*, ABS, Canberra

——1998b *1996 Census of Population and Housing: selected family and labour force characteristics, Australia*, ABS, Canberra

——1998c *1996 Census of Population and Housing: selected characteristics for urban centres and localities, Australia*, ABS, Canberra

——1998d, *Year Book Australia 1998*, Australian Government Publishing Service, Canberra

——1999 *Labour Force, Australia*, June, Catalogue no. 6203.0, Australian Government Publishing Service, Canberra

Australian Council of Social Services (ACOSS) 1997 *Jobs Pack*, ACOSS, Sydney

Australian Council of Trade Unions (ACTU) 1999 'Style at the expense of others', http://www.worksite.actu.asn.au/snapshot/outwork.htm

Australian Local Government Association (ALGA) 1997 *Designing Competitive Spaces*, ALGA, Canberra

——1998 *Working out Agreements: a practical guide to agreements between local government and indigenous Australians*, ALGA, Canberra

Badcock, B. 1984 *Unfairly Structured Cities*, Basil Blackwell, Oxford

——1994 ' "Stressed out" communities: "out-of-sight, out-of-mind"?' *Urban Policy and Research*, 12(3), pp 191–7

——1995 'Towards more equitable cities: a receding prospect?' ed. P. Troy *Australian Cities: issues, strategies and policies for urban Australia in the 1990s*, Cambridge University Press, Melbourne

——1997 'Recently observed polarising trends in Australian cities' *Australian Geographical Studies*, 35(3), pp 243–59

Bailey, J. 1975 *Theories for Planning*, Routledge & Kegan Paul, London

Barnett, F.O. 1944 *We Must Go On: a study in planned reconstruction and housing*, The Book Depot, Melbourne

Beck, U. 1997 *The Reinvention of Politics: rethinking modernity in the global social order*, trans. M. Ritter, Polity, Cambridge

Beder, S. 1993 *The Nature of Sustainable Development*, Scribe, Newham (Victoria)

Beed, C. 1981 *Melbourne's Development and Planning*, Clewara Press, Melbourne

Beilharz, P. 1994 *Postmodern Socialism: romanticism, city and state*, Melbourne University Press, Melbourne

Bell, S. 1997 *Ungoverning the Economy: the political economy of Australian economic policy*, Oxford University Press, Melbourne

Bennetts, S. 1997 'New project to spark debate on "English-speaking disease" ', *Uniken*, (University of New South Wales) no. 426, pp 1, 4

Bentley, A. 1908/1935 *The Process of Government*, Principia Press, Evanston, Ill.

Bernard, R. 1970 'Community action in a twilight area' *Journal of the Royal Institute of British Architects*, 77, pp 445–53

Berry, M. & Huxley, M. 1992 'Big build: property capital, the state and urban change in Australia' *International Journal of Urban and Regional Research*, 16, pp 35–59

Birnbauer, B. 1994 'Case-mix's damning diagnosis' *The Age*, News Extra 3 September, p. 10

Birrell, R. 1993 'Ethnic concentrations: the Vietnamese experience' *People and Place*, 1, pp 26–31

Blair, T.L. ed. 1973 *The Poverty of Planning*, Macdonald, London

Blowers, A. 1993 'The time for change' *Planning for a Sustainable Environment: a report for the Town and Country Planning Association*, ed. A. Blowers, Earthscan, London

Bonyhady, T. 1997 'Diminished democracy' *Urban Research Program Newsletter*, (Australian National University), 31, pp 1–2

——1999 'Grand Prix culture' *The Australian's Review of Books*, 4(1), pp 3–4

Bookchin, M. 1974 *The Limits of the City*, Harper & Row, New York

——1980 *Toward an Ecological Society*, Black Rose Books, Montreal

——1990 *Remaking Society: pathways to a green future*, South End Press, Boston

Boyd, R. 1960 *The Australian Ugliness*, Cheshire, Melbourne

Brady, N. 1995 'Rialto owners loaned $1m from gambling fund' *The Age*, 29 September, p. 3

——1999 'Victoria's homeless highest in nation' *The Age*, 20 May, p. 7

Brady, N. & Miller, C. 1995 'Boost for crown, windfall for state' *The Age*, 13 October, p. 1

Brain, P. 1999 *Beyond Meltdown: the global battle for sustained growth*, Scribe, Melbourne

Breheny, M. & Rookwood, R. 1993 'Planning for the sustainable city region' *Planning for a Sustainable Environment: a report for the Town and Country Planning Association*, ed. A. Blowers, Earthscan, London, pp 150–89

Buchanan, J.M. 1977 *Freedom in Constitutional Contract: perspectives of a political economist*, Texas A. and M. University Press, College Station, TX

Bunker, R. & Minnery, J. 1992 *Recent Commonwealth Initiatives in Urban Affairs*, Australian Institute of Urban Studies National Monograph no. 1, AIUS (SA Division), Adelaide

Burgmann, M. & Burgmann, V. 1998 *Green Bans, Red Union: environmental activism and the New South Wales Builders Labourers' Federation*, UNSW Press, Sydney

Burnley, I.H. 1998 'Immigrant city, global city? Advantage and disadvantage among communities from Asia in Sydney' *Australian Geographer*, 29(1), pp 49–70

Burnley, I.H. & Murphy, P. 1995 'Exurban development in Australia and the United States: through a glass darkly' *Journal of Planning Education and Research*, 14, pp 245–54

Burnley, I.H., Murphy, P. & Fagan, R. 1997 *Immigration and Australian Cities*, The Federation Press, Sydney

Butler, J.T. 1982 'A guide to town planning for Queensland secondary schools' *Queensland Planner*, Special Edition

Button, V. 1998 'Threat to shut Shell plant', *The Age*, 21 October, p. 2

Buxton, M. 1998 'How to reconcile the competing processes underlying Melbourne's spatial restructuring' *Community Planning Bulletin*, 7, pp 3, 7

Cannon, M. 1975 *Life in the Cities: Australia in the Victorian age*, Nelson, Melbourne

Capling, A., Considine, M. & Crozier, M. 1998 *Australian Politics in the Global Era*, Longman, Melbourne

Carson, R. 1962 *Silent Spring*, Riverside Press, Cambridge, MA

Carter, M. 1996 'A revolution in health care: commercial or democratic?' *Putting the People Last: government, services and rights in Victoria*, eds M. Webber & M. Crooks, Hyland House, Melbourne

Castells, M. 1977 *The Urban Question*, Edward Arnold, London

——1978 *City, Class and Power*, Macmillan, London

Castles, F.G. 1985 *The Working Class and Welfare: reflections on the political development of the welfare state in Australia and New Zealand, 1890–1980*, Allen & Unwin, Sydney

Castles, S., Kalantzis, M., Cope, B. & Morrisey, M. 1988 *Mistaken Indentity: multiculturalism and the demise of nationalism in Australia*, Pluto, Sydney

Caulfield, J. & Painter, M. (1995) 'Urban policy and management in Sydney' *Reform and Reversal: lessons from the Coalition government in New South Wales 1988–1995*, eds M. Laffin & M. Painter, Macmillan, Melbourne

Chadwick, G. 1971 *A Systems View of Planning*, Pergamon, Oxford

Chaples, E., Nelson, H. & Turner, K. 1985 *The Wran Model: electoral politics in New South Wales, 1981 and 1984*, Oxford University Press, Melbourne

Charles, C. 1990 'Urban consolidation, an answer?' *Shelter—National Housing Journal*, (Australia), 6, pp 17–24

Christoff, P. 1998 'Degreening government in the garden state: environment policy under the Kennett government' *Environmental and Planning Law Journal*, 15(1), pp 10–32

——1999 'Regulating the urban environment' in ed. P. Troy, *Serving the City*, Sydney, Pluto Press, pp 34–59

Christoff, P. & Low, N.P. 1999 'Australian urban policy, green or mean?' *Consuming Cities: the urban environment in the global economy after the Rio Declaration*, eds N.P. Low, B.J. Gleeson, I. Elander & R. Lidskog, Routledge, London

Clark, G. & Dear, M. 1981 'The state in capitalism and the capitalist state' *Urbanization and Urban Planning in Capitalist Societies*, eds M. Dear & A.J. Scott, Methuen, London

Clune, D. 1997 'Political chronicles: New South Wales' *Australian Journal of Politics and History*, 43(3) pp 384–92

Cockburn, C. 1977 *The Local State: management of cities and people*, Pluto Press, London

Cockett R. 1995 *Thinking the Unthinkable: think-tanks and the economic counter-revolution, 1931–1983*, Fontana, London

Colebatch, T. 1999 'State's economy falling behind', *The Age*, 24 May, p. 5

Considine, M. 1990 'Managerialism strikes out' *Australian Journal of Public Administration*, 49(2), pp 166–78

Considine, M. & Costar, B. eds 1992 *Trials in Power: Cain, Kirner and Victoria 1982–1992*, Melbourne University Press, Melbourne

Considine, M. & Painter, M. eds 1997 *Managerialism: the great debate*, Melbourne University Press, Melbourne

Corbett, D. 1987 'The administrative organisation and performance of the states or how well do the states discharge their functions?' *The Australian States: towards a renaissance*, ed. M. Birrell, Longman Cheshire, Melbourne

Cosgrove, L. & Kliger, B. 1997 'Planning with a difference: a reflection on planning and decision making with indigenous people in Broome, Western Australia' *Urban Policy & Research*, 15(3), pp 211–17

Crow, R. & Crow, M. 1970 *Plan for Melbourne Part 2*, Victorian State Committee of the Communist Party of Australia, Melbourne

——1972 *Plan for Melbourne Part 3*, Victorian State Committee of the Communist Party of Australia, Melbourne

Cullen, R.B. 1988 'The role of management consultancy in implementing change in public administration', unpublished seminar paper delivered to Melbourne University Public Policy Group, Melbourne

Cullingworth, J.B. 1964 *Town and Country Planning in Britain*, Allen & Unwin, London

Cumberland County Council 1948 *The Planning Scheme for the County of Cumberland, New South Wales*, The Government Printer, Sydney

Dahl, R.A. 1961 *Who Governs? Democracy and Power in an American City*, Yale University Press, New Haven, CN.

——1985 *A Preface to Economic Democracy*, University of California Press, Berkeley

Daly, H. 1996 *Beyond Growth: the economics of sustainable development*, Beacon Press, Boston

Daly, M.T. 1987 'Capital cities' *Australia: a geography Vol. 2: space and society*, ed. D.N. Jeans, Sydney University Press, Sydney

Daly, M.T., O'Connor, K. & Stimson, R.J. 1993 'The restructuring of space economies in Australian states and metropolitan cities' *Conference Papers, 13th Meeting of the Pacific Regional Science Conference Organisation*, Whistler, British Columbia

Davidoff, P. 1965 'Advocacy and pluralism in planning' *Journal of the American Institute of Planning*, 31, pp 331–8

Davidoff, P. & Reiner, T. 1962 'A choice theory of planning' *Journal of the American Institute of Planners*, 28, pp 103–15

Davidson, K. 1999 'Why our public hospitals are so sick', *The Age*, Melbourne, 6 September, p. 17

Davis, G., Wanna, J., Warhurst, J. & Weller, P. 1988 *Public Policy in Australia*, Allen & Unwin, Sydney

Davison, G. & Fincher, R. 1998 'Urban studies in Australia: a road map and the way ahead' *Urban Policy and Research*, 16(3), pp 183–97

Dawkins, J. 1996 'In praise of regulation' *Australian Planner*, 33(1), p. 11

Day, P.D. 1987a *Planning and Practice: selected Queensland papers*, University of Queensland, Department of Town and Regional Planning, Brisbane

——1987b 'The Korean Tower' *Queensland Planner*, 27(3), inserted page

Dear, M. 1986 'Postmodernism and planning' *Environment and Planning D: Society & Space*, 4, pp 367–84

Dear, M. & Scott, A.J. 1981 'Towards a framework for analysis' *Urbanization and Urban Planning in Capitalist Societies*, eds M. Dear & A.J. Scott, Methuen, London

Demsetz, H. 1995 *The Economics of the Business Firm: seven critical commentaries*, Cambridge University Press, Cambridge

Department of Infrastructure 1997 'Consultant brief for analysis of planning system under National Competition Policy', Department of Infrastructure, Melbourne

Department of Urban Affairs and Planning (DUAP) 1998 *Shaping Our Cities*, DUAP, Sydney

——1999 *Plan Making in NSW: opportunities for the future*, DUAP, Sydney

Donaldson, L. 1995 *American Anti-Management Theories of Organization: a critique of paradigm proliferation*, Cambridge University Press, Cambridge

Dore, J. 1997 'Local government change' *Australian Planner*, 34(3), pp 158–62

Douglas, R. 1993 *Unfinished Business*, Random House, Auckland

Doyal, L. & Gough, I. 1991 *A Theory of Human Need*, Macmillan, London

Dryzek, J. 1987 *Rational Ecology: environment and political economy*, Blackwell, Oxford

Dunleavy, P. & O'Leary, B. 1987 *Theories of the State: the politics of liberal democracy*, Macmillan, London

Dunn, K.M. 1993 'The Vietnamese concentration in Cabramatta: site of avoidance and deprivation, or island of adjustment and participation' *Australian Geographical Studies*, 31(2), pp 228–45

Dunn, K.M., McGuirk, P. & Winchester, H.P.M. 1995 'Place making: the social construction of Newcastle' *Australian Geographical Studies*, 33(2), pp 149–66

Dunstan, D. 1979 'The Parameters of Government' *Australian Journal of Public Administration*, 38(1) pp 13–22

Dunstan, K. 1998 'Battle to keep public open space at Royal Park warms up', *The Age*, News, p. 17

Eckersley, R. 1992 *Environmentalism and Political Theory: towards an ecocentric approach*, UCL Press, London

——1995 'Markets, the state and the environment: an overview' *Markets, the State and the Environment*, R. Eckersley ed. Macmillan, Melbourne

Ellis, P. 1990 'The role of state government: a Queensland perspective on economic growth, industry restructuring and development' *Australian Journal of Public Administration*, 49(3), pp 221–9

Ernst, J. 1997 'Public utility privatisation and competition: challenges to equity and environment' *Just Policy*, 9, pp 14–26

Ernst & Young 1999 *Review of the Planning and Land Management (PALM) Group*, Consultant's Report, Canberra

Evans, B. 1997 'From town planning to environmental planning' *Town Planning into the 21st Century*, eds A. Blowers & B. Evans, Routledge, London

Expert Group on the Urban Environment 1996 *European Sustainable Cities*, European Commission, Brussels

Fagan, R.H. & Webber, M. 1994 *Global Restructuring: the Australian experience*, Oxford University Press, Melbourne

Falk, J., Hampton, G., Hodgkinson, A., Parker, K. & Rorris, A. 1993 *Social Equity and the Urban Environment*, Australian Government Publishing Service, Canberra

Faludi, A. 1973 *Planning Theory*, Pergamon, Oxford

Fannin, P. 1998 'Third of nation's homeless bed down in Victoria: study' *The Age*, 2 March, p. A4

Fincher, R. 1998 'Planning for cities of difference' *Renewing Australian Planning? New challenges, new agendas*, eds B. Gleeson & P. Hanley, Urban Research Program, Australian National University, Canberra

Fincher, R. & Jacobs, J. eds 1998 *Cities of Difference*, Guilford, New York

Fincher, R. & Nieuwenhuysen, J. 1998 'Introduction' *Australian Poverty: then and now*, eds R. Fincher & J. Nieuwenhuysen, Melbourne University Press, Melbourne

Fincher, R. & Wulff, M. 1998 'The locations of poverty and disadvantage' *Australian Poverty: then and now*, eds R. Fincher & J. Nieuwenhuysen, Melbourne University Press, Melbourne

Flannery, T. 1994 *The Future Eaters: an ecological history of the Australasian lands and people*, Reed, Sydney

Forester, J. 1980 'Critical theory and planning' *Journal of the American Planning Association*, 46, pp 275–86

——1989 *Planning in the Face of Power*, University of California Press, Berkeley

Forster, C. 1995 *Australian Cities: continuity and change*, Oxford University Press, Melbourne

Forster, C. & McCaskill, M. 1986 'The modern period: managing metropolitan Adelaide' *With Conscious Purpose: a history of town planning in South Australia*, eds A. Hutchings & R. Bunker, Wakefield Press/RAPI, Adelaide

Foster, C. & Plowden, F. 1996 *The State Under Stress: can the hollow state be good government?*, Open University Press, Buckingham, UK

Foucault, M. 1991/1978 'Governmentality' *The Foucault Effect: studies in governmentality*, eds G. Burchell, C. Gordon & P. Miller, Harvester Wheatsheaf, London

Foulsham, J. 1992 'Women's needs and planning—a critical evaluation of recent local authority practice' *Radical Planning Initiatives*, eds J. Montgomery & A. Thornley, Gower, London

Freestone, R. 1993 'Heritage, urban planning, and the postmodern city' *Australian Geographer*, 24(1), pp 17–24

——1996 'The making of an Australian technoburb' *Australian Geographical Studies*, 34(1), pp 18–31

Freestone, R. & Murphy, P. 1993 'Review of a debate: edge city' *Urban Policy and Research*, 11(3), pp 184–90

——1998 'Metropolitan restructuring and suburban employment centers: cross-cultural perspectives on the Australian experience' *American Planning Association Journal*, 64(3), pp 286–97

Friedmann, J. 1987 *Planning in the Public Domain*, Princeton University Press, Princeton, NJ

——1992 *Empowerment: the politics of alternative development*, Blackwell, Oxford

Frost, L. 1990 *Australian Cities in Comparative View*, McPhee Gribble, Melbourne

Frost, L. & Dingle, T. 1995 'Sustaining suburbia: an historical perspective on Australia's growth' *Australian Cities: issues, strategies and policies for urban Australia in the 1990s*, ed. P. Troy, Cambridge University Press, Melbourne

Galbraith, J.K. 1971/1967 *The New Industrial State*, Houghton Mifflin, Boston

Gallop, G. 1984 'The Burke Labor government' *Canberra Bulletin of Public Administration*, 11, pp 219–30

——1986 'Western Australia' *Australian State Politics*, ed. B. Galligan, Longman Cheshire, Melbourne

——1997 'From government in business to business in government' *Canberra Bulletin of Public Administration*, 83

Gamble, A. 1988 *The Free Economy and the Strong State: the politics of Thatcherism*, Macmillan, Basingstoke, UK

Gans, H.J. 1968 *People and Plans: essays on urban problems and solutions*, Basic Books, New York

Garreau, J. 1991 *Edge City: life on the new frontier*, Doubleday, New York

Geddes, P. 1968/1915 *Cities in Evolution: an introduction to the town planning movement and to the study of civics*, Ernest Benn, London

Gibson, K. 1996 'Social polarisation and the politics of difference: discourses in collision or collusion?' *Restructuring Difference: social polarisation and the city*, eds N. Jamieson & M. Huxley, Australian Housing and Urban Research Institute, Working Paper 6, Melbourne

Gibson-Graham, J.K. 1996 *The End of Capitalism (as we knew it): a feminist critique of political economy*, Blackwell, Cambridge, MA

Gibson, R. 1997 'We owe it all to Kennett: casino chief' *The Age*, 5 May, p. 1

Gibson, K. & Watson, S. 1995 'Postmodern spaces, cities and politics: an introduction' *Postmodern Cities and Spaces*, eds S. Watson & K. Gibson, Blackwell, Oxford

Giddens, A. 1990 *The Consequences of Modernity*, Stanford University Press, Stanford, CA

Gittens, R. 1999 'Guilt pangs of a serious economist' *Sydney Morning Herald*, 5 May, p. 15

Gleeson, B.J. 1998 'The resurgence of spatial planning in Europe' *Urban Policy and Research*, 16(2), pp 219–25

——1999 *Geographies of Disability*, Routledge, London

Gleeson, B. & Hanley, P. eds (1998) *Renewing Australian Planning? New challenges, new agendas*, Urban Research Program, Australian National University, Canberra

Goodchild, B. 1990 'Planning and the modern/postmodern debate' *Town Planning Review*, 61(2), pp 119–37

Goodman, R. 1972 *After the Planners*, Penguin, Harmondsworth

Grabow, S. & Heskin, A. 1973 'Foundations for a radical concept of planning' *American Institute of Planners Journal*, March, pp 106–14

Graham, B. 1994 'Hobart: explosion without growth' *Urban Policy and Research*, 12(4), pp 264–70

Gray, J. 1998 *False Dawn: the delusions of global capitalism*, Granta, London

Gramsci, A. 1971 *Selections from the Prison Notebooks*, International Publishers, New York

Greed, C. 1994 *Women and Planning: creating gendered realities*, Routledge, London

Green, S. 1994 'The Brumby list of the Premier's 21 top cronies' *The Age*, 6 October, p. 2

Greenhouse Challenge 1997 *Cooperative Agreements: Loy Yang Power, Hazelwood Power, Yallourn Energy, Edison Mission Energy*, Greenhouse Challenge Office, Canberra

Gregory, B. 1996 'Wage deregulation, low paid workers and full employment' *Dialogues on Australia's Future: in honour of the late Professor Ronald Henderson*, eds, P.J. Sheehan, B.S. Grewal & M. Kumnick, Victoria University of Technology, Melbourne

Greiner, N. 1985 'Address to the 38th Annual Conference of the Australian Liberal Students Federation, 14th May' cited in *Reform and Reversal: lessons from the Coalition government in New South Wales 1988–1995*, eds M. Laffin & M. Painter (1995) Macmillan, Melbourne

——1994 'Interview' December, cited in *Reform and Reversal: lessons from the Coalition government in New South Wales 1988–1995*, eds M. Laffin & M. Painter (1995) Macmillan, Melbourne

Grimshaw, P., Lake, M., McGarth, A. & Quartly, M. eds 1994 *Creating a Nation, 1788–1900*, McPhee Gribble, Melbourne

Hall, T. 1998 *Urban Geography*, Routledge, London

Hamnett, S. 1997 'Brian McLoughlin: recollections from Australia' *European Planning Studies*, 5(6), 763–4

Hamnett, S. & Freestone, R. eds 2000 *The Australian Metropolis: a planning history*, Allen & Unwin, Sydney

Hamnett, S. & Lennon, M. 1997 'Urban governance and the competitive city: planning in the '90s in Adelaide, South Australia' South Australian Planning Papers, University of South Australia, Adelaide

——1998 'Metropolitan planning for Adelaide' *Beyond the Contract State—ideas for social and economic renewal in South Australia*, ed. J. Spoehr, Wakefield Press, Adelaide

Hamnett, S., Lennon, M., Bunker, R. & Hutchings, A. 1997 'South Australian planning in the 1990s' Planning Education Foundation of South Australia, working paper no. 6, University of South Australia, Adelaide

Hannan, E. 1999 'Auditor slams state secrecy' *The Age*, 27 May, p. 1

Hanson, F. 1993 'Land and Environment Court was ill conceived' *Queensland Planner*, 33(1), p. 9

Hardin, G. 1968 'The tragedy of the commons' *Science*, 162, pp 1243–8

Harman, E. 1988 'Capitalism, patriarchy and the city' *Women, Social Welfare and the State in Australia*, eds C.V. Baldock & B. Cass, Allen & Unwin, Sydney

Harrison, P. 1974 'Planning the metropolitan areas' *Urbanization in Australia: the post-war experience*, ed. I.H. Burnley, Cambridge University Press, Cambridge

Harvey, D. 1973 *Social Justice and the City*, Edward Arnold, London

——1978 'On planning the ideology of planning' *Planning Theory in the 1980s: a search for future directions*, eds R. Burchell & G. Sternlieb, Center for Urban Policy Research, Rutgers University, New Brunswick, NJ

——1982 *The Limits to Capital*, Blackwell, Oxford

——1985 *Consciousness and the Urban Experience*, Blackwell, Oxford

——1989 *The Condition of Postmodernity*, Blackwell, Oxford

——1996 *Justice, Nature and the Geography of Difference*, Blackwell, Oxford

Hass-Klau, C. 1990 'Public transport and integrated transport policies in large metropolitan areas of Europe' *The Planner*, 76(20), pp 13–20

Haughton, G. & Hunter, C. 1994 *Sustainable Cities*, Jessica Kingsley & Regional Studies Association, London & Bristol

Hayek, F.A. 1944 *The Road to Serfdom*, Dymock's Book Arcade, Sydney

Hayward, D. 1993 'Dual politics in a three tiered state' *Urban Policy and Research*, 11(3), pp 166–80

Healey, P. 1997 *Collaborative Planning: shaping places in fragmented societies*, Macmillan, Basingstoke

Heath, R. 1999 'If young people are unhappy then planners should ask why' *Sydney Morning Herald*, 3 May, p. 15

Hempel L.C. 1996 *Environmental Governance: the global challenge*, Island Press, Washington, DC

Hilmer, F. 1993 *National Competition Policy: report of the Independent Committee of Inquiry into Competition Policy in Australia*, Australian Government Publishing Service, Canberra

Hobsbawm, E. 1995 *Age of Extremes: the short history of the twentieth century, 1914–1991*, Abacus, London

Hoch, C. 1993 'Racism and planning' *American Planning Association Journal*, 59(4), pp 451–60

Hood, A. 1997 'The not-so-level playing field: reform of significant business activities of Queensland local governments' *Local Government Law Journal*, 3, pp 64–72

Horne, D. 1987 *The Lucky Country Revisited*, Dent, Melbourne

Housing Industry Association (HIA) 1999 *Planning a National Approach to Development*, conference brochure, HIA, Sydney

Howard, E. 1946/1898 *Garden Cities of Tomorrow*, being the second edition of *Tomorrow: a peaceful path to real reform*, Faber & Faber, London, first published as *Tomorrow: a peaceful path to social reform*

Hunter, B. 1996 'Indigenous Australians and the socioeconomic status of urban neighbourhoods', Australian National University, Centre for Aboriginal Economic Policy Research, Canberra

Hunter, B. & Gregory, R.G. 1995 'The macro economy and the growth of ghettos and urban poverty in Australia', Discussion Paper no. 325, Centre for Economic Policy Research, Australian National University, Canberra

——1996 'An Exploration of the relationship between changing inequality of individual, household and regional inequality in Australian cities' *Urban Policy and Research*, 14(3), pp 171–82

Hunter, F. 1953 *Community Power Structure: a study of decision-makers*, University of North Carolina Press, Chapel Hill, NC

Huxley, M. 1994 'Planning as a framework of power: utilitarian reform, enlightenment logic and the control of urban space' *Beasts of Suburbia: reinterpreting cultures in Australian suburbs*, eds S. Ferber, C. Healy & C. McAuliffe, Melbourne University Press, Melbourne

Industry Commission 1995 *Implementing the National Competition Policy: access and price regulation*, Australian Government Publishing Service, Canberra

——1996 *State, Territory and Local Government Assistance to Industry*, Australian Government Publishing Service, Canberra

Innes, J. 1995 'Planning's emerging paradigm: communicative action and interactive practice' *Journal of Planning Education and Research*, 14(3), pp 183–90

International Union for the Conservation of Nature and Natural Resources (IUCN) 1980 *World Conservation Strategy*, Gland (Switzerland)

Iveson, K. 1998 'Putting the public back into public space' *Urban Policy and Research*, 16(1), pp 21–33

Jackson, K.T. 1985 *Crabgrass Frontier: the suburbanization of the United States*, Oxford University Press, New York

Jackson, S. 1997 'A disturbing story: the fiction of rationality in land use planning in Aboriginal Australia' *Australian Planner*, 34(4), pp 221–6

Jacobs, H.M. 1995 'Contemporary environmental philosophy and its challenge to planning theory' in *Planning Ethics: a reader in planning theory, practice and education*, ed. S. Hendler, Center for Urban Policy Research, Rutgers University, pp 83–103

Jacobs, J. 1961 *The Death and Life of Great American Cities*, Vintage Books, New York

Jakubowicz, A. 1984 'The Green Ban movement: urban struggle and class politics' *Australian Urban Politics*, eds J. Halligan & C. Paris, Longman Cheshire, Melbourne

Jary, D. & Jary, J. 1991 *Dictionary of Sociology*, HarperCollins, London

Johnston, D. 1995 'Hospital debt crisis' *Herald Sun*, 31 May, p. 7

Johnston, R.J., Gregory, D. & Smith, D.M. eds 1994 *The Dictionary of Human Geography*, 3rd edn, Blackwell, Oxford

Jones, M.A. 1983 *The Australian Welfare State: growth, crisis and change*, Allen & Unwin, Sydney

Keeble, L. 1983 *Town Planning Made Plain*, Construction Press, London

Kellow, A 1995 'The Environment' *Reform and Reversal: lessons from the coalition government in New South Wales 1988–1995*, eds M. Laffin & M. Painter Macmillan, Melbourne

Kelly, P. 1992 *The End of Certainty: the story of the 1980s*, Allen & Unwin, Sydney

Kendig, H. 1997 'Ageing and the built environment', paper presented to conference on 'Equity, Environment, Efficiency: Urban Australia. Celebration of Max Neutze's contribution to Australia', Urban Research Program, Australian National University, Canberra, 8–10 December

Kenny, C. 1993 *State of Denial: the government, the media, the bank*, Wakefield Press, Kent Town, SA

Keynes, J.M. 1931/1926 *Essays in Persuasion*, Macmillan, London

Kilmartin, L. & Thorns, D.C. 1978 *Cities Unlimited: the sociology of urban development in Australia and New Zealand*, George Allen & Unwin, Sydney

Kilmartin, L., Thorns, D. & Burke, T. 1985 *Social Theory and the Australian City*, George Allen & Unwin, Sydney

King, A. 1997 'The changing face of Australian poverty: a comparison of 1996 estimates and the 1972–73 findings from the Commission of Inquiry', NATSEM Discussion Paper no. 23, Canberra

——1998 'Income poverty since the early 1970s' *Australian Poverty: then and now*, eds R. Fincher & J. Nieuwenhuysen, Melbourne University Press, Melbourne

Kirner, J. 1988 'Address to the Regional Office Staff of the Ministry of Education, Geelong' detail quoted in *The Age*, 7 November

Kirwan, R. 1992 'Urban form, energy and transport: a note on the Newman-Kenworthy thesis' *Urban Policy and Research*, 10(1), pp 6–23

Laffin, M. 1995 'The public service' *Reform and Reversal: lessons from the Coalition government in New South Wales 1988–1995*, eds M. Laffin & M. Painter Macmillan, Melbourne

Laffin, M. & Painter, M. 1995 'Introduction' *Reform and Reversal: lessons from the Coalition government in New South Wales 1988–1995*, eds M. Laffin & M. Painter, Macmillan, Melbourne

Lagan, B. 1999 'Murder most bizarre' *Sydney Morning Herald*, 29 May, New Review section, p. 39

Lal, D. 1998 'From planning to regulation: towards a new dirigisme?' *Australian Competition Policy: deregulation or reregulation?*, eds D. Lal, A. Moran, D. Briggs, R. Scheelings, A. Fels & P. Allport, Institute of Public Affairs, Melbourne

Lane, M. 1997 'Aboriginal participation in environmental planning' *Australian Geographical Studies*, 35(3), pp 308–23

Larritt, C. 1996 'Victoria on the move, move, move' *Putting the People Last: government, services and rights in Victoria*, eds M. Webber & M. Crooks, Hyland House, Melbourne

Lawrence, D.H. 1923 *Kangaroo*, Thomas Seltzer, New York

Leavitt, J. 1981 'The history, status and concerns of women planners' *Women and the American City*, eds C. Stimpson, E. Dixler, M. Nelson & K. Yatrakis, University of Chicago Press, Chicago

Lindblom, C.E. 1959 'The science of muddling through' *Public Administration Review*, Spring, Reprinted in A. Faludi (1973) *Readings in Planning Theory*, Pergamon, Oxford.

——1968 *The Policy-Making Process*, Prentice-Hall, Englewood Cliffs, NJ

Lindblom, C.E. & Cohen, D.K. 1979 *Usable Knowledge, Social Science and Social Problem Solving*, Yale University Press, New Haven & London

Little, J. 1994 *Gender, Planning and the Policy Process*, Pergamon, Oxford

Little, F., Morozow, O., Rawlings, S.W. and Walker, J.R. 1974 *Social Dysfunction and Relative Poverty in Metropolitan Melbourne*, Melbourne Metropolitan Board of Works, Melbourne

Llewelyn-Davies, R., Weeks, J., Forestier-Walker, J. & Bor, W. 1977 *Unequal City, Final Report of the Birmingham Inner Area Study*, HMSO, London

Lloyd, C.J. & Troy, P.N. 1981 *Innovation and Reaction: the life and death of the Department of Urban and Regional Development*, Allen & Unwin, Sydney

Long, S. 1999 'For richer, for poorer' *The Australian*, Weekend 9–10 January, pp 21–3

Low, N.P. 1991 *Planning, Politics and the State*, Unwin-Hyman, London

——1995 'Regulation theory, global competition among cities and capital embeddedness' *Urban Policy and Research*, 13(4), pp 205–22

Low, N.P. & Gleeson, B.J. 1998 *Justice, Society and Nature: an exploration of political ecology*, Routledge, London

Low, N.P., Gleeson, B.J., Elander, I. & Lidskog, R. eds 1999 *Consuming Cities: the urban environment in the global economy after the Rio Declaration*, Routledge, London

Luscombe, L.H. ('Veritas') 1945 *Australia Replanned*, Ruskin Press, Melbourne

McConnell, G. 1967 *Private Power and American Democracy*, Alfred Knopf, New York

McConnell, S. 1981 *Theories for Planning*, Heinemann, London

McDermott, J. 1991 *Corporate Society: class, property and contemporary capitalism*, Westview Press, Boulder, CO

McDonald, P. & Matches, G. 1995 *Places for Everyone: social equity in Australian cities and regions*, Australian Urban and Regional Development Review, Research Report no. 1, Department of Housing and Regional Development, Canberra

McGregor, C. 1999 'The great divide' *Sydney Morning Herald*, Spectrum, 27 February, pp 1, 6

McInerney, J. 1998 'Local government planning and legislative reform' *Australian Planner*, 35(3), pp 143–6

McKay, H. 1993 *Reinventing Australia: the mind and mood of Australia in the 90s*, Angus & Robertson, Sydney

McLoughlin, J.B. 1969 *Urban and Regional Planning: a systems approach*, Faber & Faber, London

——1984 'Studying planning in practice: an expedition to an academic outback' *Australian Planner*, 25, pp 3–12

——1987 'The origins and evolution of the Royal Australian Planning Institute' *The Planner*, 26, pp 14–18

——1991 'Urban consolidation and urban sprawl: a question of density' *Urban Policy and Research*, 9(3), pp 148–56

——1992 *Shaping Melbourne's Future? Town planning, the state and civil society*, Cambridge University Press, Melbourne

——1994 'Centre or periphery? Town planning and spatial political economy' *Environment and Planning A*, 26, pp 1111–22

McLoughlin, J.B. & Huxley, M. eds 1986 *Urban Planning in Australia: critical readings*, Longman Cheshire, Melbourne

Maher, C. 1994 'Residential mobility, locational disadvantage and spatial inequality in Australian cities' *Urban Policy and Research*, 12(3), pp 185–91

Maher, C., Whitelaw, J., McAllister, A., Francis, R., Palmer, J., Chee, E. & Taylor, P. 1992 *Mobility and Locational Disadvantage within Australian Cities: social justice implications of household relocation*, Australian Government Publishing Service, Canberra

Mahony, S. 1997 'Microeconomic reform meets land use planning—National Competition Policy and the privatisation of land use decisions', unpublished paper supplied by author

Mannheim, K. 1951 *Freedom, Power and Democratic Planning*, Oxford University Press, Oxford

Manning, P. & Hardman, M. 1975 *Green Bans*, Australian Conservation Foundation, Melbourne

Mant, J. 1978 'South Australia' *Urban Management Processes*, ed. P.F. Ryan, Australian National Commission for UNESCO, Canberra (proceedings of seminar held in Adelaide, 22–25 August 1977)

Marginson, S. 1994 'Government and schooling in Victoria', unpublished paper, available from the author at the Centre for the Study of Higher Education, University of Melbourne, Melbourne

Marsh, J. 1998 'Mosque ban anger grows' *Sydney Morning Herald*, 30 October, p. 5

Marx, K. 1976/1846 '*The German Ideology*' in *Collected Works, Vol. 5*, Lawrence & Wishart, London

Marx, K. 1976/1867 *Capital, Vol. 1*, Penguin, Harmondsworth

Maser, S.M., Riker, W.H. & Rosett, R.N. 1977 'The effects of zoning and externalities on the price of land: an empirical analysis of Monroe County, New York' *Journal of Law and Economics*, 20, pp 111–32

Maximiles Consulting 1997a 'Planning Systems Performance Review', discussion paper no. 1, Maximiles Consulting, PO Box 320, Stepney, SA

——1997b 'Planning Systems Performance Review', discussion paper no. 2, Maximiles Consulting, PO Box 320, Stepney, SA

——1997c 'Planning Systems Performance Review', discussion paper no. 3, Maximiles Consulting, PO Box 320, Stepney, SA

Mees, P. 1998 'The malling of Melbourne?', unpublished paper, Faculty of Architecture, Building and Planning, University of Melbourne, Melbourne

Melbourne Bid 1997 *Melbourne 2006 Commonwealth Games Bid*, Information Package (pages not sequentially numbered) Melbourne 2006 Commonwealth Games Bid, Melbourne

Melbourne and Metropolitan Board of Works (MMBW) 1981 *Metropolitan Strategy Implementation*, MMBW, Melbourne

Memon, P.A. & Gleeson, B.J. 1994 'Reforming planning legislation: a New Zealand perspective' *Urban Policy and Research*, 12(2), pp 82–9

Mills, C.W. 1956 *The Power Elite*, Oxford University Press, Oxford

Milner, A. 1993 *Cultural Materialism*, Melbourne University Press, Melbourne

Ministry of Housing and Local Government (UK) 1969 *People and Planning: Report of the Committee on Public Participation in Planning*, HMSO, London (The Skeffington Report)

Modern Melbourne Committee 1969 *Plan for Melbourne Part 1*, Victorian State Committee of the Communist Party of Australia, Melbourne

Mollenkopf, J.H. 1983 *The Contested City*, Princeton University Press, Princeton, NJ

Molotch, H. 1976 'The city as a growth machine: toward a political economy of place' *American Journal of Sociology*, 82(2), pp 309–32

Moon, B. 1995 'The SEQ 2001 Project is DEAD: long live vested interest!' *Queensland Planner*, 35(3), pp 24–9

——1998a 'Reforming the Queensland land-use planning legislation' *Australian Planner*, 35(1), pp 24–31

——1998b 'Privatising the land-use debate' *Queensland Planner*, 38(1), pp 18–19

Moore, B. 1978 'Administrative Chronicle: New South Wales' *Australian Journal of Public Administration*, 37(2), pp 189–90

Moore, D. 1993 'Reversing the rorts: shifting jobs and services to the private sector' *The Australian Rationalist*, 35, pp 7–17

Moriarty, P. 1998 'Inequality in Australian cities' *Urban Policy and Research*, 16(3), pp 211–8

Moriarty, P. & Beed, C. 1991 'Equity, transport and greenhouse' *Urban Policy and Research*, 9(3), pp 141–7

Morris, L. 1999 'Flight of the battlers' *Sydney Morning Herald*, Spectrum, 22 May, pp 1, 4

Moser, S.T. & Low, N.P. 1986 'The central business district of Melbourne and the dispersal and reconcentration of capital' *Environment and Planning A*, 18, pp 1447–61

Mowbray, M. 1994 'Wealth, welfare and the city: developments in Australian urban policy' *Urban Policy and Research*, 12(2), pp 91–103

Mowbray, M. & Stubbs, J. 1996 'Manufactured home estates: extended housing options or benchmarking cities?' *Urban Policy and Research*, 14(2), pp 129–43

Munro, A. 1993 'Reinventing planning: an overview of the women and planning conference' *Urban Futures*, 3(3), pp 62–3

Mullins, P. 1995 'Households, Consumerism and Metropolitan Development' ed. P. Troy, *Australian Cities: issues, strategies and policies for urban Australia in the 1990s*, Cambridge University Press, Melbourne

Murphy, P.A. & Watson, S. 1997 *Surface City: Sydney at the millennium*, Pluto, Sydney

Murphy, P.A. & Wu, C.-T. 1998 'Governing global Sydney: from managerialism to entrepreneurialism', conference paper presented at the 'Intercity Networks' meeting, Taipei, April 1998

Myer, R. 1999 'Gravy Train Worth $419 Million' *The Age*, 29 May, Business, p. 1

Nader, R. 1999 'Open Letter to Mr W.H. Gates', published on the Internet by Third World Network

National Housing Strategy 1991 *Australian Housing: the demographic, economic and social environment*, Australian Government Publishing Service, Canberra

——1992 *Housing Location and Access to Services*, Australian Government Publishing Service, Canberra

National Population Inquiry 1975 *Population and Australia: a demographic analysis and projection*, Australian Government Publishing Service, Canberra

Neilson, L.R. 1997 'Improving the financing of metropolitan areas', paper presented to OECD/Sweden workshop 'Governing metropolitan areas: institutions, finance and partnerships', copy available from author, Centre for Developing Cities, University of Canberra, ACT, 2601

Neutze, M. 1977 *Urban Development in Australia*, George Allen & Unwin, Sydney

——1978 *Australian Urban Policy*, George Allen & Unwin, Sydney

——1997 *Funding Urban Services: options for physical infrastructure*, Allen & Unwin, Sydney

NSW (New South Wales) Government 1997 *Local Government Amendment (Ecologically Sustainable Development) Act 1997*, Department of Local Government Circular to Councils 97/75, Government Printer, Sydney

——1998 *Environmental Guidelines: State of the Environment Reporting by Local Government Promoting Ecologically Sustainable Development*, Department of Local Government Circular to Councils 98/29, Government Printer, Sydney

Newman, P. 1992 'The compact city: an Australian perspective' *Built Environment*, 18(4), pp 285–300

——1997 'Greening the city: the ecological and human dimensions of the city can be part of town planning' *Eco-City: healthy communities, healthy planet*, ed. M. Roseland, New Society, Gabriola Island, BC

Newman, P. & Kenworthy, J.R. 1980 'Public and private transport in Australian cities: I. an analysis of existing patterns and their energy implications' *Transport Policy and Decision Making*, 1, pp 133–48

——1989 *Cities and Automobile Dependence: an international sourcebook*, Gower Technical, Aldershot, Hants

——1992 *Winning Back the Cities*, Australian Consumers' Association/Pluto Press, Sydney

Nicholls, B. 1994 'Victoria' *Metropolitan Planning in Australia*, ed. The National Capital Planning Authority, Australian Urban and Regional Development Review, Workshop Papers no. 3, Canberra

Nijkamp, P. & Perrels, A. 1994 *Sustainable Cities in Europe: a comparative analysis of urban energy-environmental policies*, Earthscan Publications, London

Nillumbik Shire 1997 *Municipal Strategic Statement*, Shire of Nillumbik, Melbourne

Nozick, R. 1974 *Anarchy, State and Utopia*, Blackwell, Oxford

O'Brien, P. 1991 'WA Incorporated and the origins and development of West [sic] Australia's Executive State' *The Executive State: WA Inc and the Constitution*, eds P. O.'Brien & M. Webb, Constitutional Press, Perth

O'Connor, M. ed. 1994 *Is Capitalism Sustainable? Political economy and political ecology*, Guilford Press, New York

O'Connor, K.B. & Stimson, R.J. 1995 *The Economic Role of Cities, Economic Change and City Development 1971–1991*, Urban Futures Research Program, Australian Government Publishing Service, Canberra

O'Connor, K.B., Stimson, R.J. & Taylor, S.P. 1998 'Convergence and divergence in the Australian space economy' *Australian Geographical Studies*, 36(2), pp 205–22

Orchard, L. 1992 'Urban Policy' *The Bannon Decade: the politics of restraint in South Australia*, eds A. Parkin & A. Patience, Allen & Unwin, Sydney

——1995 'National urban policy in the 1990s' *Australian Cities: issues, strategies and policies for urban Australia in the 1990s*, ed. P. Troy, Cambridge University Press, Melbourne

Osborne, D. & Gaebler, T. 1993 *Reinventing Government: how the entrepreneurial spirit is transforming the public sector*, Plume, New York

Page, B. 1995 'Political Chronicles: New South Wales' *Australian Journal of Politics and History*, 41(3), pp 449–54

Painter, M. 1987 *Steering the Modern State: Changes in central coordination in three Australian state governments*, Sydney University Press, Sydney

——1995 'Microeconomic reform and the public sector' *Reform and Reversal: lessons from the Coalition government in New South Wales 1988–1995*, eds M. Laffin & M. Painter, Macmillan, South Melbourne

Papadakis, E. 1993 *Politics and the Environment: the Australian experience*, Allen & Unwin, Sydney

Paris, C. ed. 1982 *Critical Readings in Planning Theory*, Pergamon, Oxford

Paris, C. & Williams, P. 1986 'Planning, urban crisis and urban management' *Urban Planning in Australia: critical readings*, eds J.B. McLoughlin & M. Huxley, Longman Cheshire, Melbourne

Parker, R.S. & Troy, P.N. eds 1972 *The Politics of Urban Growth*, Australian National University Press, Canberra

Parkin, A. 1995 'Political chronicles: South Australia' *Australian Journal of Politics and History*, 41(3), pp 465–72

Parkin, A. & Patience, A. eds 1992 *The Bannon Decade: the politics of restraint in South Australia*, Allen & Unwin, Sydney

Parkin, A. & Pugh, C. 1981 'Urban policy and metropolitan Adelaide' *The Dunstan Decade: social democracy at the state level*, eds A. Parkin & A. Patience, Longman Cheshire, Melbourne

Paterson, J. 1976 'The changing nature of planning: from Philosopher King to Municipal Dog Catcher', plenary paper delivered at the Fourteenth Biennial Congress of the Royal Australian Planning Institute, Adelaide, 15–19 August

——1977 'Urban Management: the Australian context' *Urban Management Processes*, ed. P.F. Ryan, Proceedings of the seminar held in Adelaide, 22–25 August, Australian National Commission for UNESCO, Australian Government Publishing Service, pp 7–14

——1988 'A managerialist strikes back' *Australian Journal of Public Administration*, 47(4), reprinted in *Managerialism, The Great Debate*, eds M. Considine & M. Painter (1997) Melbourne University Press, Melbourne

——1993 'Beyond case payments: a new paradigm for Australian health and welfare', Speech: October, reported in J. Thwaites & A. Refshauge, 'Competition and Health Care' *Putting the People Last, Government, services and rights in Victoria*, eds M. Webber & M. Crooks (1996) Hyland House, South Melbourne

Paterson, J.P., Yencken, D. & Gunn, G. 1976 *A mansion or no house: a report for UDIA on consequences of planning standards and their impact on land and housing*, Urban Development Institute of Australia (Victoria), Melbourne

Peattie, L. 1968 'Reflections on advocacy planning' *Journal of the American Institute of Planners*, 34, pp 80–8

Peel, M. 1995 'The urban debate: from "Los Angeles" to the urban village' *Australian Cities: issues, strategies and policies for urban Australia in the 1990s*, ed. P. Troy, Cambridge University Press, Melbourne

Pennington, M. 1999 'Free market environmentalism and the limits of land use planning' *Journal of Environmental Policy & Planning*, 1(1), pp 43–59

Pepper, D. 1993 *Eco-socialism: from deep ecology to social justice*, Routledge, London

Plumwood, V. 1999 'Ecological ethics from rights to recognition: multiple spheres of justice for humans, animals, and nature' *Global Ethics and Environment*, ed. N.P. Low, Routledge, London

Polanyi, K. 1975/1944 *The Great Transformation*, Octagon Books; Farrar, Strauss & Giroux, New York

Prime Minister's Urban Design Task Force 1994 *Urban Design in Australia*, Australian Government Publishing Service, Canberra

Property Council of Australia (formerly Building Owners' and Managers' Association

(BOMA)) 1996a *Planning for Change: recommendations for Australia's development systems*, BOMA, Sydney

——1996b *States of Progress: an audit of planning and development control legislation in Australia's states and territories*, BOMA, Sydney

——1997 *Unfinished Business: prospects for an intergovernmental agreement on development control*, PCA, Sydney

Public Transport Users' Association of Victoria 1995 *Wrong Way, Go Back: the alternative to Melbourne's freeway explosion*, 247 Flinders Lane, Melbourne, VIC 3000

Pusey, M. 1991 *Economic Rationalism in Canberra: a nation-building state changes its mind*, Cambridge University Press, New York

Putnam, R. 1993 *Making Democracy Work*, Princeton University Press, Princeton, NJ

Rabinowitz, F. 1969 *City Politics and Planning*, Atherton Press, New York

Radbone, I. 1992 'Public sector management' *The Bannon Decade: the politics of restraint in South Australia*, eds A. Parkin & A. Patience, Allen & Unwin, Sydney

Rawls, J. 1971 *A Theory of Justice*, Harvard University Press, Cambridge, MA

Reade, E. 1987 *British Town and Country Planning*, Open University Press, Milton Keynes

Rhodes, R.A.W. 1996 'The new governance: governing without government' *Political Studies*, 44(4), pp 652–67

Rittel, H.J.W. & Webber, M.M. 1973 'Dilemmas in a general theory of planning' *Policy Sciences*, 4, pp 155–69

Roberts, G. 1999 '"Tacky" Gold Coast loses its holiday lustre' *Sydney Morning Herald*, 8 May, p. 15

Robertson, D. 1986 *The Penguin Dictionary of Politics*, Penguin, London

Robinson, K. 1993 'Blood out of a stone? Community involvement in new regional planning mechanisms in Queensland' *Queensland Planner*, 33(1), pp 13–16

Rose, R. 1979 'Ungovernability: is there fire behind the smoke?' *Studies in Public Policy*, 16, Centre for Policy Studies, University of Strathclyde, UK

Roseland, M. ed. 1997 *Eco-City: healthy communities, healthy planet*, New Society, Gabriola Island, BC

Rothbard, M.N. 1973 *For a New Liberty*, Macmillan, New York

Roweis, S.T. 1981 'Urban planning in early and late capitalist societies: outline of a theoretical perspective' *Urbanization and Urban Planning in Capitalist Society*, eds M. Dear & A.J. Scott, Methuen, New York

Royal Australian Planning Institute (RAPI) 1997 'Memorandum to all National Councillors and Division Presidents', prepared by E. Wensing, 19 May, RAPI, Canberra

Russell, B. in collaboration with Dora Russell 1923 *The Prospects of Industrial Civilization*, George Allen & Unwin, London

Saegert, S. 1981 'Masculine cities and feminine suburbs: polarized ideas, contradictory realities' *Women and the American City*, eds C. Stimpson, E. Dixler, M. Nelson & K. Yatrakis, University of Chicago Press, Chicago

Sandercock, L. 1977 *Cities for Sale: property, politics and urban planning in Australia*, Melbourne University Press, Melbourne

——1979 *The Land Racket: the real costs of property speculation*, Silverfish, Canberra

——1983 'Educating planners: from physical determinism to economic crisis' *Urban Political Economy: the Australian case*, eds L. Sandercock & M. Berry, George Allen & Unwin, Sydney

——1998 *Towards Cosmopolis: planning for multicultural cities*, Wiley, Chichester, UK

Sandercock, L. & Berry, M. 1983 *Urban political economy: the Australian case*, George Allen & Unwin, Sydney

Sandercock, L. & Forsyth, A. 1992 'A gender agenda: new directions for planning theory' *American Planning Association Journal*, 58(1), pp 49–59

Sarkissian, W. 1976 'Planning as if women mattered: the story of Brown Hills' *Makara*, 3(3), pp 9–12

Sarkissian, W. & Sidhu, M. 1993 'Brown Hills revisited' *Urban Futures*, 3(3), pp 6–7

Schumpeter, J.A. 1943 *Capitalism, Socialism and Democracy*, Allen & Unwin, London

Scott, A.J. & Roweis, S.T. 1977 'Urban planning in theory and practice: a reappraisal' *Environment and Planning A*, 9, pp 1097–119

Scott, G.M. 1992 'Economic policy' *The Bannon Decade: the politics of restraint in South Australia*, eds A. Parkin & A. Patience, Allen & Unwin, Sydney

Seebohm, K. 1992 'Contested terrain in the urban landscape: homosexual space in inner-city Sydney', paper delivered at the Inaugural Joint Conference New Zealand Geographical Society and Institute of Australian Geographers, University of Auckland, 27–31 January, Auckland

Self, P. 1993 *Government by the market? The politics of public choice*, Macmillan, Basingstoke, UK

——1995 'Alternative urban policies: the case for regional development' *Australian Cities: issues, strategies and policies for urban Australia in the 1990s*, ed. P. Troy, Cambridge University Press, Melbourne

——1998 'Democratic planning' *Renewing Australian Planning? New challenges, new agendas*, eds B. Gleeson & P. Hanley, Urban Research Program, Australian National University, Canberra

——1999 *Rolling Back the Market: economic dogma and political choice*, Macmillan, Basingstoke, UK

Shields, R. 1989 'Social spatialization and the built environment: the West Edmonton Mall' *Environment and Planning D: Society and Space*, 7(2), pp 147–64

Sibley, D. 1995 *Geographies of Exclusion: society and difference in the West*, Routledge, London

Simmie, J. 1974 *Citizens in Conflict: the sociology of town planning*, Hutchinson, London

Smerdon, H. 1992 'The Queensland Agenda for Reform' *Public Sector Reform under the First Goss Government*, ed. G. Davis, Royal Institute of Public Administration (Queensland Division) and Centre for Australian Public Sector Management, Griffith University

Socialist Alternative Melbourne Collective 1985 *Make Melbourne Marvellous! A draft for wide discussion on socialist alternative Melbourne 2000*, Communist Party of Australia, Melbourne

Solomon, I. 1998 'Turn back: more infrastructure disasters ahead' *The Age*, 22 October, p. 15

Sorenson, A. & Day, R. 1981 'Libertarian planning' *Town Planning Review*, 52, pp 390–402

Soule, G. 1933 *A Planned Society*, Macmillan, New York

Spearitt, P. 1995 'Suburban cathedrals: the rise of the drive-in shopping centre' *The Cream Brick Frontier: histories of Australian suburbia*, ed. G. Davison, Monash University Publications in History no. 19, Melbourne

Spearitt, P. & DeMarco, C. 1988 *Planning Sydney's Future*, Allen & Unwin, Sydney

Spiller, M. 1999 'From victim to vanguard, the remaking of regional planning in Australia', paper delivered to Royal Australian Planning Conference, Darwin, 19–22 September

Steering Committee for the Review of Commonwealth/State Service Provision 1998 *Report on Government Services, vol. 1*, Industry Commission, Melbourne

Stein, P. 1998 '21st century challenges for urban planning: the demise of environmental planning in New South Wales' *Renewing Australian Planning? New challenges, new agendas*, eds B. Gleeson & P. Hanley, Urban Research Program, Australian National University, Canberra

Stephenson, G. 1995 *Compassionate Town Planning*, Liverpool University Press, Liverpool

Stilwell, F. 1974 *Australian Urban and Regional Development*, Australia & New Zealand Book Co., Sydney

——1980 *The Impact of the Current Economic Crisis on Cities and Regions*, Mitchell College of Advanced Education, Bathurst

——1993a *Reshaping Australia: urban problems and policies*, Pluto Press, Sydney

——1993b 'Economic rationalism: sound foundations for policy?' *Beyond the Market: alternatives to economic rationalism*, eds S. Rees, G. Rodley & F. Stilwell, Pluto Press, Sydney

——1997 'Globalisation and cities: an Australian political-economic perspective', Urban Research Program Working Paper no. 59, Australian National University, Canberra

——1999 'Land, inequality and regional policy' *Urban Policy and Research*, 17(1) pp 17–24

Stimson, R., Shuaib, F. & O'Connor, K. 1998 'Population and employment "hot spots" and "cold spots" in the Australian space economy, 1986 to 1996', paper presented to ANZRSAI Annual Conference, Tanunda, South Australia, pp 21–3, September

Stone, B. 1997 'Taking 'WA Inc' seriously: an analysis of the idea and its application to West Australian politics' *Australian Journal of Public Administration*, 56(1), pp 71–81

Stretton, H. 1970 *Ideas for Australian Cities*, Georgian House, Melbourne

——1976 *Capitalism, Socialism and the Environment*, Cambridge University Press, Cambridge

——1977 'Business and government' *Australian Journal of Public Administration*, 36(1), pp 64–74

——1987 *Political Essays*, Georgian House, Melbourne

Stull, W.J. 1975 'Community environment, zoning, and the market value of single-family homes' *Journal of Law and Economics*, 18, pp 535–57

Sykes, T. 1993 'How the banks lost $28 billion' *Australian Business Monthly*, October

Tawney, R.H. 1981/1944 'We mean freedom' *The Attack and Other Papers*, Spokesman Press, Nottingham, UK

Thomas, H. 1994 'The New Right: "race" and planning in Britain in the 1980s and 1990s' *Planning Practice and Research*, 9(4), pp 353–66

Thomas, H. & Krishnarayan, V. 1994 '"Race", disadvantage, and policy processes in British planning' *Environment and Planning A*, 26, pp 1891–910

Thompson, D. 1986 *Flaws in the Social Fabric: homosexuals and society in Sydney*, Allen & Unwin, Sydney

Thompson, E., Painter, M., Wheelwright, T. & Mutch, S. 1986 'New South Wales' *Australian State Politics*, ed. B. Galligan, Longman Cheshire, Melbourne

Town and Country Planning Association of Victoria (TCPA) 1997 *A Charter for Planning*, TCPA, Melbourne

Troy, P. 1978 *A Fair Price: the Land Commission Program 1972–1977*, Hale & Iremonger, Sydney

——1981 ed. *Equity in the City*, George Allen & Unwin, Sydney

——1995 'Introduction' ed. P. Troy, *Australian Cities: issues, strategies and policies for urban Australia in the 1990s*, Cambridge University Press, Melbourne

——1996a 'Introductory remarks' *The End of Public Housing?*, ed. R. Coles, Urban Research Program, Australian National University, Canberra

——1996b *The Perils of Urban Consolidation*, The Federation Press, Sydney

——1998 'Lowering the standard', unpublished paper, Urban Research Program, Australian National University, Canberra

——1999 'Urban institutions' *Serving the City*, ed. P. Troy, Pluto Press, Sydney

Tullock, I. 1995 'Political Chronicles: Victoria' *Australian Journal of Politics and History*, 41(3), pp 454–60

——1996 'Political Chronicles, Victoria' *Australian Journal of Politics and History*, 42(3), pp 415–19

van der Pijl, K. 1998 *Transnational Classes and International Relations*, Routledge, London

Vann, G. 1991 'President's message: the 1990s—a decade for planning?' *Queensland Planner*, 31(3), p. 2

Victoria, Government 1993a *Towards Prosperity*, Government Printer, Melbourne

——1993b *Agenda 21: Foreword*, Government Printer, Melbourne

——1994 *Creating Prosperity*, Government Printer, Melbourne

——1995 *Living Suburbs: a policy for metropolitan Melbourne into the 21st century*, Department of Infrastructure, Melbourne

Vuchic, V. 1981 *Urban Public Transportation: systems and technology*, Prentice-Hall, Englewood Cliffs, NJ

Wackernagel, M. & Rees, W.E. 1996 *Our Ecological Footprint: reducing human impact on the earth*, New Society Publishers, Gabriola Island, BC

Walker, D. 1995 'Victorians should use more electricity, says US Buyer' *The Age*, 7 November, p. 3

Walker, R.G. 1995 'State finances and financial management' *Reform and Reversal: lessons from the Coalition government in New South Wales 1988–1995*, eds M. Laffin & M. Painter, Macmillan, Melbourne

Walmsley, D.J. & Weinand, H.C. 1997 'Is Australia becoming more unequal?' *Australian Geographer*, 28(1), pp 69–88

Wanna, J. & Weller, P. 1995 'Structuring influence: executive governance at the local level' *Power and Politics in the City: Brisbane in transition*, eds J. Caulfield & J. Wanna, Macmillan, Melbourne

Waring, M. 1988 *If Women Counted: a new feminist economics*, Macmillan, London

Warner, S.B. 1966 *Planning for a Nation of Cities*, MIT Press, Cambridge, MA

Waste, R.J. 1987 *Power and Pluralism in American Cities: researching the urban laboratory*, Greenwood Press, New York

Watson, S. 1993 'Work and leisure in tomorrow's cities' *Beyond the Market: alternatives to economic rationalism*, eds S. Rees, G. Rodley & F. Stilwell, Pluto Press, Sydney

Watson, S. & Gibson, K. 1995 'Postmodern politics and planning: a postscript' *Postmodern Cities and Spaces*, eds S. Watson & K. Gibson, Blackwell, Oxford

Watson, S. & McGillivray, A. 1994 'Stirring up the city: housing and planning in a multicultural society' *Metropolis Now: planning and the urban in contemporary Australia*, K. Gibson & S. Watson, Pluto Press, Sydney

Webber, M. & Crooks, M. eds 1996 *Putting the People Last: government, services and rights in Victoria*, Hyland House, Melbourne

Webber, M. & Rigby, D. 1996 *The Golden Age Illusion: rethinking postwar capitalism*, Guilford, New York

Wensing, E. 1998 Open letter to delegates at 'Renewing Australian Planning' forum, 10 June, Planning Integration Consultants, 6 Charlick Place, Nicholls, ACT 2913

Wensing, E. & Davis, R. 1998 'Letter to editor' *Australian Planner*, 35(1), pp 3–4

Wensing, E. & Sheehan, J. 1997 'Native title: implications for land management', The Australia Institute, Discussion Paper no. 11, Canberra

Wettenhall, G. 1994 *Australian Cities and Regions: a national approach*, Australian Urban and Regional Development Review, Melbourne

Whiteford, P. 1995 'Does Australia have a ghetto underclass?' *Social Security Journal*, June, pp 6–19

Whittaker, S. 1996 *National Local Sustainability Survey*, Occasional Paper no. 3, Environs Australia, Canberra

——1997 'Are Australian councils "willing and able" to implement local Agenda 21?' *Local Environment*, 2(3), pp 319–28

Wildavsky, A. 1973 'If planning is everything, maybe it's nothing' *Policy Sciences*, 4, pp 127–53

Wilenski, P. 1988 'Social change as a source of competing values in public administration' *Australian Journal of Public Administration*, 47(3)

Wilmoth, D. 1987 'Metropolitan Planning for Sydney' *Urban Australia: planning issues and policies*, eds R. Bunker & S. Hamnett, Mansell, New York/Nelson, Melbourne

Wilson, J., Thompson, J. & McMahon, A. 1996 *The Australian Welfare State*, Macmillan, Melbourne

Winston, D. 1957 *Sydney's Great Experiment: the progress of the Cumberland County Plan*, Angus & Robertson, Sydney

Wiseman, J. 1998 *Global Nation? Australia and the politics of globalisation*, Cambridge University Press, Melbourne

Wolch, J. 1990 *The Shadow State: government and the voluntary sector in transition*, The Foundation Center, New York

World Commission on Environment and Development (WCED) 1987 *Our Common Future*, Oxford University Press, Oxford

Wotherspoon, G. 1991 *'City of the Plain': history of a gay sub-culture*, Hale & Iremonger, Sydney

Wright, I. 1995 'The PEDA Bill' *Queensland Planner*, 35(3), pp 12–14

Wright, L. 1998 'Aussie battlers number in millions' *Canberra Times*, 4 June, p. 3

Yearbury, K. 1997 'Planning for the new millennium', Queensland Environmental Law Association Seminar 27 on the Draft Integrated Planning Bill, September

Yeatman, A. 1994 'The reform of public management: an overview' *Australian Journal of Public Administration*, 53(3), pp 285–95

Yiftachel, O. 1991 'State policies, land control and an ethnic minority: the Arabs in the Galilee, Israel' *Environment & Planning D: Society & Space*, 9, pp 329–52

——1995 'The dark side of modernism: planning as control of an ethnic minority' *Postmodern Cities and Spaces*, eds S. Watson & K. Gibson, Blackwell, Oxford

Young, I.M. 1990 *Justice and the Politics of Difference*, Princeton University Press, Princeton, NJ

Young, J. 1990 *Post Environmentalism*, Belhaven Press, London

Zifcak, S. 1997 'Managerialism, accountability and democracy: a Victorian case study' *Australian Journal of Public Administration*, 53(3), pp 106–19

Glossary

These definitions are for technical terms used in the text. The terms appear in boldface at their first mention in the book and we have indicated at the end of each definition the chapter in which the term first appears.

Assimilation   The attempt to make newcomers to a country conform to some idea of normal behaviour in that country. The imposition of a supposedly universal set of values to govern social behaviour. Thus in the 1950s migrants to Australia were expected to see themselves as 'Australians', conforming to norms which had developed in the predominantly Anglo-Celtic culture of a British colony. (*Chapter 3*)

Cold War   The period from shortly after the end of World War II (1945) until approximately the fall of the Berlin Wall in 1989, when America and the Soviet Union vied for military supremacy in many local theatres of politics (Europe, Africa, Indochina, Latin America) but without direct military confrontation—or 'hot' war—between America and the Soviet Union. The 'arms race' between the two 'superpowers' to develop the most destructive nuclear capacity was accompanied by the 'Truman doctrine' (after the American president) of containment of the vast Soviet empire, and the establishment of NATO (North Atlantic Treaty Alliance) in the West and the Warsaw Pact, which cemented the military alliance of the Eastern bloc. (*Chapter 6*)

Fast-tracking   An application for approval for development of land and/or buildings normally has to go through a process of examination under the relevant regulations. The process may involve public review and appeal, which can take a considerable time. In order to encourage development of particular large-scale projects, the normal process may be curtailed to reduce the time between application and final approval, sometimes with the intervention of the state planning minister; this is called the 'fast track'. (*Chapter 4*)

Fordism The period of growth of the world economy after World War II organised around the principles of mass production of consumer goods (exemplified by cars), relatively high wages permitting mass consumption (the principle established by Henry Ford), the factory discipline of the production line, established gender relations in which the male was the principal 'breadwinner', the growth of social protection afforded by the institutions of the welfare state, and a world economy stabilised by exchange rate controls which fixed the value of currencies against the US dollar. The remnants of a colonial system remained in which the world economy was organised into a developed industrial core supplied by raw materials from peripheral countries. The term 'Fordism' was first used in a theoretical context by the Italian political economist Antonio Gramsci. (*Chapter 7*)

Gentrification The movement of new investment in housing into areas, often environmentally degraded, occupied mainly by the poor. Such investment is attracted by the potential of the area to meet a demand from higher income earners—as with the demand for the accessibility provided by inner-city living. Hence the idea that the 'gentry' become new residents. Gentrification is often carried out by investment companies, but it may also be pioneered by prospective owner-occupiers buying cheaply into poorer areas. (*Chapter 3*)

Governance The manner or function of governing, viewed as rule, influence or regulation with authority. Governance most often refers to the manner of rule of the state, but it may also refer to regulating the proceedings of any organisation, such as a business corporation (corporate governance). (*Chapter 1*)

Government The system of governing, viewed as rule, influence or regulation with authority. Most often it refers to the body of persons governing a state. Thus rule through an institutional system, sometimes inscribed in a constitution, constitutes a government. (*Chapter 1*)

Labour force participation rate The labour force includes people aged 15 years and over who are either (a) employed or (b) unemployed and actively looking for work. The labour force participation rate is the labour force expressed as a percentage of the civilian population aged 15 years and over (ABS 1999). The rate moves upwards when more people are actively looking for work, and downwards when discouraged work-seekers stop looking. (*Chapter 5*)

Land value increment The amount by which the exchange, or market, value of a plot of land increases as its use changes from rural (e.g. agricultural) to urban (e.g. residential). Owners of land on the edge of a city can make large gains in market value as the urban fringe pushes outwards in response to demand for, say, new housing. If government is responsible for zoning land, a government may raise the market value of land by simply rezoning it. As urban growth is a social process and not due to any action on the part of the individual land owner, it is sometimes claimed that the land value increment should return to society either by a tax or by social ownership of land for new development. (*Chapter 4*)

Multiculturalism A policy position that recognises the political virtue of having many different cultures and their value systems in a society. Multiculturalism values the existence of such cultures and seeks to uphold and encourage—even celebrate—their existence, as long as they are consistent with support for the basic political institutions of the host society. The assumption is that the basic political institutions provide a framework for a wide variety of cultural values to flourish in civil society. (*Chapter 3*)

Outsourcing The practice of having work performed for an organisation by a private firm for profit under contract. Some outsourcing has always been undertaken by business corporations which 'subcontract' out certain tasks they have to carry out for a customer. In the 1990s business outsourcing of all but 'core' work became more commonplace. Most importantly, government bodies began to engage increasingly in outsourcing and were sometimes required to do so by government directive. (*Chapter 4*)

Place marketing The practice of publicly offering the qualities of a place, such as a city or government territory, as a good place for business investment. The underlying assumptions of place marketing practices are that localities (e.g. cities) are competing among themselves for a limited amount of investment, that business investment in the area is the most important way of improving the welfare of the people living there, and that businesses will be persuaded to invest once they know about the qualities of a place on offer. Comparative or competitive advantage is stressed. Government policies may be designed to favour business. (*Chapter 5*)

Suburbanisation The process of outward spread of residential population in towns and cities from higher-density residential areas to lower-density 'suburbs' on the growing edge of the city. Suburbanisation takes place as land owners and developers seek to meet a perceived demand for more space in, and especially around, the home. Sub-urbanisation is also driven by the desire of persons to form separate households and their ability to pay for separate accommodation from the family home. In the process, formerly agricultural land is converted to urban (e.g. housing, commercial) use. (*Chapter 2*)

Unemployment   That part of the workforce which desires paid work but cannot obtain it. The usual way of measuring unemployment is either by the number of people registering as unemployed in order to apply for income support from the state, or by the number of people who say they are out of work and desire paid employment on the day of the national census. There is considerable difficulty in measuring precisely what activities should count as 'work' or 'employment', as well as the period spent 'out of work' that should count as a period of unemployment. (*Chapter 2*)

Name Index

Subject Index